OCR HISTORY A A2

Civil Rights in the USA 1865–1992

David Paterson | Doug Willoughby | Susan Willoughby | Series editors: Martin Collier | Rosemary Rees

www.heinemann.co.uk

✓ Free online support
✓ Useful weblinks
✓ 24 hour online ordering

01865 888080

Official Publisher Partnership

Heinemann is an imprint of Pearson Education Limited, a company incorporated in England and Wales, having its registered office at Edinburgh Gate, Harlow, Essex, CM20 2JE. Registered company number: 872828

www.heinemann.co.uk

Heinemann is a registered trademark of Pearson Education Ltd

Text © David Paterson, Doug Willoughby and Susan Willoughby 2009

First published 2009

12
10 9 8 7 6 5

British Library Cataloguing in Publication Data is available from the British Library on request.

ISBN 978-0-435-31266-4

Typeset by TechType
Original illustrations © Pearson Education Ltd, 2009
Illustrated by TechType
Cover design by Pearson Education Ltd
Cover photo/illustration © Bridgeman Art Library/Museum of the City of New York, USA
Edited by Kirsty Taylor
Index compiled by Catherine Harkness
Printed in the UK by Ashford Colour Press Ltd, Gosport, Hants.

Acknowledgements
The author and publisher would like to thank the following individuals and organisations for permission:

Photographs
© Getty Images/Hulton Archive: p. 10; © Corbis: p. 13; © Rex Features/CSU Archives/ Everett Collection: p. 17; © Corbis: p. 18; © Mary Evans/Illustrated London News: p. 34; © Getty Images/MPI; © PA Photos/AP: p. 18 (top); © Getty Images/Hulton Archive: p. 18 (bottom); © Getty Images/MPI: p. 67; © Mary Evans/Interfoto: p. 73 (top); © Corbis/ Flip Schulke: p. 73 (bottom); © Getty Images/William Lovelace/Express: p. 75; © Topfoto: p. 79; © Magnum Photos/Bruno Barbey: p. 82; © Getty Images/Keystone: p. 83; © Library Of Congress, LC-USZC4-5956: p. 103; © Library Of Congress, LC-USZ62-75205: p. 112; © Corbis/Underwood & Underwood: p. 122; © Library Of Congress, LC-USZ62-97542: p. 124; © Corbis/Oscar White: p. 126; © Library Of Congress/Dick DeMarisco, LC-USZ62-126870: p. 137; © Topfoto: p. 144; © Library Of Congress/Lowther & Schreiber, LC-USZ62-63378: p. 153; © Topfoto: p. 162; © Getty Images/MPI: p. 172; © Corbis: p. 174; © Corbis/Bettman: p. 188; © Corbis: p. 190; © Corbis Bettman: p. 202; © Rex Features/CSU Archives/Everett Collection: p. 206; © Corbis/Bettman: p.210; © Corbis/Bettman: p. 221; © Library Of Congress/Keppler & Scwarzman, LC-USZC2-1051: p. 227; © Corbis: p. 231; © Corbis/Underwood & Underwood: p. 239; © Getty Images/Lambert: p. 252; © Library Of Congress/Warren K Leffler, LC-U9-32955-26: p. 267; © Corbis Bettman: p. 276

Written sources
p. 16, p. 26: Extracts from 'The Longman History of the United States of America' by Hugh Brogan. Published by Longman. Used by kind permission of Longman a division of the Pearson Group; p. 43: Extract from 'Better Day Coming' by Adam Fairclough is used by kind permission of Penguin Group (USA); p. 58: Extract from 'Sweet Land of Liberty' by Robert Cook. Published by Longman. Used by kind permission of Longman a division of the Pearson Group; p. 74: Reprinted by arrangement with The Heirs to the Estate of Martin Luther King Jr., care of Writers House as agent for the proprietor New York, New York. Copyright 1963 Dr. Martin Luther King Jr; copyright renewed 1991 Coretta Scott King; p. 76: The Unfinished Journey by William H. Chafe. Used by kind permission of Oxford University Press; p. 96: Black Civil Rights in America edited by Kevern Verney, June 2000. Reprinted with the kind permission of Taylor and Francis Books UK; p. 121: Article from the United Mine Workers Journal used by kind permission of the Mine Workers Journal; p. 159: 'The Sisterhood: The True Story of Women Who Changed the World, 1988' © Marcia Cohen; p. 245: Speech by Pauline Sabin; p. 276: Extract from 'The Power of Positive Women' by Phyllis Schlafly.

Every effort has been made to contact copyright holders of material reproduced in this book. Any omissions will be rectified in subsequent printings if notice is given to the publishers.

Websites
There are links to relevant websites in this book. In order to ensure that the links are up to date, that the links work, and that the sites are not inadvertently linked to sites that could be considered offensive, we have made the links available on the Heinemann website at www.heinemann.co.uk/hotlinks. When you access the site, the express code is 2664P.

CONTENTS

HOW TO USE THIS BOOK

This book is primarily designed to meet the requirements of OCR A2 History Unit F961 Option B: Civil Rights in the USA 1865–1992. It is divided into four sections each of which examines an aspect of how civil rights developed over the period. These are: African-American rights, Labour rights, Native American and Women's rights.

Features

There are many features in the margins of the book which are directly linked to the text and will help stimulate the students' imagination and enhance the overall understanding of the period.

Key Terms – these pick out and define key words.
Key People – these give a brief biography of important people.
Key Ideas – these pick out important ideas, either of the time or of historians studying this period.
Key Events – these give a brief overview of important events.
Key Places – these give a brief explanation of why certain areas are important for this topic.
Key Concepts – these communicate understanding by organising information and theories about the past.

There are questions to consider at the end of each chapter which will help students to build up knowledge of the period and exam-style questions at the end of each section.

Exam Café

The text in the book is supplemented by an exciting **Exam Café** feature. The Exam Café is split into three areas: Relax, Refresh, Result!

- **Relax** is a place for students to share revision tips.
- **Refresh** your memory is an area for revising content.
- **Result** provides examiner's tips and sample answers with comments.

Planning and Delivery Resource

The Civil Rights chapter of this resource contains guidance and advice for the OCR specification. There are student worksheets which help to build up skills for the examination requirements. This also contains an Exam Café with more tips, sample answers and detailed examiner commentary.

INTRODUCTION

The United States of America 1865–1992 – the study in context

This book explores the struggle for civil rights of four groups of Americans – African Americans, Trade Unions and Labour, Native Americans and Women. Whilst there are clear differences in the efforts of all four to establish their rights, each was affected by the wider context in which their campaigns took place. Some knowledge of this is, therefore, helpful to gaining a deeper understanding of the factors that promoted or inhibited their progress.

The period from 1865 until 1992 is a dynamic and challenging one in the history of the USA. In 1865, the United States of America could be described as a fledgling nation having only existed since 1783 and having just emerged from a potentially destructive **civil war** that threatened its continued existence. By 1992, the USA had become a well-established super-power on the world stage.

The domestic front

On the domestic front, our period of study saw dramatic territorial expansion, economic growth and social change that transformed the United States of America from the original thirteen states (the former British colonies) with a predominantly white population of British origin, to a culturally and ethnically diverse nation of fifty states stretching from coast to coast. The ancestors of the native white population of the US were predominantly from Protestant sects that had migrated to the US in the seventeenth century to escape persecution, Puritans and Quakers, for example. This is especially true of those living in the northern, east coast states (e.g. Massachusetts, Connecticut, Pennsylvania). In some instances, these were intolerant of other faiths, particularly Roman Catholicism and Judaism. Their beliefs also influenced their attitudes to many aspects of life such as issues of morality, home and family. The influx of significant numbers of Roman

KEY EVENTS

The American Civil War (1861–65) was the outcome of the attempt by the **southern states** (the Confederacy, see pages 9 and 10) to establish independence from the federal government. The remaining states of the Union fought to maintain the unity of the states within the USA. The Confederacy was defeated. The Civil War destroyed the economy of the south and left a legacy of hatred and mistrust on both sides of the divide. See Chapter 1 for more information.

KEY PLACES

The southern states who made up the Confederacy were Virginia, North and South Carolina, Georgia, Alabama, Florida, Tennessee, Arkansas, Louisiana, Texas and Mississippi.

KEY EVENTS

Massive immigration In 1870, the population of the USA was 39,818,449. By 1990, it had grown to 249,975,000.

Catholic immigrants from Ireland and Italy, along with the Jewish communities from Russia in the late nineteenth and early twentieth centuries, contributed significantly to native white hostility. The emancipation of the black slave population in the southern states of the US after 1863, together with massive immigration before 1929 which brought greater religious as well as cultural diversity, challenged the existing native white population and the government of the USA to address the principles of freedom and equality that were embodied in the Declaration of Independence in 1776. This underpinned the original US Constitution and Bill of Rights drawn up after the American colonists won their independence from Britain. The struggle, therefore, for the recognition of equality and civil rights that are the subject of this book, has its origin in these crucial developments.

Foreign Policy

In the period from 1865 until 1941, the federal government adopted a policy of isolationism believing that its main priority was governing the USA and avoiding involvement abroad. The support given to the allies in the First World War was a brief departure from this. Foreign policy became of increasing importance in the second half of the twentieth century with the imperative to prevent the spread of communism as the Soviet Union sought to establish spheres of influence during the Cold War and with nuclear proliferation. For the USA, involvement in Vietnam from 1959, the expansion of its nuclear capability and its involvement in the 'space race' also absorbed ever larger proportions of federal expenditure. This impacted on projects at home that required not only the attention and support of the President and the federal government but also substantial federal funding to facilitate the improvement of disadvantaged groups, for example African Americans, Native Americans and the poor.

The obsession with communism had already manifested itself at home in the **Red Scare** of the 1920s. A second intense period of anti-communism dates from the late 1940s until the mid 1950s and was characterised by a fear of the presence of Soviet spies in the US and suspicion of communist influence on American institutions and individuals. Sometimes referred to as the Second Red Scare, in the early 1950s it became known as **McCarthyism** after Joseph McCarthy, the US Republican Senator who became notorious for his zeal in rooting out alleged subversive individuals or organisations. Leaders of any kind of protest could arouse suspicion of being socialists or communists and attract condemnation for 'un-American' activities. African American and trade union leaders were particularly vulnerable as were university academics and some in the entertainment industry.

Government and politics

Some knowledge of the structure and working of the federal system of government in the US (see page 9 and diagram on page 4) is vital to understanding many of the terms and references in this book. In comparison with the working of other democracies, the US system was deliberately structured to ensure that there were checks and balances on the power of individuals or groups. For example, the system of voting can mean that **Congress** is made up predominantly of members from one party whereas the President can belong to another. This can impact on the power of a President to introduce change successfully. It was also constructed to leave a considerable amount of power in the hands of the government of each state. Whilst only the federal government can decide on foreign policy and national taxation, state legislatures have the power to make the laws that operate in each state. Consequently, for example, some women had voting rights in some states at certain points in this period that others did not have. All constitutional laws passed by Congress were only enforceable at state level when they had been **ratified** by three quarters of the total number of states. 'States' rights' affected all the groups in this study to a greater or lesser extent but were especially significant in the struggle of African Americans for their civil rights.

The progress made by those groups seeking their civil rights depended, to some extent, on which of the two parties were in power. During the period from 1865 until 1913, government was dominated largely by the Republican Party with the exception of the years 1865–69, 1885–89 and 1893–97 when a Democratic President was elected. On the

KEY TERMS

Congress The federal legislature (parliament or law-making body) of the USA. It consisted of two houses with near equal powers, the democratically elected House of Representatives with numbers proportionate to population, and an indirectly (until 1913) elected upper house, the Senate, which had two representatives per state regardless of population. For legislation to be successful both houses had to pass any proposal.

Ratified Accepted and given assent.

KEY CONCEPTS

States' rights Each individual state was originally all powerful. The birth of the United States involved states voluntarily giving up some of their power to a federal government. Many Americans, particularly southerners, believed they had the right to retain as many powers as possible – especially in domestic matters. During this period the states' rights argument was repeatedly used to defend a state law which the federal government tried to override or to prevent a federal law being passed.

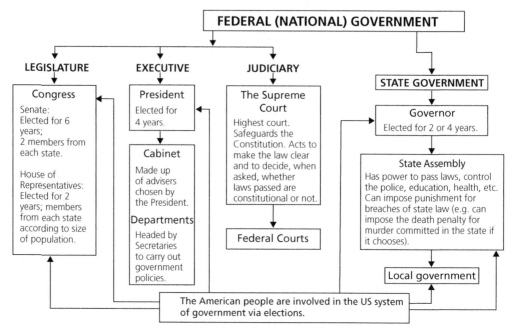

The US system of government.

other hand, elections were frequently close and power was often balanced between the parties in Congress. The period of Reconstruction (1865–77) saw the struggle to re-establish the integrity of the United States following the Civil War. Civil rights were extended to the newly emancipated slaves during this period though not upheld. In the closing decades of the nineteenth century, federal and state governments were largely preoccupied with the social and economic impact and implications of industrialisation, as well as the tensions caused by large scale immigration. The responses to these issues characterised what came to be known as the Progressive era by the turn of the century. Historians divide politics of the twentieth century into three eras or orders. Progressive Order (1900–33), The New Deal Order (1933–late 1960s) and The Divided Order which covers the last third of the twentieth century and into the early twenty–first century.

The Progressive Order was a response to the effects of industrialisation and was characterised by a willingness to engage with political and social reform, especially during

the years between 1900 and 1917. This gave some impetus
to the causes fought for by women. For much of this
period, with the exception of the period from 1912 until
1920, the Republicans were in power. A characteristic of
Republican and Democrat politicians at the time was that
they were largely of white, Anglo-Saxon, Protestant origin.
This impacted on African-Americans and other non-whites
who were segregated, on women and on immigrants who
occupied a second class position. (It is significant that it
was the Democratic president, Woodrow Wilson
(1913–20) who introduced and supported the Nineteenth
Amendment in 1919 giving women the vote although
Wilson and the Democrats continued to oppose black civil
rights.) The Wall Street Crash (1929) destroyed the
credibility of the Republicans and brought the Progressive
Order to an end.

The inauguration of Franklin Roosevelt as President
marked the beginning of what is termed the 'New Deal
Order' which survived until the late 1960s. The Democrats
became the majority party with labour unions and women
enjoying increasing political awareness and involvement.
The Democrats became associated with the willingness of
federal government to solve economic and social problems.
However, it can be over-simplistic to categorise the position
of the different leading parties too neatly. The position
taken by politicians within one party on some issues could
be opposed. Southern Democrats, for example, were
traditionally anti-trade unions and black civil rights and
did not always support reform measures in Congress. The
inclination of successive Democratic governments to
attempt to impose their will abroad in this period
ultimately weakened the administrations of the day at
home. The prolonged war in Vietnam contributed
significantly to the end of the Democratic ascendancy.

A significant feature of the years known collectively as The
Divided Order was the way in which no political party
controlled the period as the presidency and the majority in
Congress passed backwards and forwards between the
candidates of both parties. It was characterised by the way
in which the White House and Congress were in
competition with each other when the majority in the
latter was not of the same party as the President in the

White House. As politicians of both parties became increasingly more hungry for votes, greater attention had to be paid to the issues that most affected their electorate. Cultural and lifestyle issues such as abortion became more important than ever before with political implications.

What is meant by 'civil rights'?

Civil rights are those rights which citizens in a democracy are entitled to expect. These include the right to vote, to equality of opportunity (to education, to work and to self-improvement, for example), the right to receive the protection of the law and to be judged fairly by the courts. Civil rights guarantee the liberty of the individual, including the freedom of thought, action, speech and expression. All of these were enshrined in the Constitution and the Bill of Rights and its amendments but remained open to interpretation. This is the role of the Supreme Court. As the highest court in the USA, it is an integral part of the system of government established in 1783, having the task of safeguarding the rights and freedoms embodied in the Constitution and ensuring that any laws that are passed do not violate its terms. The judges to the Supreme Court are nominated by the President. Their appointment must then ratified by the Senate. This serves as a limit on the power of the President and is a further example of the checks and balances built into the Constitution to set parameters to the exercise of power for each of its parts, preventing any one part from becoming too powerful. One of the prime functions of the Supreme Court is still to interpret the Constitution as it applies to specific cases that are brought before it and also the terms of laws passed by Congress and State legislatures to ensure that they are in keeping with the rights and freedoms guaranteed by the Constitution. It then passes judgement on alleged violations which, in turn, become points of reference for subsequent similar cases. At various times throughout our period, African Americans, Trade Unions, Native Americans and Women all appealed to the Supreme Court as the most effective means of making progress in securing their civil rights.

Section 1: African Americans 1865–1992

The section on African American civil rights has as its starting point the abolition of slavery in 1865 and the subsequent amendments to the Constitution which, in theory, ensured equality of the African-American race under the broad umbrella of civil rights such as equality under the law and the right to vote. In practice many of their promised freedoms failed to last or did not even materialise, particularly in the southern states, where blacks faced segregation, discrimination and violence.

From the end of the first decade of the twentieth century, campaigning to gain black civil rights became more organised and widespread. This coincided with the start of a substantial movement of the African-American population north, where segregation and discrimination were more variable and less embedded into the political and economic system. The period after 1945, especially until the late 1960s, was notable for advances in civil rights for black Americans. A powerful movement campaigned in a disciplined, determined and successful way for the rights that had been given under the Constitution to become a reality. They found a Supreme Court and some members of Congress as well as at least two Presidents now more sympathetic to their claims. They were able to overcome severe white resistance from the south. Thus by 1970 much of the political and legal equality so long denied African Americans was becoming a reality, even in the Deep South.

However, social and economic questions, such as housing and unemployment, remained disproportionately a problem among African Americans, as well as a frequent lack of real educational equality. The minority of blacks who were 'making it' in the ultimate land of opportunity, however, was steadily rising and by 1992, African Americans were starting to play a much more significant part in the US political system beginning, in some cases, to realise the 'American Dream'.

CHAPTER 1

1865–77 'Standing in the sun'

How far did black Americans acquire civil rights in the period of Reconstruction?

Hypothesis:

- African Americans gained legal civil rights between 1865 and 1870 through constitutional amendments and acts of Congress: however, in practice some of these rights did not materialise and by 1877 they were starting to lose what rights they had.

INTRODUCTION: WHAT WAS THE ATTITUDE TOWARDS SLAVERY IN THE USA UP TO ITS ABOLITION IN 1865?

What was the early history of African Americans in the New World?

The original enslavement of African men and women in the USA dates from the seventeenth century. By the end of the eighteenth century the trade in human beings across the Atlantic Ocean had increased the African-American population to twenty per cent of the total population of the thirteen original states of America. As the cotton-based economy of the southern states grew during the nineteenth century, so did the states' dependence on slave labour.

The shared experience of slavery united African peoples, whose cultural origins were extremely diverse. In slavery the foundations were laid for the eventual emergence of a sense of identity and cultural pride.

In northern states the morality of slavery was hotly disputed from the start. A smaller number of African Americans lived here and the majority appeared to be free men and women: they possessed full civil rights of citizenship, including (for men) the right to vote. However,

KEY CONCEPTS

Civil Rights remained theoretical In the north, free black people frequently faced intimidation when they attempted to register to vote in elections so they could not always exercise their rights. Craft unions in the north excluded them from skilled work. Aggressive competition for work from Irish immigrants in the cities and unrelenting discrimination ensured that black males were confined to menial work, whilst black women were mainly confined to work as domestic servants. Even after the emancipation of all slaves in 1865, a common theme during the next 100 years was the difference between the Civil Rights granted in theory and those actually granted in practice.

KEY TERMS

Abolitionist Movement The earliest movement demanding abolition of slaves dates from 1817, when the American Colonization Society demanded a gradual emancipation of the slaves with compensation for their owners. Most supporters of abolition resided in the northern states.

KEY TERMS

Federal system A Federal system is a form of government where there is more than one source of authority; in the case of the USA, a combined government for all the states in Washington and governments within the states themselves, each having their own defined areas of authority over citizens. This is in contrast to a unitary system where all power flows from the top.

KEY PEOPLE

Abraham Lincoln (1809–65) Born in Kentucky in modest circumstances he joined the Republican Party in 1856. Opposing the spread of slavery but not calling for its outright abolition he was elected as President at the end of 1860. President throughout the Civil War he insisted at first that the fight was to preserve the Union but changed his emphasis in 1863 when he issued the Emancipation Proclamation (see page 10).

KEY TERMS

Confederacy The eleven states that tried to secede (break away from) the United States: Alabama, Arkansas, Georgia, Florida, Louisiana, Mississippi, South and North Carolina, Virginia, Tennessee and Texas. They formed their own system of government giving each state some independence but combining militarily in an attempt to beat off northern forces.

these **rights often remained theoretical.** In spite of the support that the **abolitionist movement** received in the north, a significant proportion of the population was hostile to African-American equality; some even owned slaves.

What was the background to the outbreak of civil war?

Abolitionist feelings continued to grow stronger in the north in the mid-nineteenth century but it would require constitutional change to destroy slavery: within the political system, the president did not have the power to do this alone. The **federal system** was still weak and the real power rested with the state governments. However, in 1854 the Republican Party, with its base of support in the north, was formed as a party opposed to slavery. By contrast the Democrat Party, strong in the south and especially among plantation owners, was split over the question.

The struggle between the north and the south reached a climax over the issue of extending slavery to the newly settled territories in the west. **Abraham Lincoln's** view was that if it remained contained in the original southern states, it could eventually be ended. Despite his reassurances that he had no plans to interfere with slavery, the south did not believe Lincoln and states began seceding from (leaving) the Union at the end of 1860 and forming their own **Confederacy.** When southern leader Jefferson Davis laid claim to the arms stores in South Carolina at Fort Sumter, conflict broke out between north and south. Few, however, would have anticipated that this would be the start of four years of bloody struggle in civil war.

What was Emancipation and what was its effects?

Lincoln had insisted at the start of the war that it was the question of secession and not slavery being fought over, but his policy changed during 1862. He issued the **Emancipation Proclamation** stating that black people could no longer be owned as property by others and were free to leave their masters. Helping to accelerate a movement that had already begun, the Proclamation resulted in slaves continuing to leave their plantations in increasing numbers.

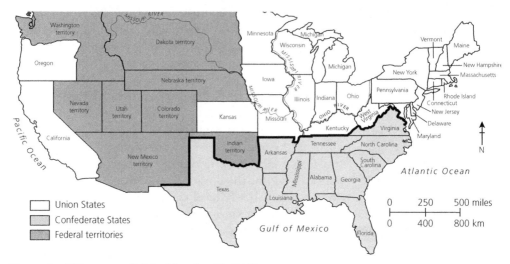

How the US states divided in the Civil War.

Union States
Confederate States
Federal territories

In 1865 all slaves in the country were formally freed with the passing of the Thirteenth Amendment to the Constitution, days before the formal **ending of the Civil War** in early April. This was a turning point in the progress of African Americans towards securing a better life since it established their freedom in law and provided them with some basic human rights.

Black Americans celebrating the Emancipation Proclamation in 1863.

10   African Americans 1865–1992

Formal ending of the Civil War This occurred on 9 April 1865 when Commander Robert E. Lee surrendered to the northern military chief Ulysses S. Grant at the Appomattox Courthouse, Virginia.

Lincoln's assassination
On 14 April 1865, Lincoln went to Ford's Theater in Washington DC, with his wife and friends. During the third act, an assassin, John Wilkes Booth, entered the President's box and shot him in the back of the head. Booth sympathised with the Confederate cause and resented Lincoln's policy towards Confederate rebels. Lincoln died in the White House the following morning. Booth was hunted down and probably shot by Union troops, although it has also been suggested that he may have shot himself. Eight others were charged with plotting the President's death and four were hanged for the crime including Mary Surratt, the first woman in US history to be executed.

They could now:

- have their plantation marriages legalised,
- worship freely in their own churches,
- own property,
- become educated,
- travel freely.

However, the unleashing of around three and a half million former slaves into society made the nature of emancipation and the question of civil rights for the free slaves a major issue in the post-war period. Moreover, the uncertainties that lay ahead were compounded by the **assassination of President Lincoln**.

What was the situation in the south in 1865?

The period immediately following the end of the Civil War was crucial in determining the future prospects for freed slaves. The short-term gains that were made during this period came largely as a result of the policies of the ruling Republican government. Some of these were then lost. The more lasting gains achieved in the following century were largely as a result of the efforts of black Americans themselves.

At the end of the Civil War the southern states were devastated: buildings, roads and railways had been destroyed, law and order was not restored for months or even years after the formal end of hostilities and the police and court systems had broken down everywhere. Churches and schools stood derelict.

From the time of the Emancipation Proclamation at the start of 1863 it was clear that military victory for the north would involve them forcibly imposing the abolition of slavery on the defeated white southerners. Slavery had been a major part of southern society so its removal would mean significant changes to the south's way of life.

1865–77 'Standing in the sun.' How far did black Americans acquire civil rights in the period of Reconstruction?

11

WHAT WERE THE CHANGES IN THE LEGAL AND POLITICAL STATUS OF AFRICAN AMERICANS AFTER 1865?

What were the prospects for black civil rights at the end of the Civil War in 1865?

There were two broad questions:

1. **Apart from the abolition of slavery what other rights were likely to be given?**

   Would the **freedmen** gain the right to vote, be completely equal under the law and acquire employment opportunities? Would they be able to integrate into white southern society on an equal basis? Would the rights implied by the Emancipation Proclamation and the Thirteenth Amendment abolishing slavery become a reality?

2. **By what means would these rights be granted?**

   How far would the victorious northern states continue to control the south after the end of the conflict and try to **reconstruct** a southern society without slavery? Would the federal system return and states regain their considerable independence in domestic affairs? Who would determine the kind of settlement to be made – the US Congress or the President? Would white southerners accept the amended system?

Before Congress re-commenced its duties in November 1865 prospects for further African-American civil rights looked limited, especially because of the attitude of the new President, **Andrew Johnson**. However, in the subsequent struggle between Johnson and the Congress, the latter was eventually the victor and more rights were granted.

What amendments and laws were passed to aid civil rights?

Further amendments to the Constitution were to be passed, which in theory at least gave African Americans substantial civil rights. The Fourteenth Amendment, ratified in 1868, gave all freed blacks their United States

Equal protection under the law Amendment Fourteen made clear the right to citizenship of all those born (or naturalised) in the US and that their rights could not be removed without '*due process of law*'. Section two made it clear that if the southern states tried to stop blacks voting, their punishment would be to receive a smaller representation in the Federal House of Representatives. But this later clause was never properly implemented.

The Civil Rights Act of 1866 This should have guaranteed legal equality to blacks but more radical Republicans were worried that white southerners were already planning to undermine the position of African-American voters. For instance the Act could well face a legal challenge on the grounds that it was unconstitutional because it infringed states' rights. This is why civil rights' supporters in Congress decided on the Fourteenth Amendment in 1867, thus hoping to remove any doubts about the legality of equal treatment for African Americans.

Andrew Johnson.

citizenship and **equal protection under the law**. Then in 1870 the Fifteenth Amendment forbade the denial of the vote to any man on the basis of colour, race or 'previous condition of servitude'.

Congress also passed some ordinary laws that just required a simple majority in the two Houses of Congress. **The Civil Rights Act of 1866** excluded Native Americans but asserted that all other races including African Americans were full citizens of the United States, even if they had previously been slaves. In March 1867 Reconstruction went further than political gestures when Congress passed a Military Reconstruction Act, dividing the south into **military districts.** Constitutional conventions (see page 16) would set up new state governments.

Now, in theory, the African American possessed the civil rights essential to make progress in American society; freedom of movement and employment, equality under the law and the right to vote.

Who was responsible for the Reconstruction policy?

The initiative for these changes had been taken by the more radical wing of the Republican Party. Congressmen such as **Thaddeus Stevens** and Charles Sumner acknowledged that blacks played a vital part in the American economy: their role must now be accepted on equal terms with full rights of citizenship.

President Johnson's policy differed from the radical Republicans. He wanted to re-admit the southern states to the union and so return to pre-war relations (minus slavery) with what seemed like, to many other northerners, indecent haste. Men such as Stevens and Sumner felt that Reconstruction –with all that implied for black civil rights – must be controlled from the north. If Johnson's policy were followed they feared white southerners would effectively control their own Reconstruction. This would be to the detriment of the welfare of African Americans.

However, the **radical Republicans** also had a powerful principle on their side; all people had the right to live out the 'American dream' and the radicals promoted their belief that this should apply to former slaves, and everyone should be given the right to vote, the right to own land, access to education and legal equality. The application of these principles would form the centre of discussion for the next 100 years in the ongoing debate about civil rights, though it did not yet mean that rights would be extended to black women as much as black men (see Section 4).

Johnson issued thousands of pardons to southern rebels so that many influential rich planters were able to reassert their authority. Though he insisted on the south ratifying the abolition of slavery (the Thirteenth Amendment to the Constitution) Johnson said nothing about the civil rights of the freed slaves, allowing the southern states to develop their own Black Codes (see page 21) to limit African-American civil rights.

Why did President Andrew Johnson's policy of Reconstruction fail?

The majority of northern politicians saw political advantage in smashing the power of the southern landowners who supported the Democrat party. Northern Republicans could easily convince themselves that rebellious Democrats were a dangerous breed and that Republican dominance was desirable. This more moderate Republican group was not as passionately in favour of civil rights for black people as Sumner and Stevens were, but it was happy to go along with it if it brought political advantage. Would not **enfranchised** blacks vote Republican? Not for the last time, hopes for party advantage played a part in civil rights policy towards African Americans. Stevens' and Sumner's strong policy on granting civil rights to African Americans was now implemented with profound consequences for the south.

Although Johnson could not prevent the passing of any constitutional amendments he exercised his Presidential right of **veto** on all the major pieces of congressional legislation. However, such was the strength of his opponents that the vetoes were overridden with two-third majorities in Congress. The battle between Congress and President continued until Congress determined on **impeachment of the President**: this failed but it weakened Johnson politically and he saw out the remaining year of his Presidency quietly. It meant that Reconstruction could continue in the way that radical Republicans wanted.

ADJUSTING TO FREEDOM

Emancipation had become a reality for African Americans: they had gained personal freedom to marry, travel and express their religious faith. However, would they also receive the rights to education and property and equal employment opportunities? These were complex questions

KEY TERMS

Enfranchised Being given the right to vote.

Veto To have the power of veto is to use one's position to reject a proposal that the majority support. In the American Constitution a President can veto a Bill passed through Congress if he dislikes it. However, this veto is limited. If both Houses of Congress re-pass the Bill with a two-thirds majority, the President has to accept it. This is what happened to President Andrew Johnson a number of times in 1866/7.

KEY EVENTS

Impeachment of President Johnson An impeachment is a trial of someone in authority for a serious offence involving 'high crimes and misdemeanours'. It is normally the only way of removing a President from office. The House of Representatives act as the prosecutor, the Senate as jury. The Chief Justice of the Supreme Court chairs the proceedings. When Johnson dismissed his able and successful War Secretary Edwin Stanton, Republicans felt Johnson was trying to sweep away any opposition to using his powers as Commander in Chief and impose his own policies by force. Johnson was acquitted by one vote.

dependent on political circumstances, economic prosperity and the structure of society at the time.

How far did black Americans gain political rights?

Over 700,000 black men were now enrolled to vote. These newly liberated people had a major role in electing members to the **Conventions** that had been set up by Congress. By the spring of 1868 these organisations had established civil rights for blacks on equal terms with whites. Black representatives were now in the position of possessing real political power, sharing it with pro-northern **scalawags** or actual northern **carpetbaggers**. At the end of the 1860s, the sun appeared to be shining for African Americans. They had gained greatly from Republican policies even if the motives behind these had sometimes been the punishment of Confederates. However real political power for black men was limited as they were not elected in proportion to their numbers.

Were civil rights more apparent in the north?

Although there was some movement north after 1865 (see Chapter 2) the numbers of blacks outside the south remained quite small, less than five per cent of the northern population until after 1877. Also, their right to vote and equality of opportunity in the north sometimes remained theoretical as it had before emancipation. But as historian Hugh Brogan has pointed out:

> 'their importance is not to be measured in numbers. Their existence … meant that in parts of America the principle of human equality was still acknowledged.'

Some had their lives transformed as a result of the freedoms they acquired and this served eventually as an inspiration for black southerners to claim the same rights.

One area where northern blacks could take advantage of additional opportunities was in politics. Some took the opportunity to move south to pursue their careers and federal political careers also became possible. In the 1870s twenty-two blacks were elected to Congress, twenty to the House of Representatives and two (from Mississippi) to the

Blanche K. Bruce (1841–98) Born into slavery in Virginia he moved to Mississippi in 1869, becoming a landowner and local politician and obtaining the support of a number of leading white Republicans in the state government. He served on a number of important government committees and in 1888 he gained some support for his nomination to run for the vice presidency.

Frederick Douglass (1817–95) was the leading black opponent of slavery in the years immediately before the Civil War. An escaped slave, he became active in the Anti-Slavery Society and set up his own anti-slavery newspaper. After emancipation he refused the offer of running the Freedman's Bureau, disapproving of the policies of President Johnson. Instead he took part in many speaking tours arguing the case for black rights, actively protesting about the growing discriminatory practices.

Support of freed slaves The Bureau's help included finding homes and employment and providing food, education and medical care. Schools were set up and new hospitals were built funded by a mixture of Congressional funds and missionary societies.

Blanche K. Bruce.

Senate. One of these, Hiram Revels, a minister of religion, sat for only one year. **Blanche K. Bruce** who sat for the full six-year term from 1875–81 was more significant. Here was the first black leader who had an important political career after the Civil War. However, he lacked support from others and was unable to help increase civil rights for blacks in general. The only other black leader with a substantial national reputation was **Frederick Douglass**. However, although he lived on until 1895 and held a number of public offices, Douglass never had the impact after 1865 that he had clearly possessed before the civil war. There would be a substantial wait for another black leader who held important political positions, which many saw as an essential precondition of sustained African-American progress in civil rights.

How did the Freedman's Bureau develop?

Apart from voting, the vast majority of blacks played no part in the political process but the progress of a few freedmen in government contrasted with the condition of the rest in ordinary life. Many were now technically free but homeless and unemployed. There were organisations to assist them, the most notable being the Freedman's Bureau. This was set up by the federal government in March 1865 to **support freed slaves** in the short term and to provide a basis for their long-term security. Crucially, the Bureau supported the work of **black self-help groups** in providing education for black children and adults supported financially by philanthropic organisations in the north.

The Bureau performed surprisingly well in difficult circumstances. Its head, **General Oliver Howard**, proved a forceful leader. Their traditional curriculum would train black lawyers, scientists and teachers; indirectly it would train future black leaders. However, these educational advances were only for a minority of African Americans: by 1890, 65 per cent of black American school-aged children in the south were still unable to write, compared with 15 per cent of white children. The lack of equality in educational opportunity was to be a major grievance for the next 100 years.

With the decline of radical Republicanism, Congress would not renew its mandate and the Bureau closed in 1872. It was a sign that the north was beginning to lose its enthusiasm for constant interference with matters in the south.

To what extent did African Americans lack land?
In addition to education it was land that was frequently most lacking because capital was in short supply and only white merchants and planters possessed the necessary outside links to obtain it. Many African Americans merely became wage-earning labourers. With industrial development slow compared to the north, and blacks usually lacking the experience and education for anything

Self-help groups These self-help groups were comprised of freedmen who joined together their meagre earnings to buy land and disused buildings in order to provide schools and to employ teachers who came mainly from the north. This compensated for the failure of the impoverished post-war southern state governments to provide education for all but especially for black, school aged children.

General Oliver Howard (1830–1909) Played a distinguished military role in the Civil War, much of it after losing an arm. He was made head of the Freedman's Bureau in May 1865 and was noted for his lack of corruption and genuine interest in the welfare of the emancipated slaves. One of his enduring achievements was to support newly established Colleges for African-American education such as Fisk University in Nashville, Tennessee, as well as setting up his own University in Washington.

A racist poster from 1866 encouraging people to oppose Congressional legislation to extend the powers of the Freedman's Bureau.

more ambitious, the most common route was to **sharecropping**.

An alternative might have been to grant the African American absolute ownership of some land. There had been a vision of **forty acres and a mule** for all freedmen but this idea was never properly implemented. The amnesties President Andrew Johnson granted meant that land was returned to the white owners from whom it had originally been confiscated. Immediately after 1865 there was little prosperity for anyone in the south. In the Civil War this area had lost a third of its mules and horses and 50 per cent of its agricultural machinery. Cotton production took nearly fifteen years to return to pre-Civil War levels.

Were black Americans still oppressed?

Here the difference between the rights of African Americans in theory and in practice is noticeable. They had to make do with sharecropping contracts which were frequently one-sided. They had no control over the materials they bought and found that, because he supplied all the tools and animals, the white master demanded higher and higher proportions of the final crop. So, the ex-slave frequently had to resort to borrowing money at crippling rates of interest. The **crop-lien** system tended to encourage a one crop economy – cotton. Relationships between the races were not helped by these developments. African Americans felt they had been cheated in the agreements and resented close supervision. Whites claimed that the supervision was necessary because blacks did not work hard enough. The vast majority of black people in the south remained at the bottom of the economic pile: many white southerners were determined that they would stay there.

How good were black prospects and quality of life?

Although educational opportunities were increasing they were still limited. For many African Americans there seemed no escape from a life of poverty and, in practice, they had few civil rights. Employment in industry was often discouraged because it might threaten white employment and the nature of the work meant that blacks and whites would labour in close proximity to each other. Some black people looked for work in southern cities such as New Orleans, Louisiana and Memphis, Tennessee. Emigration to the north was as yet a trickle (see next chapter) and not a practical proposition for the vast majority. Housing generally remained of a primitive quality for most African Americans. The freed slaves themselves realised what they needed. It was eloquently summarised by the **South Carolina's Freedmen's Convention in 1865**.

After the closing down of the Freedman's Bureau in 1872, federal government support for education came to an end. The fear of violence was evident – a real and justifiable fear that would do much to prevent many African Americans from attempting to initiate their own changes to the system and lowered their quality of life. Nearly 100 years later the fear was still there.

Even with some protection from the north all these weaknesses meant that from the first moments after their emancipation, blacks were ill equipped to deal with southern white resentment at their freedom, their crude racist attitudes, their economic exploitation and, not infrequently, their violent conduct towards those who, not long before, had been their slaves. The relative economic weakness of the south would impact most on the poorer sections of the community where African Americans were disproportionately represented.

South Carolina's Freedmen's Convention The appeal ran as follows: '*We simply ask that we be recognised as men; that we have the right of trial by jury of our peers; that schools be established for the education of colored children as well as white … that no impediments be put in the way of acquiring homesteads for ourselves and our people; that in short we are dealt with as others are – in equity and justice.*' Quoted in Adam Fairclough, *Better day Coming.*

WHITE REACTION TO BLACK FREEDOM

How did white southerners use the law to maintain their supremacy?

The policy of granting civil rights to ex-slaves greatly alienated many white southerners. The result was that when southern politicians had a chance to regain political control of their states in the 1870s, they set about reversing the progress that African Americans had made. Many found it psychologically impossible to see blacks as equals. This remained a consistent viewpoint of many southern whites for at least 100 years.

De jure means the official position in law.

De facto means the actual position in reality.

The Slaughterhouse Case
In judging a case concerning a meat monopoly, the federal Supreme Court decided that the rights of citizens should stay under state rather than federal control. It ruled that the Fourteenth Amendment to the Constitution protected a person's *individual* rights but not his or her state *civil* rights, that is rights granted at the discretion of the civil government, the state. In the future these latter rights would be eroded. This was the first of a number of victories for advocates of states rights that would impede the granting of civil rights to African Americans.

Ulysses S. Grant A leading northern general in the American Civil War becoming commander-in-chief of the Union forces in 1864. Turning to politics he was elected as Republican President in 1868. He broadly accepted the early Reconstruction policy and when re-elected in 1872 he promised to do his best to see former slaves achieve the equal civil rights he felt they deserved but still did not possess. However, his second term in office was dogged by financial scandals which undermined his authority.

At first, black civil rights in the south had looked secure in theory (***de jure***) even if how far they would acquire these rights in practice (***de facto***) was uncertain. It became a constant theme of civil rights' campaigners that the rights blacks acquired in this period remained theoretical only. As W.E.B. Du Bois (see page 38) remarked later, the ex-slave '*stood a brief moment in the sun*' before it went behind a large cloud for a prolonged period. The amendments to the Constitution in 1868 and 1870 had seemed clear enough. Also the Bill of Rights in the US Constitution emphasised individual freedom. However, another distinctive American emphasis was on freedom of interference from government. When Reconstruction finally ended in 1877 and southern states regained political control over their own territory, the legal use of the concept of 'states' rights' would enable white southerners to retain their old way of life and limit the rights of African Americans. Court judgements would be used to deprive blacks of some of the rights they possessed.

Even when challenged in the federal courts the removal of civil rights for blacks were frequently upheld, ultimately by the federal Supreme Court. As early as 1873 the **Slaughterhouse Case** was an omen.

It is significant that the mid-twentieth century leap forward in obtaining greater civil rights for black people was partly stimulated by more favourable Supreme Court verdicts. However, for the moment, the new President **Ulysses S. Grant** proved compliant to radical Republican wishes in regard to Reconstruction.

What do the Black Codes tell us about southern attitudes to race?

The Black Codes set up in 1865/6 were an early indication of southern white attitudes to the newly freed slaves. The southern state legislatures were determined to keep them in an inferior position. Their nightmare vision of marauding blacks taking white women and white livelihoods played on the fears and insecurities of the time. Some artfully argued that the Codes were an advance for blacks, bridging the gap between slavery and freedom. Although many aspects of these codes were soon nullified by the military commanders that moved into the south, many northerners were alarmed at what it revealed about southern attitudes to black rights. As the African-American leader Frederick Douglass remarked, most black people were *'free from the individual master but a slave of society'.*

What did the regulations say?

The Black Code regulations varied from state to state. However, they did possess some common features across all southern states. One was the wide definition of a **'negro'**. One eighth of black blood was sufficient for this. Marriages were allowed, with previous relationships often regularised as a result, but inter-racial unions were outlawed. Property could be owned, though rarely afforded, and legal rights were limited. While a black person could testify in court, draw up a contract and sue if it was not kept, they were barred from giving evidence against a white person, or serving on juries. They were not permitted to vote and if education was allowed it would be in segregated schools. These codes anticipated measures taken after 1877 when the southern states had regained more independence.

How prevalent was segregation up to 1877?

The attitude of most southern whites to the treatment of black people was to keep the races apart if at all possible. Whilst formal segregation did not occur until the 1880s and 1890s in the south, **many aspects of it were apparent from the start** of African-American 'freedom' in 1865. Clearly this segregation was often of the *de facto* rather than the *de jure* kind and was formalised later (see Chapter 6). However, the examples of educational segregation after 1865 are a revealing insight into southern mentality. It was asserted that in mixed schools African-American children would corrupt white children. In any case, whites argued, blacks could not benefit from as high a level of education as whites.

As to the overall desirability of segregation, southern white views initially varied. There had been mixing of the races under slavery, sometimes sharing houses and churches and, in a patronising way, some of the planter class wished to maintain this close contact with blacks as long as they were kept in their place.

KEY TERMS

Negro The commonly used word for the African American up to the 1960s. 'Negro' was originally seen as a politer name to the vulgar alternatives, but black consciousness in the 1960s and 1970s felt that 'negro' had too many associations with slavery, oppression and segregation, and so replaced it with 'black'. More recently African American has been used as a means of indicating a person's ethnicity while emphasising shared heritage.

KEY CONCEPTS

The start of formal segregation Recent research has cast doubt on the views of eminent historian C. Vann Woodward (1974) that segregation did not really develop until the 1880s: in South Carolina and Mississippi it was common earlier.

KEY TERMS

Ku Klux Klan (KKK) A terrorist organisation founded by Nathan Forrest and active mainly in the southern states which advocated white supremacy. Ku Klux related to the Greek Kuklos - a drinking bowl.

KEY EVENTS

Atmosphere of racial hostility and terror The activities of the KKK reflected the tense inter-racial atmosphere prevalent in the south during the time of Reconstruction. In Memphis in May 1866 there were three days of violence after a collision between two horse-drawn carriages with black and white drivers. 46 were killed and five women raped. In New Orleans the following July, African-American soldiers travelling to vote were attacked: 34 people were killed and over 100 injured: these were merely the worst examples.

KEY CONCEPTS

Democrat control of the south Democrats were the dominant party in the south after 1865, Republicans being widely hated for being responsible for their defeat in the Civil War. The largely successful campaign to prevent African Americans voting meant that, once the northern influence retreated in the 1870s, the south became a virtual one-party state – a Democrat one.

Why was separate religious worship so significant?

One of the few real freedoms afforded after 1865 was in liberty of worship. At first their churches were something of an escape from the unpleasant life many African Americans still led outside them, but later they were to become a vital base to help moves towards equality, providing moral and religious guidance and encouragement, as well as being a significant centre for campaign meetings and administration. Organisations linked to the church often gave blacks their first taste of self-help activity and the sense of acting together as a community that would be so noticeable in the later civil rights movement. Moreover, black ministers were to emerge as clear leaders of their communities.

What were the aims of the Ku Klux Klan?

One organisation, the **Ku Klux Klan** (KKK), saw terror rather than encouragement as the way to enforce separation of the races. First formed in December 1865 in Tennessee reacting to the threat of black freedom, it was specifically set up to oppose any attempt to try to persuade newly enfranchised blacks to vote Republican and guarantee the supremacy of the white race. By 1867 it asserted that whites were *'endowed with an evident superiority over all other races'* and that their dominion over others was God-given. The violent atrocities that it committed were unprecedented and were directed not only against black people themselves, but also at anyone who supported them or furthered their cause. These supporters (often white Republicans) would feel the full force of the KKK's prejudice and hatred with frequent assaults.

While the first Klan did not last long **the atmosphere of racial hostility and terror** it had helped to foster remained a crucial fact of life in the south and a major impediment to the development of black civil rights.

How did the US party system not help civil rights for black Americans?

It was assumed that African Americans would vote for their Republican liberators and so make **Democrat control of the south** more difficult. While blacks did indeed support

Republicans when they could, especially at first, many were eventually prevented from voting at all (see Chapter 2) and so Democrats dominated the south until at least the 1960s. Ironically, in the end it was a Democrat President (Lyndon Johnson) and a Democrat Congress which were responsible for ending white supremacy during the 1960s in the south: but for nearly 100 years Democratic political dominance of the southern states was seen by the white community as a guarantee of their way of life and the maintenance of segregation.

How did northern control end?

As the 1870s progressed, the northern Republican hold on the south began to weaken in President Grant's second term, 1873–77. The Freedman's Bureau came to an end and states began to throw off their military control. With the death of Stevens (1868) and Sumner (1874) the will to keep a vigilant eye on the south was weakening.

By the early 1870s most southern states had accepted their new constitutions and developed their own **Redemption governments**. Now it was apparent that slavery would not return, interest in the welfare of African Americans waned. Many northerners were embarrassed with what they heard about carpetbagger corruption and scandals within Grant's own administration. It was argued that the US was a decentralised country that should let each system of government get on with its business with minimum interference from the federal government. While Congress did pass a **Civil Rights Act** in 1875 it was not enforced and later it was declared unconstitutional by the Supreme Court in 1883. As early as 1876 the Court had ruled one of the Enforcement Acts unconstitutional in *US v. Cruikshank.*

What was the 'Compromise' of 1877?

The formal end of the system came after the Presidential election of November 1876. The contest between the Republican Rutherford B. Hayes and the Democrat Samuel J. Tilden was extremely close and some votes for the **Electoral College** were disputed. An Electoral Commission found in favour of Hayes whose path to office was smoothed when an agreement (later known as the

Redemption governments Democrat controlled governments that developed in the southern states from 1870 onwards to replace governments imposed by the north after 1865. They were said to have saved or 'redeemed' the traditional south.

In 1877 only three states (Florida, South Carolina and Louisiana) still had radical governments and northern troops. Back in 1868 when Georgia had attempted to expel its black members of the **state legislature** it was forced by the radical Republican government to take them back; but in 1874 when white southern Democrats in the state next door devised the Mississippi plan to prevent blacks from voting, no action was taken.

State legislature The parliament or law–making body elected in each state of the USA. In the federal system it has the right to pass laws on a wide range of domestic affairs.

Civil Rights Act 1875 This was motivated by increasing concern about the growing moves to formalise segregation in some southern states and the Act made it clear that equal rights applied to public areas such as places of entertainment, drinking houses and public transport.

Following a riot in Louisiana which left seventy African Americans and two white people dead, over a hundred white men were arrested by Federal authorities. They were freed when the Supreme Court ruled that the Enforcement Act empowered federal officers to take action only against states and not against individuals.

KEY TERMS

Electoral College The Constitutional system of electing an American President. Elected members of an Electoral College meet to cast their votes for the candidates for the two offices. The successful candidate will usually have received the votes of the majority of members of the College but, occasionally, as in 1876 (and also 2000) the winner takes all system can result in the candidate who has a narrow majority in the popular vote actually losing the election.

Compromise) agreed that the Democrats would accept him as President, even though he had not won the popular vote, providing he promised to withdraw remaining troops from the south. Reconstruction had ended: so had the brief period of optimism regarding civil rights for black Americans.

CONCLUSION

What civil rights had black people gained by 1877?

- Slavery had gone forever.
- There was freedom of movement and freedom to marry.
- Briefly, in the period of 'sunshine' African Americans had been given the right to vote and in a few cases a significant political role, though these rights were soon to end in the southern states.
- Educational opportunities in all states became a reality for thousands of blacks for the first time, though the overall standard of this lagged well behind the white race.
- They had made full use of the right to freedom of worship.

BUT

- Most lacked land, capital or other lucrative employment opportunities: they often ended up working for their former masters.
- The majority of men found themselves barred from voting by 1877 and political opportunities were closed off.
- They lived in fear of intimidation and violence, especially if they attempted to assert their rights.
- More formal segregation of the races was beginning.

What had caused the failure of Reconstruction and the loss of civil rights for black Americans?
- The weakness of southern Republicans contrasted with the determined opposition of most southern whites to accept the concept of civil equality for African Americans.

1865–77 'Standing in the sun.' How far did black Americans acquire civil rights in the period of Reconstruction?

25

- In the north the loss of interest in the welfare of blacks in the south affected many states – racism was increasing there as well: this was fatal to black peoples' chances of maintaining their existing civil rights let alone gaining more.
- Many northerners wished to reconcile whites in the north and south. In 1876/7 this meant ending Reconstruction to avoid the dangers of a re-igniting of the civil war conflict.
- The whole mentality of American freedom ironically worked against the survival of black peoples' civil rights. Federal government intervention on a large scale would have been necessary to preserve, maintain and increase them and to many this was unacceptable.

'It was convenient for Presidents, Senators and Congressmen, few of whom would have made convincing crusaders, to seek the co-operation of the southern leaders, rather than their destruction.'

Hugh Brogan, *Longman History of the United States of America*, 1985

QUESTIONS TO CONSIDER

1. How far did African Americans gain civil rights in Constitutional terms in 1865–77?

2. What problems did black people face working the land in the south after 1865?

3. What barriers stood in the way of black Americans obtaining equality of opportunity between 1865 and 1877?

CHAPTER 2

'Up from slavery'

How far did black civil rights fail to develop between 1877 and 1915?

Hypothesis:

- African Americans lost rather than gained civil rights in this period.

Introduction

After the end of Reconstruction in 1877 the civil rights which had been granted to black people were vulnerable to a growing racist tide of opinion that was at its most intense and virulent in the south but which also had an impact on the growing number of African Americans now living in the north. Poverty was still the norm for the majority of blacks and the development of institutionalised segregation in the south ensured that civil rights were reduced rather than increased in this period. Moreover, the acceptance of white supremacy for the time being was encouraged by the leadership of Booker T. Washington. However, a minority of blacks did make economic progress and, by the end of the period, organisations had been set up to challenge the status quo.

ECONOMIC AND SOCIAL CONDITIONS FOR BLACKS

What was the nature of southern rural poverty?

Throughout this period most African Americans remained in the rural south. Sharecroppers received artificially low prices for their produce and their 'masters' insisted they continue to grow cotton or tobacco. It was an advantage to have cheap workers for such **labour intensive crops.** This gave many freedmen a living but meant they failed to benefit **from the diversification of southern farming**. It also meant they suffered more than most when the **boll weevil** reached the southern states in 1892 and damaged the cotton crop.

'Up from slavery.' How far did black civil rights fail to develop between 1877 and 1915?

27

Despite this rural poverty there was a **slow movement towards more landownership** amongst blacks although the vast majority were still sharecroppers. By 1910, 25 per cent of black farmers owned their land, and their standard of living was rising. However, the economic and social climate in which most blacks lived was not conducive to the awareness and development of civil rights. Day-to-day survival was more important. They had freedom of movement but this was at the expense of stability.

In 1900, almost 90 per cent of African Americans still lived in the south, only one per cent less than 1870. Most migration was from rural areas in the south to the developing southern towns and cities to seek employment. Once there, workers were generally excluded from the rapidly growing textile factories by racist employers anxious to avoid both the perceived tension of blacks and whites working together and the anxiety with which many whites were becoming obsessed: their belief in the undesirability of black men working in close proximity to white women.

How far did black businesses develop in the south?

One of the ironies of formal segregation was that it encouraged the development and the extension of black self-help communities. This now went beyond the churches which had always been at the centre of black community life and blacks sometimes even formed their own trade unions, (see Chapter 6 from page 110). At first capital was lacking for blacks to develop their own businesses but this difficulty could be overcome. African-American enterprises had a guaranteed market and developed **parallel businesses** to their white equivalents serving the black community in fields such as hairdressing and restaurants. Fortified by black ministers, lawyers and other professionals, a small black middle class was developing. Black newspaper editors, reporters and readers gave testimony to their growing literacy rate.

These developments laid the foundations for later civil rights activity led by educated leaders with power and respect in their own communities. However, as Cook (1998) points out, whilst '*a fair degree of dignity and autonomy was imparted by the developing institutions, they offered no concrete threat to the existing socio-economic order on which white dominance was based'.*

What was life like for those who moved north?

Before the First World War some ten per cent of African Americans took advantage of the freedom of movement by leaving the south: for example, small groups of African Americans moved into the New York district of Harlem from the 1880s onwards. The first black **ghetto** had begun to develop. Blacks were frequently barred from trade unions (see Section 2) and returned from work to poor quality but pricey housing.

In the north blacks would find there was no legally determined segregation but they frequently experienced discrimination and their range of employment opportunities, quality of housing, low level of education and effective confinement to specific areas, meant their quality of life did not significantly improve. Also interracial violence remained a prominent feature of their lives. However, there was a greater possibility of franchise in the north and their combined votes were capable of determining the outcome of elections at local levels. There was also a strong black culture developing.

THE DEVELOPMENT OF FORMAL SEGREGATION IN THE SOUTH

How did the Jim Crow laws develop?

Segregation of the races in the south was developing even before the end of Reconstruction in 1877 and was particularly noticeable in the states most heavily populated with African Americans – Mississippi and Alabama.

Jim Crow segregation laws developed rapidly between 1887 and 1891, when eight southern states introduced formal segregation of the races on trains, three of them extending this to waiting room facilities. Train carriages had actually been informally separated in the south for some years before this. It all re-enforced the school segregation laws (common to the southern states) which

KEY TERMS

Ghetto A section of a city occupied by one social or racial group.

Jim Crow Originally a character in an early nineteenth-century minstrel act, the term became a mildly offensive way to refer to black people in a rather stereotyped way. The term then became more fixed towards the end of the century to describe the discriminatory practices of the southern states.

'Up from slavery.' How far did black civil rights fail to develop between 1877 and 1915?

29

had developed immediately after the Civil War in the late 1860s and 1870s.

After 1891 **segregation** laws were formally and rapidly extended to cover **public places** of all kinds.

How significant were the theories of racial superiority?

The movement of African Americans to southern towns helps to explain the developments of segregation laws. Blacks could now rub shoulders much more freely in the unskilled labour market with whites, who saw them as economic competitors needing to be put in their place. Whites feared a new generation of post-slavery African Americans would assert their claims to equality if given the opportunity. This played on the prejudicial feelings of many poorer whites in southern society. The emotional view of this group was that blacks were the natural underclass and there they must stay; they would do whatever it would take to ensure this happened.

This instinct was re-enforced by the increasingly prevalent climate of racism just before 1900. Theories of **social Darwinism** asserted a hierarchy of races. This would provide any pseudo-scientific justification necessary for discrimination against black people (and other non-whites).

That feelings were so intense was connected with the rise of a popular sensationalist press with publications that perpetuated a black stereotype which included laziness, intellectual weakness and a tendency to violence if provoked. White southerners who had doubts about the wisdom or morality of segregation were persuaded that separation could reduce the clear racial tensions of the time and avoid bloodshed.

On these grounds, not educating blacks beyond a certain level was defended and where separate facilities for the different races were provided they would officially be of the same standard but in reality those for blacks were poorer than their white equivalents. Despite the constitutional amendments after the Civil War, southerners were confident that the Supreme Court would not rock their segregation boat and for a time they were proved correct. Earlier decisions such as the Cruikshank case (see pages 24–25) suggested Supreme Court interpretations would favour white supremacist theories.

This confidence was confirmed by the ***Plessy* v. *Ferguson*** Supreme Court case of 1896 which ruled the racial segregation of railway carriages as constitutional and which acted as a **legal precedent** for segregation in all forms of public life. In theory this meant that facilities for whites and blacks must be separate but equal; in reality, they were separate and black facilities were of a lower standard.

THE LOSS OF THE FRANCHISE

Black civil rights and the vote: what was the historical background?

Running parallel to increasing segregation in the 1880s was a campaign to prevent blacks from exercising their civil right to vote. Back in the time of Reconstruction, radical Republicans felt blacks would naturally side with them as their Republican liberators rather than their Democrat oppressors. So, many African-American men had gained the right to vote, some assuming political office. This had rankled with white southerners. Their continuing psychological inability to see the black race as equal was compounded by the fact that the race they so despised had, for a short time under Reconstruction, allied with northern 'intruders' and southern 'traitors' to exercise real political power in the south.

What measures were taken to remove black voting rights?

The Fifteenth Amendment of 1870 (see also Section Four) had outlawed voting discrimination on grounds of race: but it had not outlawed discrimination because of gender or property ownership. So, southern state governments devised complex rules and imposed additional voting requirements which were technically non-racial.

KEY EVENTS

Plessy **v. *Ferguson* 1896 as a legal precedent**
Homer Plessy was a light skinned mulatto (person of mixed race), legally classed as black, who sued after being denied a seat in an all-white railway carriage. The justices decided 8–1 against him that segregation was constitutional. They ruled that separation in itself did not imply inferior treatment. Only Justice John Harlan dissented. His argument that '*our constitution is color blind and neither knows nor tolerates classes among citizens*' was confined (for the moment) to the realms of legal theory. The *Plessy* case created a situation whereby similar cases would look to this *preceding* case as its legal guideline. Thus, in *Cumming* v. *Board of Education* in 1899 the separate but equal principle was extended to schools, even though here the greater amount spent on white schools made a mockery of true equality.

- **Poll Tax** – Before polling, the voter had to make a monetary payment which had to be made well in advance.
- **Property qualifications** – Some states also imposed rules which meant that only those who owned their own home were allowed to vote.
- **Literacy tests** – In Mississippi, literacy tests of 1880 included being able to interpret a section of the Constitution. This process could be arranged so that the questions for uneducated whites were simpler than those for their African-American equivalents.
- Where **primaries** existed to choose party candidates, southern states made moves to ensure all voters were white.
- **Grandfather Clauses** – This was an effective measure to eliminate black but not white votes. The franchise was granted to adult males providing their fathers or grandfathers had voted before Reconstruction, that is before 1867 and the growth in the black franchise.

The change was not immediate and spread at different rates across the southern states. However, by 1910 the near elimination of the African American vote was all but complete in the south.

Why was there no sympathetic reaction in the north to the loss of black civil rights?

Democratic President **Grover Cleveland** did not question white supremacy. However, even Republican controlled Congresses and Republican Presidents were not prepared to interfere: they maintained the Compromise of 1877. The federal system in the USA made the relative independence of the individual states in domestic affairs secure on questions such as voting qualifications or local segregation arrangements. In addition, the position was re-enforced by verdicts of the southern dominated Supreme Court.
Mississippi v. *Williams* in 1898 ruled the Mississippi poll tax and similar devices were constitutional and did not breach the Fifteenth Amendment. This cleared the way for even stricter conditions. The decision undermined black voting rights in the same way that *Plessy* v. *Ferguson* had given the green light to their segregation.

KEY TERMS

The Progressive Movement The Progressives believed that aspects of American society (especially corruption among the very rich) needed reforming. Despite this, Progressives had little to say about civil rights for African Americans.

KEY PEOPLE

Theodore Roosevelt (1858–1919) Elected Vice President in 1900, he became President the following year after the assassination of President McKinley. He supported the Progressive movement but did not really address the question of black civil rights. Despite this, he was criticised by white supremacists for holding official meetings with Booker T. Washington, of whose work he clearly approved.

William Howard Taft (1857–1930) succeeded Roosevelt as President but his style seemed dull and he lacked Roosevelt's political skill. Taft took little interest in black civil rights, regarding it (like most Presidents of the time) as a question of states' rights.

Thomas Woodrow Wilson (1856–1924) was elected President in 1912 and re-elected in 1916. He held typical racist views prevalent in the south at the time. This meant he did not appoint (indeed he dismissed) African Americans or associate with their leaders. He appointed segregationist southerners to his administration, who proceeded to segregate employees by race in the growing number of government agencies.

Even the **Progressive Movement** failed to take action. In the words of Fairclough (2001), as far as northerners were concerned, '*what happened in the south, a region of diminishing economic and political significance, was of secondary importance*'. President **Theodore Roosevelt** showed a passing interest in the conditions of African Americans by discussing matters with black leader Booker T. Washington (see marginal note) as did his successor **President Taft**: but even this ended in 1912 with the election of a southern President, **Woodrow Wilson**. After he entered the White House all black advisors in the federal government were dismissed and executive departments of governments became segregated areas.

OPPRESSION

What did lynching involve?

Southerners did not just rely on the law to deny civil rights to blacks. The period between 1880 and 1910 saw the height of a lynching campaign against African Americans. White mobs would take an African American man and submit him to beatings and torture before murdering him, usually by hanging. After the Civil War and especially the end of Reconstruction, the majority of lynching took the form of attacks on southern black men.

It was alleged that the victim had committed a serious crime such as raping a white woman, an action so vile that it was claimed justice could not wait for the courts but had to be dispensed immediately there and then. This was racism at its rawest and grossest: its removal of legal rights absolute. Moreover, lynching was sometimes regarded as a public event which even children occasionally attended. Southern state governments and police forces did little to stop it.

Cases were rarely brought to court and, if they were, the all-white juries would not convict. As was intended, the constant climate of fear had a huge impact on the whole black community. To speak out against it or oppose it was unusual and extremely brave.

'Up from slavery.' How far did black civil rights fail to develop between 1877 and 1915?

33

A sketch published in the *Illustrated London News*, 8 August 1863, showing a mob lynching a black person in New York's Clarkson Street.

How did Ida B. Wells oppose lynching?

One notable exception was **Ida B. Wells**. She challenged two myths: firstly she showed that alleged rape was often not the cause of lynching and, secondly, she called into question the idea of total white female innocence in some of the alleged rapes. If the first accusation was infuriating to white prejudice, the second was intolerable. After publishing her opinions Wells had to leave her home town of Memphis, Tennessee and move to New York, where she immediately expanded her views in **T. Thomas Fortune's** publication *New York Age*. She continued her message, speaking to branches of the newly formed (1896) National Association of Colored Women.

Given the reforming atmosphere of the progressive era she was frequently received sympathetically. But she failed to gain any commitment from Congress or President for a federal anti-lynching law so that the problem could be tackled in the federal courts. The southern defence, that a federal anti-lynching law would interfere with states' rights, always won the day.

Ida B. Wells (1862–1931) She was born of slave parents in Mississippi. Her campaign against discrimination began in 1884 when she refused to give up her seat on a train to a white man. She was forcibly removed but subsequently sued the railroad company. Her personal courage is particularly highlighted by her public opposition to lynching after some friends who owned a successful grocery store were lynched for 'rape', led by the white owners of a rival store. She was also a staunch advocate of women's rights and of the vote for women (see page 225).

T. Thomas Fortune (1856–1928) Born into slavery in Florida, from 1883–1907 he was editor of the *New York Age*, protesting against the treatment of African Americans. He formed the Afro-American League at the start of 1890 to defend black civil rights, arguing it was '*time to call a halt*' to accommodation. But it collapsed in 1893 through lack of funds. It was later revived as the Afro-American Council in 1898 with Fortune as President. Later he became a supporter of Marcus Garvey (see pages 48–50), edited the *Negro World* from 1923–28 (see pages 48–49). He coined the term Afro-American.

What do lynching and convict leasing reveal about southern white attitudes?

The obsession with rape of white women by black men (figures for which were wildly exaggerated) is revealing. It was feared that liaisons between the races could lead to a mulatto nation and destroy the whole concept of rigid segregation which was developing. At the same time as measures were introduced for segregation and discrimination in voting, southern states introduced miscegenation (literally mixture of races) laws banning inter-racial sexual relations.

A less well known manifestation of hatred was convict leasing. Bankrupt governments would lease out convicts for cash to businessmen, who therefore acquired a useful form of cheap labour. With very long hours the working conditions, especially in the mines, were appalling, the discipline severe, the workers underfed. The system seemed to be an attempt to retain slavery by other means and was much more common in areas of higher black population.

CASE STUDY: BOOKER T. WASHINGTON AND THE CONDITION OF THE AFRICAN AMERICAN

Booker T. Washington (1856–1915) Born into slavery in Virginia and of mixed race parentage, Washington was part of the first generation of children who benefited from the new educational opportunities available after emancipation in 1865. The penniless Washington was so grateful for the opportunity which he received at Hampton that he determined to dedicate his life to ensure that as many members of his race as possible received the same chance. He ran the Tuskegee Institute from 1881 until his sudden death.

It is hardly surprising that some African Americans accepted their situation for the time being and developed a pragmatic approach. Demands for civil rights would be put on hold and a longer term strategy of developing and strengthening their own community would come to the forefront. This was embodied in the career and philosophy of **Booker T. Washington**.

Early life: how did Washington establish his career?

After studying, Washington became a teacher and decided to form his own institute in 1881, in Tuskegee, Alabama. Building up a major organisation he showed powers of administrative ability, leadership and great vision. His personal standards of morality remained high and there was no trace of the financial corruption so noted for this period elsewhere in the USA. He expected others to follow his example. Cleanliness, thrift, punctuality, sobriety and hard work would be notable features of Tuskegee.

'Up from slavery.' How far did black civil rights fail to develop between 1877 and 1915?

35

The development of his Institute coincided with Jim Crow laws, the campaigns to prevent black men voting and the rise in lynching. Washington considered a number of responses to these problems. The idea of African Americans returning to Africa was quickly rejected on the twin grounds of impracticality and lack of desire. However, easy assimilation of the races on equal terms with civil rights for all, seemed even less plausible in the climate of the south in the 1880s and 1890s. Nor was he convinced that a move to the rapidly industrialising north (while appropriate in some individual cases) was the overall answer. He noted that white northerners generally preferred the employment of immigrants from Europe to offering job opportunities to their American brothers and sisters. At the very least, he argued, the black man should acquire some skills first. Reconstruction had caused problems for inexperienced African Americans who had suddenly been given power.

At Tuskegee the emphasis was on literacy and numeracy and practical skills, rather than more theoretical, intellectual accomplishments. As Washington argued, '*cast down your bucket where you are*'. He recruited high quality teachers and inspired other institutions to model themselves on Tuskegee.

Washington realised that the basics learnt at Tuskegee might eventually lead some to follow a more academic education later, as he would have provided the basic education necessary for them to start something more scholarly. He did not think that practical work was all that they were capable of, he just viewed it as a starting point.

What was the importance of the Atlanta Speech in 1895?

In a speech at Atlanta, Georgia in 1895 Washington argued that if whites could regard blacks as potential economic partners rather than dangerous political opponents the race question would eventually be defused.

Vice President William Taft, Booker T. Washington and Andrew Carnegie outside the Tuskegee Institute during the Institute's 25th anniversary celebrations in 1906.

Segregation would be accepted for the time being. '*In all things that are purely social we can be as separate as the fingers, yet one as the hand in all things essential to mutual progress*'. The emphasis for black people should be on education and economic opportunity rather than agitating for social equality in general and voting rights in particular.

The speech had an instant impact. The ideas expressed became known as the Atlanta Compromise, an attempt by blacks to reach an **accommodation** with the white dominated south. Coming six months after the death of Frederick Douglass (see page 17), it catapulted Booker T. Washington into the leadership of the southern black community. Douglass had toned down his campaigns in his later years and had not led any prominent protest against the segregation and voting laws that were undermining the position of African Americans shortly before his death. Also, the absence of any other outstanding black figure at this time, the continuing success of Tuskegee, and the apparent fruitlessness of a more confrontational policy, paved the way for Washington's pre-eminence.

How did Washington cement his reputation?

One of Washington's greatest triumphs here was to gain the interest of President Theodore Roosevelt (see page 33). Roosevelt frequently consulted Washington on African-American questions and invited him to tea in the White House.

In 1900 Washington organised the Negro Business League, to act as a national centre for black chambers of commerce. The publication of Washington's autobiography *Up From Slavery* in 1901 further added to his fame.

What were the arguments of Washington's critics?

By 1901 Washington had a growing number of critics from the African-American community. They argued that he seemed to accept the idea of white supremacy and was making no attempt to challenge the lower social position of the African American. It was true that Washington was not using his position to challenge either the wilder, violent side of control (the lynching mentality) or the political control of stopping blacks from voting. Washington irritated his detractors by playing down the importance of the ballot. The dramatic improvements in the living standards of the African-American community after the Voting Rights Act was finally passed in 1965 (see page 74–75), bears out their criticism.

Despite Washington's efforts, the educational gap between black and white was widening. After 1900, rapidly increasing spending on white schools was not matched in the African American sector.

W.E.B. Du Bois came to regard Washington's views as limited and even dangerous for the future development of the black race. In 1903 his book, *The Souls of Black Folk*, was published with a chapter entitled '*Of Mr Booker T. Washington and Others*'. De Bois, believed that what Washington was suggesting was necessary but hardly sufficient to provide a base for black advances. He was concerned that Washington's approach seemed to have nothing to say about the disastrous developments of segregation and the loss of the franchise.

Did Washington change his views?

Washington was hurt by these criticisms. Over-sensitive and finding debate with men like Du Bois difficult, the Tuskegean leader resorted to accusations of jealousy and political ambition against his opponents. However, Washington's admirers remained sufficiently numerous that, for a time, he could afford to dismiss his critics. In his later years Washington became aware that his policy was not working. The lack of progress in civil rights and the violent unforgiving attitude of many southern whites to black people seemed to ignore the genuine progress made by some African Americans. In private he gave money to finance challenges to segregation laws and, while rarely writing them himself, he encouraged others to publish articles critical of the way separate development and legal treatment of blacks was progressing. He felt that too much

William Edward Burghardt Du Bois (1868–1963) Born in Massachusetts, the son of free black parents, he acquired a PhD from Harvard University, the first African American to do so, in 1895. A prolific writer on the black condition and an early sociologist, he helped to found the Niagara movement in 1905 and National Association for the Advancement of Colored People in 1909 (see pages 40–42). He then moved away from the NAACP's approach. In the McCarthyism era after 1945, he was persecuted as a suspected Communist: this experience actually made him into one and his views had completely changed from his younger days. He emigrated to Ghana in 1961.

open criticism could undermine his position of strength in the white community.

Conclusion: What was the contribution of Booker T. Washington to civil rights?

- His own advancement from slave to College Principal provided an inspiring example for his fellow African Americans.
- Washington set strict standards of behaviour and self-discipline which were extremely valuable for his students.
- Between 1895 to at least 1905 and arguably for a further ten years, he was the main leader and spokesman of the black race in the USA.
- He developed many valuable contacts for the African American race in the white dominated political world of the US.
- His long term aim was to show the white race by example that blacks could equal them in qualities such as hard work and practical skills.

BUT

- His policy appeared to accept the lower position for blacks in American society that many blacks and some whites felt was unacceptable.
- He focused on working within the system, rather than trying to change the system itself.
- His negative view of the importance of the vote for African Americans brought him much criticism.
- After 1905 his position as leader of America's black population was increasingly questioned by the African Americans themselves though he remained popular with many whites.
- Washington's suspicion – even paranoia – regarding criticism of him produced further questioning of his effectiveness as a black leader. He had done little for civil rights.

'Up from slavery.' How far did black civil rights fail to develop between 1877 and 1915?

39

THE DEVELOPMENT OF A BLACK CIVIL RIGHTS MOVEMENT

What was the Niagara movement?

Washington was criticised by writers such as Du Bois and the editorials in the *Boston Guardian* written with verve, style and a touch of satire by **William Monroe Trotter**, who denounced Washington's policies as accommodationist. Du Bois and Trotter helped to found the Niagara movement in 1905, which developed from a meeting held in Canada, in the city of Niagara Falls. Meeting by the great waterfall tied in with the '*mighty current of change*' they believed was required in the American approach to the welfare of its black citizens. They wanted a campaign to restore voting rights and to abolish all discrimination. It was a rejection of Washington's cautious approach, and put the emphasis on protest to demand civil rights.

Niagara was never likely to become a mass movement. Du Bois and many others (though not Trotter) had an academic approach to the question of black civil rights and, though they praised working people, did not always relate to them. Washington was likely to become too confrontational. Also, from the start Niagara lacked money and effective organisation and achieved little that was concrete. It was superseded by the development of the NAACP (see below). However, it did outline clear principles of the belief in black equality, particularly legal equality, as well as equal employment and educational opportunities. It was well supported by women and it backed the campaign for women's suffrage and demanded an end to the convict lease system, a clear illustration of how this system was regarded as racist in its application (see page 35).

How did the NAACP begin? The Springfield Riot and its effects

Nevertheless the Niagara movement had provided an impetus to the growing number of blacks who wished to challenge the Booker T. Washington approach. The trigger for change was a serious race **riot at Springfield**, Illinois in 1908. As a direct response to this, a meeting was held in

National Association for the Advancement of Colored People (NAACP) Founded in 1909 the year after the Springfield riot, it was the first successful, nationwide, civil rights organisation to campaign systematically for black civil rights and gain a large membership of both black and white supporters. It remained a peaceful and Constitutional organisation. Its successes were rarely spectacular but it played a significant long-term role in the fight for the legal end of segregation.

National Conference of the Negro The following statement was issued: '*Often plundered of their just share of the public funds, robbed of nearly all part in the government, segregated by common carriers, some murdered with impunity , all treated with open contempt by officials they are held in some states in practical slavery*'.

New York where Du Bois teamed up with other **leading African-American civil rights campaigners,** both black and white, to form the first proper civil rights organisation, the **National Association for the Advancement of Colored people (NAACP)**. Meeting at the **National Conference of the Negro** in May 1909 they issued a passionate denunciation of the treatment of African Americans. Du Bois, unlike some other black leaders such as William Monroe Trotter, was keen to see as many white people as possible join the movement. He was becoming convinced that the American academic community was starting to reject the flawed science behind racial superiority and that they could lend their weight to the campaign for equality and civil rights.

How did the NAACP operate as a civil rights organisation?

The aims of the NAACP were to investigate racism, publicise it, suggest positive solutions and take legal action to enforce the law and the Constitution to ensure civil rights in general and equality of opportunity in particular. It adopted a constitutional approach to lawsuits believing, that many of the measures taken against African Americans violated the constitutional amendments passed between 1865 and 1870. Others agreed: for the first time a Supreme Court ruling backed their case. In 1915 in the legal case *Guinn* v. *US* the grandfather clauses in the state constitutions of Maryland and Oklahoma were outlawed.

The swift early impact of the NAACP inspired the development of the Nation Urban League, set up in 1911 to look after the welfare of African Americans in northern cities. Though not directly a civil rights organisation and having little impact in the south, the NUL did campaign against discrimination in jobs and housing. Despite the presence of Du Bois, most of the early leaders of the NAACP were white, which led to debate about the whole question of race co-operation in the fight for equality. It was a discussion still going on in an amended form in the 1960s. Du Bois played a crucial role in the NAACP: he edited its magazine *Crisis* for over twenty years. The increasing circulation of this magazine began to fulfil necessary ingredients for civil rights success: greater

'Up from slavery.' How far did black civil rights fail to develop between 1877 and 1915?

41

awareness, not least in the north, of the black predicament, powerful arguments for change and the refusal of African Americans to accept their lot.

CONCLUSION: HOW FAR HAD AFRICAN AMERICANS LOST RATHER THAN GAINED CIVIL RIGHTS BETWEEN 1877 AND 1915?

- The active political role at lower (and occasionally higher) levels of government that some African Americans gained in the south during Reconstruction had disappeared. There were no African Americans in Congress by 1915 or even in state legislatures.
- The right of the black man to vote had been systematically removed in the south (and on occasions less systematically in the north) by a series of state laws of doubtful constitutional validity but upheld by the legal system.
- It was extremely difficult to challenge white political domination, especially in the south.
- As blacks disappeared from voting registers they lost any right to serve on juries and give their own race any chance of legal equality.
- Violent threats in general and lynching in particular, produced a climate of fear in many black communities which impoverished their quality of life even if they were not directly attacked themselves.
- Segregation laws had formalised, cemented and increased a separation of the races in the south. The development of public transport in this period merely produced additional opportunities for the more humiliating forms of segregation.

It is true to say that:

- Equal opportunities in education had never existed for African Americans.
- There had never been a chance of a fair trial if the colour of your skin was not white.
- Chances of receiving a formal education did increase for blacks in this period but not as much as for whites.

However, there were a few encouraging signs:

- African Americans were still free to leave the south and were doing so in increasing numbers.
- The Tuskegee machine had improved economic opportunities for African Americans.
- By the end of the period a civil rights protest movement had begun to be developed with the NAACP.

- With the sudden death of Booker T. Washington in 1915 and the increasing impact of the world war, thousands were now joining the organisation and the wisdom of blacks meekly accepting their oppression was being increasingly challenged.

> *'By 1900 the south's black population was more powerless than at any other time since the death of slavery.'*
>
> Adam Fairclough, *Better day Coming*

QUESTIONS TO CONSIDER

1. Why did more formal segregation of African Americans develop in the south after Reconstruction?

2. In what ways did Booker T. Washington's critics feel that he impeded the development of black civil rights?

3. Why did a more organised civil rights movement develop after 1908?

'Up from slavery.' How far did black civil rights fail to develop between 1877 and 1915?

43

CHAPTER 3

1915–41 'A nation within a nation'?

How far were the foundations laid for black civil rights?

Hypothesis:

- Presidents, Congress and the Supreme Court gave only limited support to black Civil Rights at this time.

MIGRATION AND THE FIRST WORLD WAR

The Great Migration: Why did blacks move north?

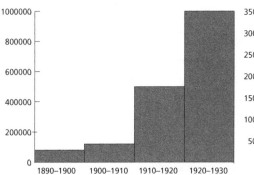

Graph showing the number of African Americans moving north.

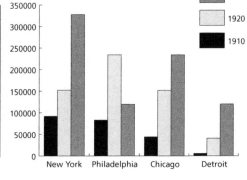

African-American movement to major cities in the north.

As the graphs show, the numbers of African Americans moving north dramatically increased after the First World War. Indeed, the impact of the First World War on the United States was felt long before the country entered the conflict in 1917. In 1914 two factors increased employment opportunities in the north – there was a sudden drying up of the European immigrant labour force and the armaments industry was expanding rapidly to supply the war combatants (see Chapter 6, page 110). Black workers now poured in from the south and this did not stop with the ending of the war in November 1918

The melting pot The idea
that all the different peoples
living in the United States
would minimise their
differences in cultural, racial
and religious background to
integrate harmoniously,
producing an American
identity. The question of
whether this kind of
integration was superior to
maintaining equality though
respecting cultural and other
differences between the
various groups was becoming
a major discussion point,
which is still debated today.

KEY IDEAS

**African Americans
served with distinction**
The 369th Infantry division –
the 'Harlem hellfighters'
produced the first two black
American soldiers to receive
the French gallantry medal,
the Croix de Guerre. No black
soldier was convicted of
disloyalty during the war.

KEY EVENTS

**Chicago race riots July
1919** A teenage black boy
accidentally drifted towards the
'whites only' section on Lake
Michigan beach. He was
stoned, and then drowned.
Thirteen days of sporadic
violence followed when Irish
and Polish workers attacked
the city's black ghettos, leaving
23 black and 15 white people
dead and 1,000, mainly black,
families homeless. This frenzied
reaction indicated that race
hatred could be just as virulent
in the north and was not
confined to those of Anglo-
Saxon origin.

since the rapid growth of the American economy in the
1920s continued the demands for more workers.

In the south, segregation, inequality and lack of the
franchise partly caused this acceleration in migration to the
north as did rigid segregation and discrimination, and the
climate of fear engendered by lynching. Moreover, in the
south, African Americans were constantly made to feel
inferior. Feelings of insecurity were strong and blacks were
sacked at the merest excuse. Economically, sharecroppers
were poorly off and increasingly badly affected by the
ravages of the boll weevil (see page 27). At the same time
there were pull factors attracting people north. People who
were already there sent stories south about better
conditions, voting rights and steady employment. But
unlike some of the immigrants from Europe they did not
integrate into **the melting pot** so easily.

What were the experiences of those African Americans who went to war?

Over 350,000 blacks served in the First World War,
although only 40,000 of these saw active service and 1,300
black officers were commissioned. About half of those
drafted went to France. They **served with distinction** in
segregated regiments fighting alongside French colonial
troops rather than their fellow Americans. The experience
broadened their horizons on the question of racial equality.
This process would occur again on a larger scale in the
Second World War but even at this earlier stage it
stimulated campaigning for more equality.

POST WAR DIFFICULTIES

Why was 1919 such a difficult year?

White soldiers returned home to find that their jobs had
been taken – many by African Americans. This tension
produced a brief but intense period of social unrest, with
race riots in Chicago. Ghettos rapidly developed in many
cities as more and more African Americans arrived and
housing covenants prevented blacks from moving outside
the area where they had first settled. It seemed that
'unofficially' segregation had moved north as the Chicago

riots had persuaded the authorities that segregation was necessary to keep the peace. For many blacks, freedom of movement in the sense of choosing a home had disappeared.

Was life in the north better for black Americans?

Though the problems were different in nature from the south, African Americans found civil rights in the north very limited. The ghetto had a direct effect on education. Neighbourhood schools became segregated *de facto* rather than *de jure* because of population patterns. Much less money was spent on education for black children and they rarely had the privilege of being taught by the most successful teachers (see Chapter 4). There was also severe discrimination in employment particularly in clerical work and the more skilled unionised trades (see Chapter 6, page 110). There were some advantages for blacks living in the northern states. Unlike the south, lynching was not publicly condoned and was therefore less common; if blacks were on the voting register (which they were in many northern states) they were also eligible to be jurors. Trials were sometimes fairer and more open. The institutional racism normal in the south was much patchier in its application in the north. However, there was still segregation, discrimination and, in places, desperate poverty for blacks. In short, in the north African Americans were the victims of *de facto* rather than *de jure* discrimination. This led to a lack of confidence, frustration and bitterness to the extent that it could be argued that life was little better in the north for many of the poorer and less well-qualified African Americans.

Did movement north increase black consciousness?

Just as segregation had encouraged the development of a separate black culture and way of life in the south, so the less formal *de facto* rather than *de jure* segregation in the north encouraged a similar process. There was an out-pouring of writers, poets, musicians and painters from black society. Indeed, the 1920s became known as the 'Jazz age'. Many of the talented black people discovered during this period emerged from the poverty and squalor of Harlem and other impoverished areas, so that the

KEY TERMS

Black consciousness Acute awareness of your black racial identity, partly caused by a society that treated people in an inferior manner because of your racial background. It led many to investigate their own racial roots and to emphasise their own cultural heritage.

A bus showing the areas for whites at the front and blacks at the back.

Harlem Renaissance An out-pouring of artistic talent by blacks in the 1920s and 1930s in literature, the visual arts, theatre and music. African-American artistic performers were now praised by critics and publicly acknowledged. Leading figures included Paul Robeson (actor and singer), Langston Hughes (poet), Louis Armstrong (trumpeter and bandleader), Bessie Smith (singer), James Van Der Dee (photographer), Aaron Douglas (painter) and Duke Ellington (composer). For the first time there were black people singing and writing about their experiences and desire for equality and freedom.

movement became known as the **Harlem Renaissance.** However, Harlem showed up the kind of *de facto* rather *de jure* segregation developing in the north; the top jazz nightclubs were owned and operated by whites and the only blacks allowed inside were the performers, prostitutes and kitchen hands. A significant black middle-class developed who had more educational opportunities and as a result there were more black professionals and businesses than ever before. It should be noted that these developments in the 1920s were mainly confined to black men.

A jazz group of the 1920s.

CASE STUDY: MARCUS GARVEY AND UNIA 1917–25

These social changes were briefly but effectively exploited with the emergence of a charismatic black leader, the Jamaican **Marcus Garvey**, who came to the US in 1916. He built up a rapid and dynamic following within a year but in the mid-1920s his downfall was nearly as fast. Nonetheless, he was for a few years the best-known leader of African Americans and his ideas, though seemingly unproductive at the time, were to have a considerable impact on the next generation of black leaders putting forward the idea of 'Black Power' (see Chapter 5).

What were Garvey's ideas?

Marcus Garvey was initially inspired by Booker T. Washington's work at Tuskegee. Garvey's **Universal Negro Improvement Association (UNIA)** began in 1914 in his native Jamaica. Garvey wished to go further than Washington in his approach to improving the lives of blacks including not just economic progress and white acceptance of black equality, but blacks taking control of their own affairs.

Garvey ultimately saw a return to Africa as the only solution but he always remained vague about specific details of a 'back to Africa' move. In the short term Garvey believed that blacks should concentrate on building up their own education and their own businesses. He encouraged them to have pride in themselves and their culture. His message was so well received that Garvey decided to stay and develop UNIA in the US.

Why was Garvey so successful?

In the tense atmosphere of 1917 his movement made substantial progress. In June, Garvey's speech in Harlem was wildly cheered and in December he moved his base to New York. Garvey made use of the growing interest in black newspapers to launch his own, *The Negro World*, which was partly funded by small contributions from his supporters, often northern blacks who had been earning the best wages of their lives in the last two or three years of the war. Garvey was also an effective orator who could hold

KEY PEOPLE

Marcus Garvey (1887–1940) Born in Jamaica, he originally worked as a printer leading a strike in 1908/9. He arrived in the US in March 1916 and decided to stay, founding the first American branch of his organisation UNIA in 1917, becoming quickly an important figure in the discussion over how black civil rights could best be achieved. He was imprisoned in 1925 and deported from the US in 1927. He continued his journalistic work in exile in the 1930s.

KEY TERMS

Universal Negro Improvement Association (UNIA) The aim of the organisation was to help '*the new and rising Negro give expression to his feelings*' as Garvey asserted in a speech in February 1923 and to gain for blacks '*the industrial, social, political and religious emancipation*' of the race by campaigning for equal rights and for the independence of the black race rather than it being absorbed into an equal melting pot in the US. It would not campaign to ask a white US government to improve the lives of blacks (which is what they saw the NAACP as doing) but rather encourage them to develop their own means of salvation through their own efforts and developing their own institutions, trying for example to set up factories, hotels and printing presses run by blacks.

KEY IDEAS

Ritual pageantry Garvey organised open-air parades through Harlem. He was driven in a special car wearing a military style uniform and describing himself as the 'provisional president of Africa'.

KEY TERMS

Black Eagle Star Steamship line Garvey purchased four ships for merchant navy purposes as an ambitious publicity venture and an investment opportunity for better off blacks; but after initial successes the line soon ran into financial difficulties.

KEY IDEAS

Garvey must go Garvey was attacked by Chandler Owen in his socialist magazine *The Messenger*. Garvey's black opponents in the black trade unions and the NAACP came together in a group called the Friends of Negro Freedom, to try to highlight Garvey's shortcomings as a leader to his supporters.

KEY EVENTS

Garvey left the USA In 1925 he was arrested and imprisoned for mail fraud. He claimed (possibly with some justification) that the charges against him had been trumped up by his enemies. On his release in 1929 he was deported back to Jamaica where he became briefly involved in the island's politics. Though UNIA continued, Garvey never returned to the US and their conferences in 1936–38 were held just over the Canadian border. He died in England in 1940.

a crowd. Many blacks saw him as the new leader to replace the recently deceased Booker T. Washington. The immediate post-war ferment also aided Garvey's dramatic rise. He argued that African Americans needed to be proud of their African heritage. This appealed to the ghetto-residing blacks who liked Garvey's use of **ritual pageantry** and could relate to his ideas.

What were the strengths and weaknesses of Garvey's movement?

Garvey felt that attempts by blacks at integration were pointless. But Du Bois (who changed his own views later) reflected a common opinion that Garvey was on the wrong track. However, Garvey struck a chord with working-class blacks who were starting to believe that true equality of the races in the United States would never come. His proud assertion of self-awareness was hopeful to those persecuted and living in urban squalor. Garvey's idea of a shipping line – the **Black Star line** – proved popular.

Garvey's approach had fundamental weaknesses from the beginning; he lacked a political strategy and seemed more concerned with fancy ventures than addressing immediate economic and social concerns for black people. His developments ran into economic problems. As the immediate post-war rioting and racial tension died down so ardour cooled for UNIA.

Suspicions about Garvey increased when he held talks with the KKK in 1922 and when a critical colleague, James Easton, was murdered on New Year's Day 1923. '**Garvey Most Go**' became a catchphrase and not long afterwards **he left the USA**.

What is the overall assessment of Marcus Garvey?

Garvey anticipated many of the later ideas of the Black Power movement (see Chapter 5) and had come nearer to mobilising mass black action than any other black leader up until this time. This confirmed the need for African Americans to help themselves and be concerned with **racial uplift**. It was not coincidence that the next wave of Black Power thinking began to develop at the same time as movements demanding liberation from imperial control swept Africa in the 1950s and early 1960s.

THE PROGRESS OF CIVIL RIGHTS IN THE NORTH AND SOUTH IN THE 1920S

Did the situation change for black Americans in the south?

Many black southerners were too preoccupied with making a living to be involved with civil rights movements. Lacking the educational opportunities to articulate their opposition, they found segregation a barrier to their learning. Moreover, white southerners made attempts to keep radical literature out of their states, though radical black northern newspapers did infiltrate. In this atmosphere, southern white liberals were unsurprisingly cautious. They were worried, for example, that a **federal anti-lynching law** would anger segregationist whites and undermine the liberties of the federal system which the south enjoyed.

Were African Americans ready to lead their own civil rights movement?

The steady development of a black middle class and the consequent social stratification in black society had clear implications for civil rights on the questions of leadership and solidarity. Could those who articulated the grievances of the black community find effective tactics and unite sufficiently to develop a proper movement? **Oscar de Priest** did get elected to Congress in 1928, the first African American to do so since 1900, but his was a lone voice.

What was the importance of the NAACP?

Between the World Wars (and particularly after the fall of Marcus Garvey), the organisation that embodied the civil rights campaign most clearly was the NAACP. Led by both blacks and whites, it adopted an approach more vigorous than Washington's though still legal and constitutional. It was (and remains) a national organisation with branches all over the US. It focussed on Civil Rights rather than social conditions and its Secretary in the 1920s, James Welson Johnson, targeted desegration voting rights and education.

Walter White (1893–1955)
Secretary of the NAACP
1930–55. Having
organisational and personal
skills he had good relations
with many influential white
political figures.

**The tragedy of Elaine,
Arkansas 1919** It began
with a meeting of black
people, the Progressive
Farmers and Household
Union of America, who were
demanding better money for
their cotton crops. Two white
officials who arrived at the
meeting (and may have been
trying to break it up) were
shot in disputed
circumstances. One was
wounded and one killed. As a
result, mobs of whites
attacked the local black
community. Police arrested all
blacks at the meeting and
numerous others, claiming a
'black insurrection' for which
there was no evidence. Many
blacks were wrongfully
convicted of affray. There were
many African-American
fatalities but the death toll
estimates vary from 20 to 250.
The NAACP successfully
appealed to the Supreme
Court to get the African-
Americans' convictions
overturned.

These themes were continued by the new secretary. **Walter White**, in the 1930s.

What were the policies and fortunes of the NAACP?

The NAACP believed the races should live, work and be educated together. It would take cases to federal courts (and the Supreme Court if necessary) cases that would establish the equal rights of the African American. Though non-violent the NAACP raised money to defend those accused of rioting. Lobbying rather than mass action was the central policy. One of its campaigns was for a federal anti-lynching law. Though unsuccessful, this raised awareness of the issue all over the US and contributed to the decline in lynching.

The growth of NAACP membership was rapid after 1915. By the early 1920s there were over 90,000 members, reflecting the greater interest in civil rights. But these had been exceptional times. By 1930 there had been a decline to 50,000. The NAACP developed a reputation for a cautious and bureaucratic outlook. Also, it was run by middle-class African Americans and whites and therefore it did not relate so clearly to the large deprived section of the African-American community. This was a difficult task, though, as Martin Luther King showed 25 years later, not an impossible one.

In the north, opposition to the NAACP was usually peaceful. In the south it seemed that almost the entire white community was violently against it. It discouraged many leaders of the organisation from even trying to speak in the south. The only successes for the NAACP were when they used the Courts, such as after the riots at **Elaine, Arkansas**.

How important was Communist Party support for the civil rights movement?

After the Wall Street Crash of 1929 (see Chapter 7), and the decline of UNIA, civil rights activity was at a low ebb. American Communists adopted a new militant approach. They had developed rapidly for a short period in the favourable climate when they could take advantage of

1915–41 'A nation within a nation'? How far were the foundations laid for black civil rights?

51

labour unrest around 1919–21. The party recruited about 7,000 black supporters who were either homeless and unemployed blacks in the north or segregated sharecroppers in the south and they also organised the legal defence in the case of the **Scottsboro Boys**. Their Party membership rose in 1934 when they were ordered by the Communist Soviet Union to change strategy and ally with other groups in their fight against Fascism. When a National Negro Congress was formed in 1934 it soon became influenced by the Communists but its attempts at boycotting stores where blacks were discriminated against failed to produce a large scale response.

Communist successes were few. From the start, civil rights leaders tended to distance themselves from the movement for fear of prejudice by association, a problem particularly acute after the Second World War (see Chapter 4). Trade Union leader Philip Randolph (see Chapter 7) made a sharp distinction between democratic socialism and more dictatorial Communism, though he did support the **National Negro Congress** for a time. Many others saw Communist rejection of capitalist democracy and allegiance to a foreign power, the Soviet Union, as un-American. It would take courage for African Americans to become Communist Party members and the party never succeeded in mobilising blacks on a large scale. In August 1939 when Communists approved Stalin's pact with Hitler, they lost a lot of the limited support they possessed.

WHITE REACTION

The revival of the Ku Klux Klan

The increase in resentment and fear amongst southern whites towards blacks is illustrated by the re-formation of the Ku Klux Klan in Atlanta, Georgia in 1915 organised by **William Simmons.** Communist growth, though greatly exaggerated, did aid the revival of the KKK. Even before this, however, D.W. Griffith's film *The Birth of a Nation* in 1915 was sensationally successful both in glorifying the old Klan and presenting a brutal stereotype of the African American.

Hiram Evans (1881–1966)
was also from Alabama and
ousted Simmons from the head
position of Imperial Wizard of
the KKK. Under his leadership
the target of hate was widened to
include a variety of racial and
religious groups that were not
'WASPS' –White Anglo-Saxon
Protestants.

Theodore Bilbo (1877–1947)
was born into a poor Mississippi
family. He became Mississippi
Governor 1916–20 and 1928–32
and a Senator from 1934 until
his death. In crude language he
violently opposed any votes for
black people hinting at what
should be 'done' to them if they
tried. Dubbed 'America's most
notorious merchant of hatred'.

**Eugene Talmadge (1884–
1946)** came from a Georgia
farming family and wrote
articles for agricultural journals.
Governor of Georgia 1932–36,
1940–42 and re-elected again
in 1946 but he died at the end
of the year before assuming
office. A controversial figure,
with similar racist views to
Bilbo, his own son claimed that
'one-third of Georgians would
follow him into hell while
another third wanted him in
hell'.

**None were of sufficient
calibre** Talmadge and Bilbo
were both efficient governors but
in order to win office they still
relied on the racist card more
than Long. They were popular
with the agricultural community,
Bilbo especially identifying with
the poorer white farmers.

However, after **Hiram Evans** took over as leader in 1922 the KKK widened its targets. While it was just as racist as ever, blacks were now seen as largely pitiable creatures, whose social threat to society was seen as less serious than the religious threat of Roman Catholics and Jews and the political challenge of Communism. The Klan infiltrated and split the Democrat Party in the south.

In the north the organisation remained a shady affair with limited support, but in the south its backing of capitalism, old time religion and 'traditional' American virtues meant that at its height in 1924, it claimed over five million members and had certainly risen dramatically from the 100,000 of 1921. Once again its hooded figures openly paraded the streets, burning crosses in the night and intimidating, beating, mutilating and murdering its victims. The Klan's fall was as rapid as its rise. Corruption of local officials was exposed, much to the movement's embarrassment. By 1930 barely 30,000 members remained, largely because segregation and the traditional white southern way of life did not seem threatened.

How popular were southern racist politicians?

The majority of white southerners neither supported black civil rights nor showed sympathy towards the Klan. States run by the Democrats were one party affairs which intended to maintain the status quo – segregation, cheap black labour, a white electorate suspicious of any attempt at federal interference and a one race legal system to enforce it all; in short, white supremacy.

With the exception of Huey P. Long of Louisiana, most of the southern politicians were keen segregationists. **Theodore Bilbo** of Mississippi suggested that all African Americans should return to Africa, while Georgia's **Eugene Talmadge** attacked integrated education. There is no doubting the political popularity of these men who were continually re-elected to public office. Apart from Long, **none were of sufficient calibre** not to play the race card and gained votes from uneducated, uncaring, or downright hostile racists. This kind of populist racism was to continue into the 1960s and made life more difficult for any civil rights movement.

1915–41 'A nation within a nation'? How far were the foundations laid for black civil rights?

53

The depression of the thirties meant that white working-class southern attitudes to equality of opportunity for blacks stalled at just the time when the climate of educated opinion in the US more widely, was moving in favour of racial equality. Southerners were skating on constitutionally thin ice. The *Plessy* case of 1896 (see page 31) was the backbone for the continuation of segregation on a separate but equal basis. But, quite deliberately, facilities were not equal. In 1930 for every seven dollars spent on white schools just two were spent on black schools in the south. In the following ten years statistics like these would provide the lawyers of the NAACP their method of claiming civil rights for blacks.

FEDERAL AND COURT ATTITUDES

Were US Presidents of any assistance to African American civil rights in the 1920s and 1930s?

In this period Presidents showed limited interest in the black civil rights question. Woodrow Wilson, a broken and sick man in 1921, was replaced by Warren Harding who considered that with regard to race relations the south had a *'superior understanding'* of the problem, a clear indication he was not going to intervene. After his sudden death in 1923 his replacement, **Calvin Coolidge**, took an apparently more positive line but it came to nothing. **Herbert Hoover,** the last Republican President to receive large-scale support from blacks in an election, was no friend to African-American civil rights.

With Presidents indifferent, incompetent, preoccupied or powerless and **with southern Democrats occupying leading positions in Congress,** federal intervention seemed unlikely in the twenties. When Democrat, **Franklin D. Roosevelt** was elected President in 1932 he was certainly not incompetent and not as indifferent to black civil rights as may appear at first sight. However, he argued that he was preoccupied with *'saving America'* and that, paradoxically, this rendered him powerless to do much for African Americans. In 1933 Roosevelt frankly told the NAACP Secretary, Walter White**,** that to get his **New Deal** Programme (see pages 126–30) through

KEY PEOPLE

Calvin Coolidge (1872–1933) Early on in his presidency he declared that the rights of twelve million blacks were as *'sacred'* as everyone else. However, he took a passive view of the presidency (i.e. he let Congress take the initiative).

Herbert Hoover (1874–1964) It was his attempt to appoint a racist Supreme Court Judge that the NAACP successfully opposed in 1930 (see page 51). He had resorted to the race card to win over Democrats to his Republican Party, a move as unedifying as it was unsuccessful.

KEY CONCEPTS

Southern Democrats holding leading positions in Congress Roosevelt was faced with an alliance of Republicans and more conservative Democrats against his New Deal plans. He believed passing his legislation through Congress would be impossible if he offended southern Democrats with a policy of civil rights for African Americans.

KEY EVENTS

New Deal This was a set of initiatives and programmes led by Roosevelt after he took office in 1933, to try and stimulate economic growth and employment after the depression which followed the Wall Street crash in 1929 (see pages 125–26).

Franklin D. Roosevelt (1882–1945) came from a wealthy New York family and was a distant cousin of Theodore Roosevelt. Senator (Democrat) 1910; unsuccessful vice presidential candidate 1920. In 1921 he contracted polio after which he was unable to stand unaided. Governor of New York 1928–32 when he was elected President. Although personally sympathetic to the plight of African Americans, he did little directly to help them, partly because he was dependent on southern Democrats for passing legislation. Re-elected (uniquely) three times in 1936, 1940 and 1944.

Eleanor Roosevelt (1884–1962) was the niece of Theodore Roosevelt and cousin of her eventual husband, Franklin. She became more acutely aware of racism after becoming the President's wife in 1933 and travelling around the nation. She publicly supported the NAACP's Anti-Lynching Bill in the 1930s to the embarrassment of her husband.

James Cleveland (Jesse) Owens (1913–80) was born in Alabama. After winning his medals he received no advertising endorsement deals like the white athletes. Awarded the American Medal of Freedom by President Ford in 1976.

Congress, he had to rely on southern Democratic support. If he insisted on federal action on black civil rights he would lose the support of the southern Democrats for his vital programme. It was not to be the last time that an apparently strong President felt unable to act positively on civil rights. The black civil rights movement received more encouragement from the President's wife, First Lady **Eleanor Roosevelt**. Her frequent support of black causes and black women in particular, was noticeable.

What impact did Roosevelt's New Deal have on the black community?

Blacks praised Roosevelt's attempts to encourage the raising of wages and cutting of working hours. By 1935, 30 per cent of black families were on relief compared with 10 per cent of whites. This illustrated their greater poverty but also the fair application of the policy towards them.

However, urban black unemployment rates were high (see Chapter 7). In the south the black sharecroppers were hit hard by the depression, as they were not covered by the Social Security Act or the National Labor Relations Act that assisted so many others. This was not merely bad luck. Southern Democrats had refused to vote for a measure that would particularly help blacks.

Sport and entertainment

Limited progress was being made towards the acceptance of the black race in sport and entertainment. The triumph of **Jesse Owens**, winner of four gold medals in the 1936 Olympic Games, challenged the idea of racial superiority. In films Hattie McDaniel became the first African American to win an Oscar, in Gone with the Wind in 1940. Opposition to racist theories is illustrated by the large **public protest** when black classical singer Marian Anderson was refused permission to sing in Constitution Hall, Washington by the White women's group Daughters of the American Revolution, comprised of descendants of those who fought in the War of Independence.

How helpful were Supreme Court decisions for black civil rights between 1915 and 1939?

With the federal, executive and legislative routes to aid civil rights apparently blocked, the NAACP turned to the courts and ultimately the federal Supreme Court. It was a lengthy journey. Since the end of Reconstruction, Supreme Court rulings had interpreted civil rights very narrowly (see Chapter 2). There was a success early in 1917 when, in *Buchanan* v. *Warley*, city regulations in Louisville, Kentucky concerning residential segregation were found to be unconstitutional; but the judgement had been based on property rights, something that hardly boded well for an attack on one of the largest issues in civil rights – segregation in public places.

Another favourable and more significant verdict for legal rights of African Americans came in 1923 when *Moore* v. *Dempsey* failed to uphold the death sentences of twelve blacks because their trials had been 'dominated by mobs'. The verdict may have been another factor in hastening the increasing unacceptability of lynching in the south.

Did the Supreme Court verdicts change in the 1930s?

With an increasing number of legal cases coming forward, *Trudeau* v. *Barnes* in 1933 insisted on all state appeals being exhausted before cases could come before the Supreme Court. This emphasised the slowness of the tactic of legal appeals that the NAACP had adopted.

By the late 1930s the composition of the Supreme Court was starting to change after a period of stability. As elderly justices died, Roosevelt was able to appoint more liberal ones. Between 1937 and 1941 seven of the nine were replaced and verdicts began to reflect the change. In **Gaines v. Canada (1938)** it was ruled that separate but equal facilities must be really equal. This was a promising development for the NAACP's strategy of proving that they rarely were. However, it re-emphasised the slowness of the method. The Court had not challenged *Plessy* v. *Ferguson* (1896) which had ensured the continuation of segregation.

So in the short run the Supreme Court was of limited value to civil rights campaigners. The Fifteenth Amendment forbidding voting restrictions (see page 13) continued not to be enforced. From a wider perspective it is clear that from when the Supreme Court began to rule civil rights legislation unconstitutional, in the 1870s (see Chapter 1)

KEY EVENTS

Public Protest Eleanor Roosevelt resigned her membership of the Daughters of the Revolution in protest at their action in banning Marion Anderson. In a visible act of defiance a giant, multi-racial crowd attended an open air concert given by Miss Anderson at the Lincoln Memorial.

Gaines v. *Canada* **1938**
The white-only law school of the University of Missouri denied well-qualified, black student Lloyd Gaines a place, claiming he was within reach of Universities in other states. Charles Hamilton Houston successfully argued that this violated the Constitution's 'equal protection' clause and that the University must offer him a place. On the basis of the Court's judgement in *Gaines,* NAACP lawyers pushed hard for equal salaries for black teachers which rose in the 1940s to some 80 per cent of white teachers' incomes.

right up to the 1940s, it had been unhelpful to the cause of civil rights. Its lack of commitment could be compared with the negative approach of Congress and the hesitancies and timidity of the Presidents of this time.

CONCLUSION: THE STATE OF BLACK CIVIL RIGHTS BY 1941

By the end of the 1930s progress in civil rights seemed to have come to a standstill:

- Despite the vigorous campaigning of Walter White and others, the successes of the NAACP had been limited.
- With due respect to White, no charismatic personality had emerged to replace the disgraced Marcus Garvey as a leader of African Americans.
- In federal institutions little sympathy had been shown to taking action on black civil rights by Congress, the Presidency or the Supreme Court.
- Educational inequalities were all too apparent as far less money was spent on black educational facilities than white ones.
- Blacks were still largely excluded from voting in the south.
- Without blacks on voting rolls, all-white juries rarely gave blacks justice and the same applied to white police forces.
- Although lynching was declining, the climate of fear remained.
- Housing conditions for most blacks (especially in the ghettos) were primitive. *De facto* residential segregation remained in the north and sometimes in public places as well as residential areas.
- Poverty was endemic in many black communities and discrimination in employment all-pervasive.
- *De jure* segregation was rigidly enforced in the south where white Democrat politicians frequently played the race card for electoral support.
- White opinion (especially in the south) seemed determined to maintain the existing system of race relations.

- The system of 'states rights' which helped to maintain rigid segregation in the south seemed as strong as ever.

However, there were some positive signs:

- The climate of northern liberal opinion was now rejecting the racist theories of the past.
- Blacks were starting to play a more significant role in cultural, sporting and artistic life in the US and a more substantial African-American middle-class was developing.
- Though slow in application, legal challenges by the NAACP were showing signs of progress: after all, sections of the Constitution so beloved of most Americans clearly outlawed the kind of discrimination that was still continuing.

Overall, this mainly pessimistic analysis was to change dramatically in the next twenty-five years.

> *'While the vast majority of whites retained their faith in the existing social and economic system and often remained suspicious of federal intervention in local affairs, most African Americans were too preoccupied with the day-to-day task of survival to countenance protest inside or outside the system.'*
>
> Robert Cook, *Sweet Land of Liberty?*

QUESTIONS TO CONSIDER

1. Account for the rapid rise and fall of Marcus Garvey.

2. How effective were the NAACP in aiding civil rights in this period?

3. Why did Presidents and the Supreme Court give so little support to black civil rights in this period?

CHAPTER 4

1941–65 'We shall overcome'

How far and why did black Americans gain civil rights?

Hypothesis:

• Supreme Court verdicts, Martin Luther King's campaigns and the commitment of President Lyndon Johnson were the most important factors in the acquisition of black civil rights.

Introduction

From America's entry into the Second World War in 1941 to the signing of the Voting Rights Act in 1965 there were more changes in civil rights for black Americans than before or since. In the south the transformation was particularly noticeable. Blacks went from rigid and demeaning segregation, fear of violence, a second-class education and gross legal inequalities, to a situation where solutions were being applied to these problems. It could be argued that this change was inspired by favourable Supreme Court verdicts and legislation passed by Congress but originated by the Presidency. The resistance of southern whites to these changes was considerable but they were no longer able to hide successfully behind the excuse of 'states' rights' in order to prevent change and maintain white supremacy.

Ever since the formation of the Niagara movement back in 1905 there had been civil rights organisations, civil rights meetings, civil rights leaders, civil rights demands and civil rights protests but, arguably, no great sense of a civil rights *movement,* that is a nationwide campaign with some sense of co-ordination, a mass membership and widespread support from different regions of the US social classes and ethnic groups. After 1945 a *movement* developed in a more systematic way, though it was even more apparent after 1955.

These years also produced a charismatic civil rights leader in Martin Luther King, a better funded movement, substantial public sympathy and support from all races, classes and areas of the United States, even including the south. By the early 1960s some white civil rights activists felt so passionately about the cause that they were willing to risk their life in its support. The views of white churches and church leaders had been transformed to the extent that they were becoming strong supporters of the movement, the press were devoting more print space to the cause than any other in the country and two successive Presidents showed commitment to change. All this was achieved with a non-violent, if confrontational, approach.

THE DEGREE OF CIVIL RIGHTS PROGRESS 1941–54 PART ONE: THE SECOND WORLD WAR

What were the effects of the Second World War?

As with the earlier conflict of 1914–18, the 1939–45 war had a major impact on civil rights. Black migration north **increased much more dramatically** than between 1914 and 1918. This time, the tensions and violence erupted during, rather than immediately after, the war; for example there was a **serious riot in Detroit** in 1943. Racial tensions were often greatest in the workplace and in both north and south there were strong objections to **black workers exercising authority** (see Chapter 8).

The presence of black people in the US army brought its own tensions and reinforced segregation: the races were kept apart. The Red Cross was forced to segregate the blood of black and white people. Yet in the long term, horizons were widened. For example, over 100,000 black servicemen were sent to England and their experiences were similar to their comrades in France in 1918 – they experienced life in a more equal society.

The irony of fighting Nazi racism was not lost on those who stayed in the US. Civil rights campaigners highlighted the contrast that there should have been between a racist Germany and the supposed freedom of all Americans. They emphasised that blacks should receive full civil rights at home. This was taken up by groups such as the **Congress**

of Racial Equality (CORE) which was set up by James Farmer in 1942 to protest against the segregation that was increasingly occurring in the north.

THE DEGREE OF CIVIL RIGHTS PROGRESS 1941–54 PART TWO: THE COLD WAR

The Cold War was the dominant political theme in US history in the years following 1945. This meant that any kind of radical activity or attempt to upset the status quo was questioned. This affected civil rights' supporters who showed communist sympathies or criticised the severe actions taken against others, such as singer Paul Robeson, New York Congressman **Adam Clayton Powell** and W.E.B. Bois. Even the legal and constitutional approach of the NAACP incurred suspicion despite its Secretary, Walter White, being staunchly anti-communist. It was difficult to hold meetings because the organisation might sometimes be proscribed (made illegal). Forced to fight expensive battles to establish their legality, the NAACP lost money that could have gone towards fighting civil rights' legal cases.

However, the wartime period had seen an intellectual assault on the kind of racist views that underpinned the basis of white supremacy in the USA, and which the Nazis had now discredited. Moreover, the propaganda war with the Soviet Union did continue to influence many hearts and minds in the US that action needed to be taken on African-American equality. How could the USA champion individual freedom in the world generally, while denying it to an important minority in its own country?

The nature and direction of the civil rights movement were both influenced by the anti-Communist mood. The direct protest style of CORE would suffer until **McCarthyism** was discredited and social and economic grievances of blacks were played down in favour of legal and political ones which could appeal more clearly to American values and constitutional rights. This explains why the movement ran into difficulty when advocating better housing and employment rights: these demands seemed to question the

1941–65 'We shall overcome.' How far and why did black Americans gain civil rights?

61

freedoms of property and contract, enshrined in the American Constitution.

THE DEGREE OF CIVIL RIGHTS PROGRESS 1941–54 PART THREE: FEDERAL INVOLVEMENT

What help came from the federal authorities?

Of the three federal authorities, Congress, the Supreme Court and the President, Congress was the least likely to change its stance on civil rights. It frequently had Democrat majorities and southern Democrats were unmoved by any pressure for change with regard to the anti-lynching law and most other attempts to pass mild civil rights legislation. Only if a powerful and persuasive President was able to exert his authority was it likely to take action – this would have to wait for President Lyndon Johnson in the 1960s. Despite personally being in favour of civil rights, the occupants of the White House from 1933 to 1953, Roosevelt and Truman, were too concerned with the need for southern support to launch a frontal attack on civil rights.

However, on individual issues Presidents could and did take action. This happened in areas where Presidential authority could be exerted by Executive Order rather than relying on Congressional legislation. One example was Roosevelt's reaction in 1941 to Philip Randolph's demand for action on discrimination in employment when he issued his Executive Order banning racial discrimination in federal employment and set up the Fair Employment Practices Commission to monitor this question in the future (see page 87). After Roosevelt's death in 1945, President Harry Truman (see page 133) used his authority as Commander-in-Chief of the Armed Forces to issue executive orders to desegregate the US military in 1948.

He also commissioned a **President's Committee on civil rights** in 1946 and its report identified major civil rights problems. Truman was creating a climate of opinion that made the reception of future changes much more positive than they would otherwise have been. However, no legislation followed, since the President would not have been able to persuade the Congress to pass any.

KEY TERMS

President's Committee on civil rights This was an advisory Committee set up by Truman in 1946 to report to the President personally to help him see how progress towards black civil rights could be made in a gradual and peaceful way. The 15 members were from business, education, trade unions and the churches and included a majority who favoured reform, though it did not include civil rights activists. They interviewed over 250 people and issued a Report in October 1947, *To Secure These Rights.*

What other concrete progress was made in black civil rights 1945–55?

Faced with accusations of communism after 1945, the NAACP was involved less with direct protest than it had been in the war. However, it continued to mount legal challenges to the system of segregation and discrimination, particularly with regard to fair employment, voter registration, and education:

KEY TERMS

Deep South Usually refers to the states where segregation was most embedded, Mississippi, Alabama, Georgia, South Carolina and Louisiana.

KEY EVENTS

Launched voter registration drives In the US potential voters have to take the initiative to register their qualification to vote. The registration drives, developed by civil rights organisations, focused on visiting black areas in the south informing people of their rights, encouraging them to register and, if necessary, helping them to fill in the registration forms.

KEY PEOPLE

Thurgood Marshall (1908–93) was a black lawyer who took cases regarding segregation to the Supreme Court on behalf of the NAACP and won nearly all of them (for example *Smith* v. *Allright* and *Brown* v. *Board of Education, Topeka*). In 1967, he was appointed by President Johnson as the first black Justice of the Supreme Court.

- **Employment** – By 1953, 20 states and 30 cities had adopted Roosevelt's fair employment regulations.
- **Voter registration** – Here it was a Supreme Court initiative rather than a Presidential one on which the NAACP was able to build. In 1944, its decision in *Smith* v. *Allright* outlawed all kinds of white primary in Texas. As a result, black registered voters in the USA rose from two per cent of blacks in 1940 to 12 per cent in 1947. A few African Americans managed to get elected for state legislatures (about 25) though none in the **Deep South**. In New York, Adam Clayton Powell was elected to the federal House of Representatives. The NAACP **launched voter registration drives** to use the slightly more favourable situation to get blacks on to the voting register. These, however, met with heavy resistance in Mississippi and Alabama. As in the 1920s when similar efforts had been made, campaigning for voting rights was a dangerous activity. It was particularly difficult for black women to exercise their right to register and vote and those that did, such as Mary McCleod Bethune, were the exception (see pages 238).
- **Education** – The NAACP attempted to challenge the 'separate but equal' doctrine of *Plessy* v. *Ferguson* in education. In 1949 in Clarendon County, South Carolina, an average of $179 was spent on each white child, but only $43 on each black one. The pupil-to-teacher ratio was still 20 per cent better in white schools than in black ones. The NAACP sued on behalf of the black children. **Thurgood Marshall** impressively argued why the legal system should acknowledge and tackle the lack of equality in the education system. The legal process moved slowly, however, as a number of similar cases gradually worked their way up to Supreme Court

1941–65 'We shall overcome.' How far and why did black Americans gain civil rights?

63

level. However, this strategy of legal challenges was about to pay off.

CASE STUDY: THE LINDA BROWN SUPREME COURT CASE 1954. HOW FAR WAS THIS A TURNING POINT IN THE CIVIL RIGHTS MOVEMENT?

What happened in the legal case?

The climax of the NAACP's efforts came with the *Brown v. Board of Education, Topeka, Kansas* legal verdict in 1954. The Supreme Court unanimously ruled that a black girl, Linda Brown, should be allowed to attend her nearest school (an all-white one) and that to bar her from it was unconstitutional. Chief Justice **Earl Warren** accepted **all the arguments of black lawyer Thurgood Marshall**. He said that segregation *'generates a feeling of inferiority as to their* [black peoples'] *status ... in a way unlikely ever to be undone'*. The equal protection clause of the Fourteenth Amendment (see page 13) was clearly interpreted. It required admission of all children to state schools on equal terms.

What was the immediate impact of the verdict?

The decision created an important **legal precedent** and was expected to produce major change. It did so in a number of places outside the Deep South where segregation had still prevailed up to this point. Washington DC, Baltimore, St Louis and other towns and cities now began to integrate schools but progress was not quick. By 1957 less than 12 per cent of the school districts in the south had been integrated.

There was resistance in the south to the whole principle of integration using the states' rights argument. The federal government was seen as acting dictatorially in seeking to impose its values and opinions on those in different states.

What was the long-term significance of the verdict?

Though the Brown decision had a limited immediate impact, it was a turning point. Of all the federal

The Arguments of Thurgood Marshall
Marshall was not merely asserting that black education should be given an equal status to white education with equal money spent. He argued that education should be integrated. As a witness he produced eminent black psychologist Kenneth Clark to argue that segregation produced low self-esteem among African Americans.

KEY PEOPLE

Earl Warren (1891–1974) was a lawyer and Republican politician. As Attorney-General of California between 1939 and 1943, he was active in the decision to arrest over 100,000 Japanese-Americans when war broke out in 1941. He was Governor of California from 1943 to 1953, and in that year was appointed Chief Justice of the Supreme Court by President Eisenhower. He had played a part in helping Eisenhower get elected. Eisenhower was surprised by Warren's liberal judgments on the race question, which included *Brown* v. *Board of Education, Topeka*. He later headed a commission that investigated the assassination of President Kennedy.

KEY TERMS

Legal precedent When the principles created by an important legal decision are followed in subsequent cases.

institutions, the independent judiciary (Supreme Court) showed they no longer had the political difficulties concerning positive action over civil rights that were still present in Congress and the Presidency. With this decision, the Warren Court ended the vice-like grip of the *Plessy* v. *Ferguson* (1896) (see page 31) precedent, which had dominated relations between blacks and whites ever since. By going further than merely attacking inequalities, and insisting on the psychological need for integration of the black minority, more liberal verdicts were to follow (see page 71 *Boynton* v. *Virginia*).

Moreover, the verdict gave many southern black people a belief in the American political system and Constitution that Martin Luther King and other leaders were later able to exploit effectively. It was also a vindication of the legal strategy of the NAACP. The dramatic success of the more militant, if still non-violent, civil rights movement from the mid-1950s onward has slightly obscured the vital role of the NAACP. Without its efforts to bring cases to the Supreme Court in the first place, the legal foundations on which these later struggles were built would not have been laid.

The Brown decision signalled the start of a new era, though not an era of straightforward progress. Some historians, such as Riches (1997) have criticised the Court for not following up its original verdict with a more vigorous attempt at enforcement.

SOUTHERN WHITE REACTION

How popular was segregation amongst southern whites before the Brown Case?

Up to 1954, although black people were only making modest progress in the educational, voting and economic fields, the changes were still significant enough for some resistance from southern whites. All of the old Confederate states were segregated, but the Deep South (see page 63) maintained segregation the most rigidly. Many southern politicians would often increase their racist comments when it came to election time in order to win the support of the predominantly white, prejudiced electorate.

Sharecroppers and black industrial workers employed by white people could easily be evicted and jobs lost if they were brave enough to attempt to register to vote. Few black people could take legal action against white people and fewer still could hope for a favourable verdict. Governors and state officials, including the police, were generally racist in these states and though it was relatively small compared to the 1920s, the Ku Klux Klan was still present in the Deep South. Lynching was not as common nor as public as it had been in the 1930s, but it still occurred. One of the most notorious cases was that of the **murder of Emmet Till** as late as 1955.

Many southerners still used the old argument that imposing civil rights upon them was an unacceptable breach of their freedom. In South Carolina, **Strom Thurmond** felt so strongly about Truman's desegregation of the military and his Civil Rights Commission that he deserted the Democrats at the time of the **presidential election in 1948** and ran as a Third Party candidate.

The election of 1948 had been a reminder for the Deep South that its attitude towards race and 'States' Rights' was not shared by the majority of Americans. Since the Roosevelt Presidency and the New Deal, federal power was much greater and likely to be used more frequently. States were increasingly dependent on grants from the federal government and were therefore finding it harder to oppose its demands. The resistance after the *Brown* verdict in 1954 proved the beginning of the last phase of their active opposition.

What was the effect of the Brown verdict in the south?

In the Deep South further strategies were now developed to resist the expected pressure to change their approach to race. One of these was the development of **White Citizen's Councils** which aimed to maintain segregation as much as possible. There were even signs that some southern state legislatures were passing pro-segregation measures. Mississippi and Louisiana amended their constitutions to aid the retention of segregation: the white south was clearly on the defensive.

It soon became apparent that the *Brown* ruling would have to be imposed on the southern states. This was because of the

KEY EVENTS

The Murder of Emmet Till Emmet Till was a 14-year-old black youth from Chicago who was visiting Mississippi where he was said to have made remarks to a white woman and wolf whistled. He was shot in the head and his body dumped in the river. The case excited great publicity and protest. This showed that these events were becoming rarer and that peoples' attitudes were changing. However, the case also showed the continuing lack of justice in the south. Despite clear evidence against the two alleged murderers, an all-white jury found them not guilty.

KEY EVENTS

Strom Thurmond and the presidential election in 1948 Over a million people voted for his 'states' rights' campaign but, compared to 24 million votes for Truman and 22 million for Dewey, Thurmond's support was small and localised.

KEY TERMS

White Citizens' Councils The earliest ones date from 1955 in reaction to the Brown verdict on segregated education. Aiming to maintain strict segregation in as many areas of life as possible, they waged economic warfare against anyone supporting integration and believed in defying federal court rulings if necessary. In short, they were much like the Ku Klux Klan without the costumes and the lynching.

**Dwight D. Eisenhower
(1890–1969)** was Supreme
Commander of the Allied
Forces in the Second World
War. He served two terms as
Republican President of the
USA, 1953–61. 'Ike' was a
popular figure because of his
successful military past. He
did not have strong party
views. His conception of the
Presidency was passive rather
than active; he did not favour
aggressive action except as a
last resort. His failure to take
the presidential initiative after
the *Brown* case is now seen as
one of the weaker points of
his presidency.

**Faubus' dereliction of
duty** Eisenhower and Faubus
met to discuss the situation
and President Eisenhower felt
that Faubus had deceived him
into thinking that he would
obey the court ruling. When
the black children attempted
to enter the school this time,
Faubus and his troops were
absent, but a mob of white
racists was left on the streets:
the children were forced to
leave to avoid being attacked.

extent of southern resistance, which meant that the Court's
decision would not be accepted without further opposition.
This contrasted with the north, where respect for federal
institutions was strong. The south would need **Eisenhower**
as President to enforce it but he showed little sign of action.
This was not because he was especially racist – in the District
of Columbia he outlawed any forms of racial discrimination.
His reluctance to take action elsewhere was because he was
afraid of stirring up opposition, resentment and disorder in
the south. Eisenhower made little comment on the *Brown*
verdict except to say he doubted the ability of legislation to
change minds and hearts in this area. Eisenhower's passive
approach to the problem was illustrated in 1956, when
Governor Daniel in Texas brought out his local troops, the
Texas Rangers, to prevent integration through force, and
Eisenhower did nothing.

What happened at Central High School, Little Rock?

Nevertheless, Eisenhower was moved to take action after a
clear example of southern resistance to integrated education
occurred in Little Rock, Arkansas. In 1957 Governor Orval
Faubus used National Guard troops to bar the entry of
nine black children to the Central High School after a
federal district court had ruled that the school must be
desegregated. Annoyed by what he saw as **Faubus'
dereliction of duty** and using his authority as
Commander-in-Chief, the President sent in paratroopers
(federal troops) and announced that the 10,000 troopers of
the Arkansas National Guard were to be put under federal

**Federal troops
confront a racist
student from Little
Rock Central High
School, 1957.**

control. The same soldiers who had barred the way before, now kept white protesters back and escorted the children into the school.

What happened after Little Rock?
This was the only occasion when President Eisenhower used his federal authority to intervene and enforce the Brown legal ruling. The years immediately following the *Brown* decision had shown the limitations of Supreme Court power in terms of acceptance and enforcement and, with the exception of Little Rock, the continuing caution of presidential action in the civil rights field. **The two Civil Rights Acts of 1957 and 1960** were very weak and made hardly any impact. But by this time the movement for civil rights had received a boost from below with a fresh and successful campaign, a new and dynamic leader and the emergence of an organisation to challenge the NAACP in terms of popularity, tactics, and achievements.

THE CIVIL RIGHTS EXPLOSION 1955–65

PART ONE: THE MONTGOMERY BUS BOYCOTT AND ITS SIGNIFICANCE

The Montgomery Bus Boycott: what was the background?
In the south, separation on public transport was always the most resented form of segregation. Blacks were frequently made to stand, given the poorer seats, thrown off buses for little reason and generally spoken down to or humiliated by white drivers and passengers. The majority of African Americans lived in their own out-of-town areas and needed to travel frequently to employment in town centres.

In retrospect it was not surprising that this area was where the first real breakthrough for black civil rights was achieved. Yet the boycott of the buses by black people that began in December 1955 took off in an unprecedented and unexpected (if not entirely unplanned) way. NAACP activist **Rosa Parks** was thrown off a bus for refusing to give up her seat for a white person. This seemingly small incident gave birth to a new and important phase in the civil rights movement.

KEY EVENTS

The Civil Rights Act of 1957 proposed a bi-partisan Civil Rights Commission and a new division in the Justice Department to investigate civil rights abuses in fields such as voting. In Congress, Strom Thurmond, spoke for over 24 hours against it. Senator Lyndon Johnson (see page 139) was able to steer the bill through the Senate only by watering down its provisions.

The Civil Rights Act of 1960 renewed the Civil Rights Commission, allowed judges to make special appointments of those who would help blacks on to the voting register and introduced federal criminal penalties for bombing and mob action.

KEY PEOPLE

Rosa Parks (1914–2005) was a Methodist and a member of the NAACP, who was highly regarded in the local community. Others had been arrested for similar reasons, but campaigners wanted to pick a person of impeccable character and morals, to whom breaking the law would normally be unthinkable. After the boycott, harassment by angry whites in Montgomery forced the Parks family to move to Detroit in 1957. She later set up the Rosa and Raymond Parks institute for self-development, giving career training to black youths. She was awarded the Presidential Medal of Freedom in 1996 and the Congressional Gold Award in 1999.

**Martin Luther King
(1929-68)** Born Atlanta,
Georgia. He was brought up
in a well-off family but, like
all black families, suffered
from the inequality and hurt
of segregation. He was forced
to go north to Boston to
study for a PhD. He was a
Baptist Minister in
Montgomery 1954–60 after
which he returned to Atlanta
and, while assisting at his
father's church, became a full-
time leader of the civil rights
movement. He was
assassinated in 1968.

**Southern Christian
Leadership Conference
(SCLC)** Formed in 1957 in
Atlanta with King as
president. It widened the field
of civil rights activity. The
SCLC did not take individual
members like the NAACP but
reacted to events, organising
campaigns as seemed
appropriate (also see Chapter
5).

**Ralph Abernathy (1926–
90)** Minister of First Baptist
Church, Montgomery. A loyal
follower of King, he was his
deputy in the SCLC and took
over the leadership of the
organisation after King's
assassination. A good speaker
in his own right, but he
lacked King's charisma and
authority. The livelier Jesse
Jackson eclipsed him in the
1970s (see Chapter 5).

Why did the Boycott succeed?

The boycott was not the first example of direct action protest but it was the first to be really effective. It gained the near-unanimous support of ordinary black men and women, giving them a chance to participate in an activity that involved effort but avoided danger. It was an impressive display of unity and also stamina in two senses – walking to work and persisting with the boycott for almost a year. Nearly all blacks responded to the call to make a stand. They showed they could organise a protest, and co-operate with each other with minimal white participation.

It put financial pressure on the authorities who initially unwisely refused the slightest concessions. Moreover in November 1956, after an initiative by the NAACP, the Supreme Court in *Browder* v. *Gayle* gave another favourable verdict. It ruled segregation on buses to be unconstitutional with similar reasoning to the Linda Brown case. A ripping hole had been made in the vast tent of segregation. Even better it was victory in a rigidly segregated black southern town. On news of the success King and his white supporters went on an integrated bus ride.

How far was the appearance of Martin Luther King a turning point?

Moreover, a great black leader emerged, **Martin Luther King**. Ironically chosen because he was seen as cautious, King proved to be an effective organiser, a brilliant speaker and a great motivator. Organising frequent night-time rallies in his and other local churches, he re-charged the batteries of commitment and determination. By articulating the feelings and frustrations of the black community in a clear, intelligent and persuasive way, he created a vital close link between the black civil rights leadership and the less educated African-American man and woman that the NAACP in general, and men like Du Bois in particular, had often failed to achieve. King skilfully exploited the leadership potential offered by a minister of religion who had the respect of his community. His theologically-based belief in non-violence was powerfully argued and enacted throughout his own life. True progress, he argued, could only be made when the cycle of violence and hate was broken. This set the agenda for the next ten years of civil rights protest. Within a year King had set up a new civil rights organisation, the **Southern Christian**

1941–65 'We shall overcome.' How far and why did black Americans gain civil rights?

69

Leadership Conference with **Ralph Abernathy** as his deputy. SCLC took a more confrontational line on black civil rights than the more cautious and legalistic **Roy Wilkins** of the NAACP.

THE CIVIL RIGHTS EXPLOSION PART TWO: PROTESTS WIDEN

How important were the sit-ins and Freedom Rides?

The movement now developed a new confidence and style of protest especially among younger blacks and increasing interest and sympathy from white liberals in the north. These two developments were illustrated in major protests in 1960 and 1961 – the **sit-ins** and Freedom Rides.

In Feb 1960 four black students staged a sit-in at the whites-only refreshment counter in their local Woolworth's store in Greensboro, North Carolina, which prided itself on good race relations. The state authorities hesitated, which allowed the numbers of protestors to grow rapidly. Soon the concept of the sit-in at segregated facilities had spread to neighbouring states such as Tennessee and Virginia. The demonstrations were all the stronger for their apparent spontaneity, although their success owed something to the build up of student organisations in the 1950s that made the sudden spread of protests more likely to succeed.

Ella Baker, an NAACP activist, saw the significance of these sit-ins and got Martin Luther King to come and address the students. She insisted that, rather than join the SCLC, they set up their own organisation, the **Student Non-Violent Coordinating Committee (SNCC)**. The style of protest, though non-violent, was more confrontational than the boycott as it forced a response from the authorities. If police used force to remove the demonstrators and it was roughly done then the press and the **increasingly important medium of television** would record it. In this way public support could be increased. But if the police took no action then desegregation had effectively been achieved. Cracks were now beginning to appear in the segregationist system and by the end of 1961, 810 towns in the south had desegregated facilities.

The importance of Television In 1949, one million American families had a television set; by 1960, the figure had risen to 45 million. This proved significant during the 1960s, when millions watched the horrific treatment of civil rights protesters by racist police. King and others deliberately courted this favourable publicity.

Increased white support for black civil rights
Television and the written press were making inroads into white liberal opinion in the north to the extent that active and passionate supporters of the movement were emerging. This was despite the fact that protesting whites were likely to suffer even greater violence against them for 'betraying' their race.

Robert Kennedy (1925–68) was Attorney General from 1961–64, forcefully implementing favourable Supreme Court decisions on civil rights. Senator for New York from 1964, he played a leading role in getting civil rights legislation passed. He fell out with Lyndon Johnson, especially over Vietnam. He could well have won the Democratic nomination for the Presidency but was assassinated in June 1968 when campaigning.

The Freedom Rides of 1961 re-enforced the success of the sit-ins. Taking advantage of **increased white support for black civil rights**, the idea was for blacks and whites to board inter-state buses in the north, where legally they could sit together, but remain in their places as the bus entered the south, where they would be breaking local segregation laws. This confrontational strategy was again employed effectively because of the publicity it received and the negative response from the police authorities. In Birmingham, Alabama, police ignored a white mob that attacked the riders. Favourable publicity had been achieved and CORE – the northern civil rights group (see pages 60–61) had been successfully re-vitalised to co-ordinate the event.

How did the federal government respond?
Increasingly liberal verdicts from the Supreme Court were continuing to aid the civil rights cause. The Freedom Rides had been partly inspired by the Supreme Court case of *Boynton* v. *Virginia* 1960 which outlawed segregation on all inter-state travel facilities. In opposing the Freedom Riders it was the south who seemed to be defying the law. Moreover, it aroused the interest of President John F. Kennedy's (see pages 199 and 257) federal government. From the President's point of view, southern states were failing to maintain law and order.

Kennedy's response to civil rights demands had previously been lukewarm. Like previous Presidents from the Democrat Party, Kennedy was worried about losing southern white support, but as Republican Eisenhower had shown in 1957 at Little Rock, failure to keep order would no longer be tolerated. **Kennedy's brother Robert**, the Attorney General, enforced the legal orders confirming the desegregation of all inter-state travel. Federal assistance was also on hand in 1962 when, after great difficulty and two deaths, James Meredith was escorted through the gates of Mississippi University by federal marshalls to become its first black student. Perhaps more significant a few months later was the failure of the now militantly racist Governor of Alabama, George Wallace, to prevent two black students from entering the state's University at Tuscaloosa.

1941–65 'We shall overcome.' How far and why did black Americans gain civil rights?

71

THE CIVIL RIGHTS EXPLOSION PART THREE: BIRMINGHAM AND WASHINGTON 1963

Birmingham Protest: April 1963

Martin Luther King and the SCLC were now able to take advantage of the more favourable climate for civil rights. King selected Birmingham, Alabama for a major SCLC protest. It was a bold move: Birmingham was a large and rigidly segregated city and would be a tough nut to crack but King felt that if the SCLC could succeed there, then they could succeed anywhere. Favourable signs included the strong local civil rights leadership of **Fred Shuttlesworth** and a police chief, **Eugene 'Bull' Connor** who was notorious for over-reacting and who had encouraged the violence against the Freedom Riders in the town in 1961.

On 3 April 1963 King and the SCLC arrived in the town, demanding desegregation and an end to racism in employment. Only limited progress was made at first and King was imprisoned, but he then arranged a protest march at the beginning of May which included children from local high schools. As predicted, Police Chief Connor over-reacted and ordered police dogs and water cannons to be used on the protestors. The whole world, including President Kennedy, was watching the violence as it unfolded on television. The **over-reaction** had created the publicity the civil rights movements needed.

Eventually two important conclusions were reached. The white Birmingham business community decided that a few concessions (such as abandoning segregation in many shops) was less damaging than the continued chaos and the loss of profit caused by successful boycotts. Secondly, President Kennedy decided that law and order had broken down in Birmingham and that these scenes would be repeated unless he took federal action on civil rights. In the end, Kennedy's decision was more significant for civil rights than the local and limited concessions won in Birmingham.

Fred Shuttlesworth (born 1922) A Baptist Minister who formed the Alabama Christian Movement for Human Rights in 1956. He invited King and the SCLC to Birmingham in spring 1963 for a major campaign. A strong believer in non-violent direct action, he is one of the most courageous figures in the civil rights movement. In 1963 he confronted the police dogs and fire hoses in the Birmingham demonstration head on – the force sent him flying into the air and then to hospital for a few days. From the 1980s his housing foundation has aided many poor people. He finally retired in 2006.

Eugene 'Bull' Connor (1897–1973) was Birmingham Commissioner of Public Safety, 1937–53 and 1957–63. He became known for his determination to keep segregation at all costs, and was re-elected five times.

KEY CONCEPT

Over-reaction by racist southern whites was seen as helpful for further progress on civil rights because of the publicity it caused. In the 1961/2 campaign in Albany, Georgia, King and the SCLC had been less successful when Police Chief Laurie Pritchett used effective tactics which meant that demonstrators had been quietly arrested and violence avoided.

Police dogs attacking a seventeen-year-old civil rights demonstrator in Birmingham, Alabama, 3 May 1963.

KEY CONCEPTS

Waiting no longer an option King spent around 20 short periods in jail in his protesting career, frequently for violating southern segregation laws. In Birmingham jail in April 1963 in the middle of the city's protests he wrote on scraps of paper to a group of white clergymen who had argued that blacks should be prepared to wait a little longer for civil rights; King produced a memorable reply: *'Perhaps it is easy for those who have never felt the stinging darts of segregation to say "wait".'*

The march on Washington June 1963

These violent scenes in Birmingham were now followed by significant action on civil rights. King had argued powerfully that **waiting was no longer an option**. In order to maintain the pressure, the civil rights movement organised a march on Washington on 28 August 1963 (recalling Philip Randolph's idea of 1941, see page 123). Unlike other campaigns it took place in the capital and was directed at the heart of the federal government. Also, it took place 100 years after the Emancipation Proclamation and the march culminated with King's powerful '**I have a dream' speech** in front of the memorial to Abraham

The civil rights march on Washington, 1963.

Lincoln. It was a march 'for jobs and freedom', indicating concern for black economic conditions as well as questions concerning segregation. Around **250,000 people marched** and the actions of the peaceful and disciplined protesters contrasted sharply with their opponents: in September 1963 just three weeks after the march, four black children attending Sunday school were killed in a bomb attack on a black Baptist church in Birmingham which had been used in rallies against segregation.

FEDERAL LEGISLATION

How was the Civil Rights Act of 1964 passed?

The assassination of President Kennedy in November 1963, as he was preparing a Civil Rights Bill, seemed to be a setback for the movement. However, King and the SCLC kept the pressure on early in 1964 with a strong campaign in St Augustine, Florida. Moreover, the new President, **Lyndon Johnson**, needed little persuasion to act. He skilfully exploited the shocked mood of the American people after the death of Kennedy. Using his long experience of Congress and his southern background, Johnson got together a pro-civil rights coalition of Republicans and Democrats that had eluded all previous Presidents. The **Civil Rights Act of 1964** made universal what was already happening in many areas of the US but not in the Deep South. It was a major achievement and southern resistance had been largely defeated.

How did the Voting Rights Act 1965 come about?

Now the movement focused on gaining similar legislation for voting rights. Slow but steady progress had been made in this area with voter registration drives in the 1950s and early 1960s but, in the Deep South particularly, registration rates were still low. King and the SCLC pursued a similar tactic to that followed in Birmingham and targeted a town which had a terrible record of black registration. Selma, Alabama was a place with a fifty per cent African-American population, where only one per cent of the registered electorate was black. Also, like Birmingham, Selma had a particularly volatile police chief, Jim Clark.

KEY EVENTS

King's 'I have a dream' speech The dream speech was prophetic and wide ranging: *'On the red hills of Georgia sons of slaves and former slave owners will be able to sit down together at the table of brotherhood. I have a dream today ... My four little children will one day live in a nation where they will not be judged by the color of their skin but by the content of their character ... We will allow freedom to ring from every state and every city. I have a dream today ... Every valley shall be exalted and every mountain and hill laid low, the rough places made plain and the crooked places made straight ... All of God's children, black men and white men, Jews and Gentiles, Catholics and Protestants, will be able to join hands. I have a dream today.'*

250,000 people marched to Washington About a third of them were white and it involved a very wide range of civil rights groups, including the NAACP, who were often wary of confrontational protesting. Outwardly it was an impressive display of unity and strength, though there were differences simmering underneath the surface (see next chapter).

KEY PEOPLE

Lyndon B. Johnson (1908–73) President 1963–69, having been re-elected in 1964 with a landslide victory. Though not always entirely consistent, he was one of the few southern Senators to give general support to civil rights in the 1950s.

The Civil Rights Act 1964

- There was a ban on exclusion from restaurants, stores and other public places.
- The Attorney-General could file law suits to speed up desegregation, mixed education and voting rights.
- The Fair Employment Practices Commission was now set up on a permanent legal basis.
- No racial, sexual or religious discrimination would be lawful.
- There was to be no discrimination on any federally aided programmes.
- A Community Relations Service was set up to deal with remaining disputes.

Voting Rights Act 1965

The following conditions for voter registration were made illegal:

- demonstration of educational achievement
- knowledge of any subject
- ability to interpret material
- proof of moral character.

Blacks could now register to vote on equal terms to whites.

As in Birmingham, cameras recorded the violent police charge on an attempt at a peaceful protest march led by King from Selma to Montgomery. As well as the publicity generated for civil rights supporters, this produced federal protection for a march to Montgomery. It also led to a promise by Johnson for a **Voting Rights Bill** which was duly passed in the summer of 1965. As King and the marchers arrived at the scene of the bus boycott triumph almost ten years before, President Johnson prepared to sign the Act: it seemed as though the civil rights movement was riding on the crest of a wave. As things turned out, it was about to enter a much tougher period.

Martin Luther King and his wife Coretta Scott King at a black voting rights march from Selma, Alabama, to the state capital Montgomery, 1965.

CONCLUSION

The success of the civil rights movement in this period was due to:

- The outstanding leadership of Martin Luther King and other committed leaders such as Fred Shuttlesworth and Ella Baker which led to greater black confidence to protest effectively.

1941–65 'We shall overcome.' How far and why did black Americans gain civil rights?

75

- The eventual success of the NAACP's legal tactics leading to favourable decisions from a more liberal Supreme Court.
- Increasing federal government interest in general and in particular the commitment and action from President Lyndon Johnson.
- Increasing public sympathy, especially from northern whites, due to a changing climate of opinion and media publicity about racial equality, skilfully exploited by the tactics of mass protest.
- Poor tactics from southern opponents whose violent response frequently played into the hands of the civil rights movement.
- The damaging international situation and the gathering pace of decolinisation. The USA could not compete with the USSR for support in Asia and Africa while discrimination continued at home.

At this stage the different civil rights groups, though competitive, tended to spur one another on. The movement had succeeded in gaining the moral high ground with their dignified protests and had attracted much sympathetic white support.

> 'As civil rights became part of the daily agenda of life for all Americans, and more and more white students joined their black brethren in the southern struggle, civil rights and racial equality became a focal point for the whole nation'.
>
> William H. Chafe, *The Unfinished Journey*

QUESTIONS TO CONSIDER

1. Did the Cold War help or hinder civil rights progress?

2. In what ways was the Linda Brown legal case a turning point for the civil rights campaign?

3. Compare the contributions of Martin Luther King and Lyndon Johnson to the gaining of black civil rights in 1964/5.

CHAPTER 5

Dream or nightmare?

Civil rights 1960–92

Hypothesis:

- Black civil rights were extended most fully in this period to the black middle class but many African Americans in inner cities and ghettos were still languishing in poverty.

PROBLEMS FOR THE CIVIL RIGHTS MOVEMENT AFTER 1960

Introduction

During the early 1960s (a time of rapid achievement for civil rights) life still remained difficult for many African Americans with regard to employment, housing and education. Poverty and discrimination were more acute than in equivalent white communities. For most, particularly in the northern city ghettos, the real problem areas were economic and social rather than political or legal.

Northern blacks were less committed to a non-violent solution to their problems and rarely accepted the leadership of King. They were less prepared to work through, rather than against, the existing system of government. African Americans living in the north would explode into violent protest from the mid-1960s onwards and take the question of black civil rights into uncharted territory. Two days after President Johnson signed the Voting Rights Act in August 1965, serious rioting in Los Angeles gave a violently unpleasant foretaste of things to come. The civil rights movement had suddenly entered another phase.

What were the economic and social problems facing northern blacks in the 1960s?
Unemployment and poverty

Only a minority of the USA's black population shared in

the increasing American prosperity of the early 1960s. When black people from the south were pouring into northern and western cities, unskilled job numbers were declining (see page 141). But owing to past educational discrimination these were often the only ones for which they were qualified. In the 1950s, as automation took over many factories, over a million jobs (often those held by black people) had disappeared. Yet African Americans still moved north to escape the rigid segregation of the south. By 1970 half of the USA's black population was living outside the southern states, compared with barely a third in 1950.

With employment opportunities limited, discrimination was common: black unemployment (especially amongst teenagers) had increased more than white unemployment in the twenty years after 1945. This led to greater poverty: in the country as a whole in the mid-1960s about one person in ten had an income under $5000 a year, but for black people it was one in three.

Housing
Housing was another root cause of social problems. Trapped in northern cities with **segregated housing**, indifferent education and high crime rates with no money or alternative employment, there seemed to be no escape. The process of **blockbusting** set blacks at a disadvantage and encouraged segregation.

Education
With African Americans living in confined areas, education was also *de facto* segregated. Black pupils became caught in a poverty cycle, leaving school with few formal qualifications and ill-equipped to compete in the job market, where many job opportunities were for skilled workers with formal qualifications. All this was little affected by the 1964 Civil Rights Act, which did not focus directly on economic questions. Ironically, desegregation of schools was more noticeable in the previously *de jure* segregated south.

MALCOLM X AND THE DEVELOPMENT OF BLACK POWER

Malcolm X (1925–65)
Born as Malcolm Little into a poor black family in Omaha, Nebraska. In 1931 his father, a Garvey supporter, was found murdered. In 1937 his mother was committed to a mental institution. He was unable to obtain good educational opportunities, despite showing ability in his early school days; then he mixed with criminal company in New York, turning to a life of crime and drugs. While in jail between 1946 and 1952, he underwent a conversion to the Nation of Islam that completely transformed his life. He dropped the name Little and became Malcolm X, believing Little to be the name of the slave people who owned his family, not his real name. In the 1950s he was a minister in a number of Nation of Islam temples and in 1962 became national spokesman for the organisation.

Blacks in the north never had the same degree of commitment to Martin Luther King as those in the south. By focusing on desegregation and voting rights rather than social problems, King and the SCLC were not only geographically remote from northern blacks: they did not seem to be addressing their priorities. Moreover, the Christian non-violent aspect of the movement did not strike the same cultural chords in the north. There were complaints that the march on Washington (see pages 73–74) had focussed on freedom, ignoring half of its original title, 'for *jobs* and freedom'.

What was the importance of Malcolm X?

By 1960 another black leader was coming to national attention. **Malcolm X** was from the north and was a critic of the non-violent approach to black rights. Until the winter of 1962–63 he was a prominent member of the Muslim fringe group the **Nation of Islam** (NOI). From this he heard about the **idea of black superiority**. Malcolm was proud to be black and very critical of white society. Blacks must not beg favours from the whites as he felt NAACP and SCLC were doing. Expressed in eloquent and earthy language that connected with them, Malcolm's views spread quickly among poor northern blacks. They could relate to him and his deprived background in a way that they could not to King and other southern Christian leaders. Malcolm was a quick-witted debater and had considerable power over his African-American supporters.

However, Malcolm was restricted by his leader, **Elijah Muhammed**, from speaking in direct political terms and so lacked a proper platform for campaigning for civil rights. He did his best, using the NOI journal *Muhammad Speaks* and he was an increasingly popular speaker on TV shows, at campus meetings and in magazine and radio interviews. He was dismissed from the Nation of Islam early in 1963, for failing to keep quiet on political questions and making critical comments on Elijah Mohammed's leadership. Malcolm had, in any case, become disillusioned with the movement and now embraced the mainstream Sunni

Malcolm X.

Muslim faith which gave him greater opportunities to air his views, which were very different from King's.

What did Malcolm X emphasise and how were his views received?

Malcolm disliked the emphasis on civil rights that saw desegregation and voting rights as essential to progress. He preferred to focus on the appalling economic and social conditions that his fellow blacks suffered in the inner cities, problems that he did not believe would be solved by King's approach. He rejected the idea of integration with the white community as he believed that white people were inherently racist and would never be able to apply their American democratic values to blacks. In the tradition of Marcus Garvey, Malcolm X saw black people as Africans rather than Americans but dismissed a move back to Africa because of its impracticalities. Malcolm rejected the non-violent emphasis of the mainstream civil rights movement although he claimed that he never advocated initiating violence, only the right of self-defence. He believed, for example, that it was important to protect women. However, this was in a protective if not patronising way; the Nation of Islam did not see any role of authority for women in their movement.

Martin Luther King generally avoided commenting on the Nation of Islam. Governments were similarly cautious in their comments, though the FBI kept a surveillance on Malcolm from 1960 onwards. In the last year of his life, after he was expelled from the Nation of Islam, Malcolm X was much more worried about threats from The Nation than any other. He cared little about white opinion of him and even brushed aside any attempts at praise from liberal whites: he did not believe they could really have the welfare of blacks at heart.

How far did Malcolm X's views change?

Malcolm could be cruelly dismissive of the civil rights movement but later successes in 1963 did start to make him re-think. Publicly, however, he knew he could not take a 180 degree turn. After Malcolm was dismissed by the NOI, he travelled widely in Africa and Asia where he greatly broadened his horizons, realising that many Muslims were in fact white. Ironically, he was coming

KEY TERMS

Nation of Islam The Nation of Islam (also known as the Black Muslims) was a group founded in 1930 by Wallace Fard who led it until his disappearance in 1934, when Elijah Muhammad became leader. Since Elijah's death in 1975, Louis Farrakhan has led the movement.

KEY CONCEPTS

Idea of black superiority According to the racial theories of the Nation of Islam, all people had been originally coloured black until an evil scientist, Jacoub, had inbred the palest faces to produce a different and inferior race.

KEY PEOPLE

Elijah Muhammad (1897–1975) was born Elijah Poole. As a young man he became a Muslim, and became the leader of the Nation of Islam in 1934. He was jailed for avoiding war service (the draft) between 1942 and 1946. He called for a separate homeland for black Americans, but avoided making directly political pronouncements. He was greatly revered by Malcolm X, until the latter discovered that Elijah did not personally keep to the strict moral standards he demanded of his followers.

round to the idea of co-operating with the other parts of the civil rights movement just as King was moving to a small degree in the direction of Malcolm's views (see below). Malcolm X needed time to make an impact but he received little, being assassinated by members of the Nation of Islam in February 1965. But his ideas were enormously influential in the next few years.

HOW FAR DID KING'S VIEWS CHANGE AND BLACK POWER IDEAS DEVELOP 1966–68?

King was becoming disillusioned with the lack of white response to his campaigns. He was also realising that the civil rights movement must address the social and economic problems in the north if it were to really achieve equality for black people. Desegregation and voting rights required a non-economic adjustment only, but where problems struck at the root of society and needed expensive redress – housing, education, equal pay and job opportunities – there was more resistance.

What was the Chicago Campaign?

1966 confirmed King's more pessimistic views. Invited to Chicago to run a civil rights campaign in the city, King focused on *de facto* segregation in education, employment and (especially) housing. However, the SCLC found less co-operation from fellow blacks than in the south, virulent resistance from racist whites and clever tactics from Mayor Richard Daley, more akin to the subtle Laurie Pritchett in Albany (see page 72) than the bullish Bull Connor and the cantankerous Jim Clark.

The SCLC were pelted with rocks in Marquette Park and subjected to verbal racist abuse. Mayor Daley was pleasant but evasive when meeting King and other civil rights representatives. **Chicago's housing problem had been highlighted but not solved.**

KEY CONCEPTS

Chicago's Housing problem not solved A general agreement was patched up with Daley, containing (unkept) promises about improving housing conditions in the city and introducing open housing legislation.

What was the impact of the Vietnam War on the civil rights campaign?

1966 also saw the drastic reduction in support for civil rights from Congress and President Johnson because of the

Black protestors speaking out against the Vietnam War, 1967.

Vietnam War. By 1967 King felt he must speak out against it. Its violence was a total contradiction of King's religious principles and it was diverting funds and attention from civil rights at a time when further reforms seemed possible. His strong condemnation of it in New York's Riverside Church in April 1967 severed his increasingly tenuous connections with the President.

Vietnam pushed questions of black civil rights off the front pages and leading articles of serious newspapers and magazines. No more major civil rights legislation was to pass except for the **Fair Housing Act of 1968**.

How did Black Power ideas develop?

Malcolm X's views became more popular and exerted more influence after his death even in previously non-violent civil rights groups. Those who rejected non-violence saw King as the '*tool of the white man*' and thought that blacks should be in complete control of their own destiny. Both SNCC and CORE increasingly questioned the strategy of non-violence which had not yielded much social and economic progress. Demands included a more effective and fairer implementation of the law and radical social change, especially in housing and education. Many in the Black Power movement, such as **Stokely Carmichael**, rejected help from whites and even dismissed blacks who believed in working with whites.

How serious were the riots of 1965–68?

The years 1965–68 saw widespread violence in many American cities with substantial African-American populations. The first of three 'long hot summers' of rioting, started in the Watts district of Los Angeles in

The Vietnam War This was fought between the northern (communist) and southern (capitalist) parts of Vietnam from the mid 1950s to 1975. The USA supported the South Vietnamese and became increasingly involved in what was seen as an anti-communist crusade. By 1967–68, over half a million US troops (including many blacks) were involved. Civil rights campaigners pointed out that $0.5 million was being spent on killing a Vietnamese soldier but only $35 to help each poor person in the US.

Fair Housing Act 1968 No racial discrimination was to be allowed in the sale, rent and mortgaging of properties. Johnson got this passed immediately after King's death (see over) using the emotional sympathy that would ensure its passage through Congress.

Stokely Carmichael (1941–98) was born in Trinidad but spent the years 1952–69 in the USA. He was an organiser for SNCC between 1964 and 1966, when he became chair of the organisation. In 1967, he co-wrote Black Power, outlining his vision of the role for blacks in the USA. Some of the language in his speeches was extreme such as 'smashing everything that white civilisation has created'. He left SNCC to join the Black Panthers in 1967 and the USA in 1969 to live in Guinea, changing his name to Kwame Ture.

Protestors on the burned-out streets of Watts district in Los Angeles after the race riots in 1965.

August 1965 beginning after a drunken black driver was arrested and beaten by police. 14,000 troops were required to restore order and 4,000 people were arrested. Though this was the most serious outbreak, there were many others.

How did King's views change?

King never forsook his commitment to non-violence. However, between 1965 and 1968 he became disillusioned with the American political set up and despaired of the social and economic reform he recognised was needed: *'I worked to get these people the right to eat hamburgers, now I've got to do something...to help them to get the money to buy them.'* He realised that unless these problems were dealt with, violence and rioting would continue and undermine his non-violent strategy. He moved towards the kind of socialist but non-communist views that had previously been held by Philip Randolph, planning to hold a Poor Man's March from Mississippi to Washington to protest about severe poverty still existing in the US. When he was shot on 4 April 1968 in Memphis, he was there to support the local black dustmen in their efforts to gain equal employment rights but he struggled to keep his increasingly impatient followers peaceful. After the assassination of King, his belief in non-violence was ignored and there was a whole swathe of rioting across the USA. The civil rights movement now appeared leaderless, directionless, divided and confused.

Who were the Black Panthers?

A new Black Power group had emerged in 1966 known as the **Black Panthers**. Led by **Huey Newton** and **Bobby Seale**, they wanted an end to white capitalist control in general and police brutality in particular. Their demands were economic in emphasis and were clearly influenced by Black Power ideas and Malcolm X. They developed a **ten-point programme**. Some of these points were similar to demands of more mainstream civil rights groups but others were more distinctive. While requests for mixed black and white juries was a common feature of civil rights groups, the Black Panthers demand for all-black juries indicated the greater emphasis on black distinctiveness, bordering on separation and (to some) racist feeling against whites. This was a long way from the integrationist SCLC let alone the NAACP. The fact that the Black Panthers attracted members from SNCC showed just how broken the civil rights movement had become.

Ten point programme The ten points were:

- Freedom – power to determine the destiny of the black community.
- Full employment for all.
- An end to 'robbery' of black people.
- Housing which was fit for the shelter of human beings.
- Education – they wanted the truth taught about what they saw as the 'decadent racist society' of the US.
- Black exemption from military service.
- An end to acts of brutality and murder by the police.
- Freedom for all black people held in jail.
- Fair juries – black juries for black people.
- Land entitlement as well as bread, clothing, housing, education, justice and peace.

Was Black Power a help or a hindrance to civil rights?

For a typical SCLC supporter, Black Power seemed a step back. The strategy of getting general support for civil rights for blacks from whites in general and powerful whites in particular had seemed on course, with successes in 1964 and 1965. Now it seemed that the militancy and violence

The Black Panthers A Black Power group that started in Oakland, California in 1966 and soon received national attention by armed parades of 'self defence' (against 'police brutality') in a distinctive uniform that included berets and dark glasses. For three years it was a central focus of attention in the civil rights movement and recruited several thousand members in the larger US cities. It declined in numbers and influence after members were killed in shoot-outs with police in 1969.

Huey Newton (1942–89) and **Bobby Seale (b. 1936)** Newton had little formal education and was self-taught; Seale was in the US air force. They met at San Francisco School of Law and formed the Black Panther group in Oakland, California, in 1966. In 1967, Newton was shot, arrested and convicted of violent offences. Seale had a murder charge dropped in 1971. Both moved away from their violent past in the early 1970s. Newton fled to Cuba in 1974, returning in 1977. He was shot dead in a street in Oakland in 1989. Seale ran for Mayor of Oakland in 1973 and finished second. In 1981, he wrote *Seize the Time*, a history of the Black Panther movement. He then worked to improve the social and economic conditions of a number of black neighbourhoods.

Failure of the Poor People's Campaign The march that King planned to lead to highlight poverty for all poor people in the US, eventually took place in the summer of 1968. It was poorly organised. The camp, Resurrection City, was set up within sight of the US Congress building in Washington but it became a sea of mud after heavy rain. The badly organised march offended many who had hitherto been sympathetic to the cause, some of whom were concerned by the more radical nature of the economic challenge posed by the march. Conditions were so bad that many of the protesters left early before the local police received orders to close it down.

Richard Nixon (1913–94) was Eisenhower's running mate in 1952 and became Vice President, taking a strong stand against communism. In the 1950s in the Senate he tended to take a moderately liberal line on civil rights. In 1960, he was the Republican presidential candidate, but was defeated by Kennedy. In 1968 he was elected President. Though he said he opposed new initiatives on civil rights, affirmative action and bussing were largely developed under his Presidency. His first administration was occupied mainly with foreign affairs. Re-elected in 1972, his second term was overshadowed by the Watergate scandal (a break-in to the Democratic Party headquarters).

of Black Power had ruined the movement. Yet Malcolm X and those who followed him had re-defined the civil rights question. In an approach reminiscent of Marcus Garvey, they had re-asserted the idea of being proud to be black. They wished to emphasise black culture, rather than integrating with whites in a colour-blind society. Even King in his final days referred to a new racial pride which he viewed as positive.

The big question

The different approaches and theories of Black Power and the non-violent direct action of the more mainstream civil rights movement had posed a fundamental question: did the civil rights movement aim for equality in a fully integrated society or were blacks equal but different with their own cultural traditions in music, clothes, food, hairstyles and a common slave heritage? Black Power threw up other uncertainties: what were the geographical implications of a distinct black culture? Should they have a different state to themselves or go back to Africa? Some saw solidarity in developing their own Trade Unions (see section 2).

FEDERAL REACTION TO BLACK CIVIL RIGHTS 1968–74

What was the political situation in 1968?

There were few positive signs of further civil rights reforms. The **failure of the Poor People's Campaign** (without King) had lowered the movement's public image, and the growing militancy of Black Power meant that large swathes of conservative America were against supporting further civil rights campaigns. President Johnson, a strong supporter of civil rights since he became President, had been broken by the disaster of Vietnam and he decided not to stand again for Presidential election in 1968. The new President **Richard Nixon** believed there should be a pause after the drama of the previous few years.

What were Nixon's actions?

Nixon took a strong line on law and order including firm action against the Black Panthers. He also rejected Ralph

Abernathy's demands for social reform. After some early moves there were no major civil rights initiatives in the latter years of his Presidency as Watergate increasingly dominated. He **resigned in 1974**.

As a result, overcrowding problems continued and many blacks remained poor, especially with the recession. Politically, Nixon followed a 'southern strategy', aiming to take votes from southern Democrats opposed to their party's policy on civil rights. Nixon was successful in turning some of these voters into Republicans. He also hoped to prevent them supporting the segregationist Presidential candidate George Wallace. These tactics were hardly likely to result in a pro-civil rights policy. However, previous civil rights gains had provided a momentum to ensure there was movement in two areas, employment discrimination and educational equality.

Employment

Nixon encouraged a policy of **affirmative action**. The idea was to make allowances for the lack of opportunity for the African American freed for a century but discriminated against for most of it. President Johnson had mentioned affirmative action in a speech in June 1965: '*You do not take a person who, for years has been hobbled by chains and liberate him…and then say "you are free to compete with all the others" and still justly believe you have been completely fair*'.

The idea was controversial; could discrimination of a positive kind be justified whereby blacks would be guaranteed statistical quotas for employment and educational opportunities? Also, could the lack of formal educational qualifications be overlooked in view of the lack of equality of opportunity? Civil rights figures such as the Urban League's leader, Whitney Young, thought affirmative action unwise strategically because American society was known for its emphasis on meritocracy. Lawrence Reddick of the SCLC agreed. He argued that affirmative action '*violates our principle of equality*'.

What was affirmative action in practice?

In 1969 Nixon took up the idea to tackle discrimination in the construction industry. In the Philadelphia plan contractors set targets for hiring people from minorities.

FEPC The Fair Employment Practices Commission (FEPC) was set up by President Roosevelt in 1941. It was an attempt to prevent discrimination in Government jobs and the defence industries on the basis of colour or national origins. However, the success of their regulations varied greatly and it never became a federal law across all states. Probably the most effective were the ones introduced in 1945/6 in north-eastern states such as New York and Massachusetts. Southern states were not involved until the Civil Rights Act of 1964 extended the FEPC principle to the whole of the US. After the Act, the federal government continued to take the initiative on civil rights with regulations issued for the whole country, so that the south could no longer opt out on the grounds of 'states rights'.

***Griggs* v. *Duke Power Company* 1971** With regard to the Duke Power generation plant, the Supreme Court ruled that the requirement for employees to possess a high school diploma or pass an intelligence test had been unreasonable for blacks in view of past educational discrimination against them.

The result was an increase in black workers from one to 12 per cent though it was attacked on the grounds that it was a '*rigid system of inflexible quotas*'. For once, all three powers in the American Constitution (legislature, executive and judiciary) were in harmony. Congress backed the policy, passing an Equal Opportunity Act in 1972, which gave more teeth to the Equal Opportunity Employment Commission and more power to enforce the federal guidelines in the Courts. The Supreme Court had already confirmed the validity of affirmative action in ***Griggs* v. *Duke Power Company* 1971**.

Nixon took the view that Government 'hand ups' were better than welfare 'handouts' but his other reasons for backing affirmative action were pragmatic to the point of opportunism. He though that white-dominated Trade Unions might be split by the idea and thus weakened. Above all it was clear that voting equality had arrived and therefore Nixon was courting potential Republican votes in trying to improve their employment opportunities.

Desegregation of schools: What was Bussing?

Another area that saw significant developments was education. Desegregation laws could be implemented providing the Supreme Court was still liberal enough to enforce them. Bussing was the mandatory transporting of children to areas outside their own locality to achieve a better race mix in the schools. This became a radical way to try to force racial integration and beat *de facto* segregation. Those who liked neighbourhood schools, or had racist suspicions about how their white children would be treated by blacks, often opposed it. However, by 1972, due to more effective implementation, southern schools were better integrated than many other areas of the US.

What was the importance of the Supreme Court?

Significantly, change was now coming from above. However, there had also been pressure from below. Showing greater staying power than some of the other civil rights organisations, the NAACP undertook further legal action concerning school desegregation at both state and Supreme Court level. This soon bore fruit: in the 1971 legal case *Swann* **v.** *Charlotte-Mecklenburg Board of Education* the Supreme Court upheld bussing. However, later verdicts such as *Milliken* **v.** *Bradley*, were less enthusiastic. Bussing (often unpopular anyway) began to decline. If it was enforced there was a flight of white people to all-white suburbs where there were no bussing schemes: if it wasn't, re-segregation crept back in. Schools were reflecting the attitudes of society rather than moulding them.

How far was higher education desegregated?

Desegregation of higher education was another area of struggle as some private colleges in the South maintained an effective colour-bar. The Supreme Court case of *Green* v. *Connally* 1970 made it clear that federal funds would be withheld from higher education institutions that continued to have a policy of segregation. Progress was slow, some colleges remaining predominantly black or white. In 1971 about a third of black students in the US as a whole were in their traditional (predominantly black) colleges but in the south the figure was much higher, at nearly 90 per cent.

What were the attitudes of Presidents Ford and Carter to civil rights?

In the brief time of Nixon's successor **Gerald Ford** (President 1974–77) there was only a limited change of policy on civil rights. Ford enjoyed better relations with civil rights leaders than Nixon and appointed the first black Transport Secretary to his administration, William T. Coleman. However, Ford continued to back Nixon's ROAR campaign (Restore our Alienated Rights) a movement organised by white parents in Boston to stop bussing. Ford was right to be pessimistic about capturing the black vote for the Republican Party in the election of 1976; 90 per cent of blacks voted for his Democrat challenger Jimmy Carter. The position of the two main parties on black civil rights had undergone a complete revolution in 100 years.

Jimmy Carter's (President 1977–81) inexperience of federal politics (he had previously been Governor of Georgia) was a major handicap. He was potentially better

Swann **v.** *Charlotte-Mecklenburg Board of Education* The Court ruled that since school authorities had previously used bussing to transport school pupils it was a legitimate weapon in an attempt to get a reasonable racial balance in their schools.

Milliken **v.** *Bradley* **1974** In 1974, *Milliken* v. *Bradley* stopped court-ordered bussing between white suburbs and largely black metropolitan areas. It became clear that bussing would only be allowed if there was deliberate segregation.

Gerald Ford (1913–2006) Born in Omaha, Nebraska. He was selected by President Nixon to replace Nixon's existing Vice President, Spiro Agnew, who had to resign after charges of corruption. He voted for the main civil rights bills in the 1960s. However, he was sceptical of too much federal power in this area, sometimes supporting attempts to amend the legislation in favour of greater state discretion in its implementation.

Jimmy Carter (b.1924) Rather inactive on civil rights when a young Democrat in Georgia, he took a more positive line on black equality as Governor. In 1976, he defeated Gerald Ford in the Presidential election. He was a strong supporter of black civil rights while President.

1978 Alan Baake, a white student trying to get a place at the California University Medical School, won a Supreme Court case which ruled he had been unfairly discriminated against when rejected because of his race.

Ronald Reagan (1911–2004) A Hollywood actor, born in Illinois. He lost his early liberal views after he became President of the Screen Actors' Guild. Elected Governor of California in 1966 and 1970 where he dealt forcefully with student rioting. He opposed the Voting Rights Act in 1965 as 'humiliating' to the south. As President, he tended to oppose welfare and employment programmes that particularly benefited African Americans. Elected President of the US in 1979 and re-elected 1983. Following conservative economic and social policies, his folksy style proved popular with the American electorate. Even though he was a firm anti-communist, he was President at a timewhen the relationship with the Soviet Union thawed considerably.

disposed than his predecessor to civil rights, as his Government's appointments made plain, with 37 black federal judges, twice as many as ever before. However, he lacked the popular support for further measures on civil rights for blacks, the economic stability of the Johnson years to make them realistic, and a sympathetic Supreme Court. The Court decision in *Regents of the University of California* v. *Baake* 1978 began a partial reaction away from too much affirmative action. So, the signs for further significant progress in civil rights were not looking good.

How different was Reagan's approach to Civil Rights 1981–89?

Ronald Reagan's election success in 1980 sent a man to the White House, whose views on civil rights were historically negative. Eisenhower had been largely neutral on civil rights, Kennedy slow to act, Johnson (after great achievements) ultimately distracted, and Carter ineffective. But all recent Presidents, even Nixon and Ford, had supported previous civil rights legislation in 1964 and 1965. Reagan had opposed this legislation, but now accepted, it taking the line that his administration was 'colour-blind'. But those who were not politically blind could see that this was a way of trying to resist affirmative action. Legal cases were fought by federal officials in the courts. Reagan appointed fewer blacks to the federal administration than any President since Eisenhower.

What was the effect of Reagan's welfare policies on African Americans?

Reagan's Presidency coincided with an economic slowdown. Reductions in welfare payments hit the black community particularly hard. In 1980, black people were 11.7 per cent of the population but were high recipients of Aid to Families with dependent children (43 per cent), housing subsidies (34 per cent) and food stamps (35 per cent). The measures which followed Reagan's election, impacted most severely on the poorest black families. After 1983 the economy recovered but many blacks did not share in the ensuing prosperity because they had become caught in a poverty trap at the bottom of society.

What was significant about Reagan's judicial appointments?

Reagan felt 'judicial merit' should not be sacrificed merely to acquire a more statistically representative legal profession. His appointment of conservative thinker William Rehnquist as Chief Justice of the Supreme Court in 1986 meant more cautious interpretations of civil rights legislation. Though there was no major overturning of precedent, the Court gave other rulings that modified previous civil rights changes.

What was the view of Congress on civil rights?

Quite frequently Reagan was forced to accept change because of a more liberal Congress and, like the Supreme Court, he could stall and sometimes delay change but not stop it. For instance, in 1982 when renewing the Voting Rights Act, Congress strengthened it with stricter laws concerning discrimination against groups of voters. The acceptance of the Bill by the old segregationist Strom Thurmond (see pages 66 and 68 for Thurmond's opposition) showed how public opinion had changed. In 1983 Congress insisted on making Martin Luther King's birthday a public holiday: Reagan agreed reluctantly. In 1988, Congress also strengthened the 1968 Fair Housing Act and in the same year passed the **Civil Rights Restoration Act** over Reagan's veto.

George H.W. Bush and civil rights 1989–92

In his Presidential campaign, Reagan's successor, **George H.W. Bush**, had stigmatised Michael Dukakis, his Democrat challenger, for being soft on (frequently black) crime. Bush vetoed a Civil Rights Bill which made it easier to challenge job discrimination as a 'quota measure' before later allowing it to become law. Only 6.9 per cent of his judicial appointments were from racial minorities. His **appointment of Clarence Thomas** to the Supreme Court in 1991 was a cunning political move. Though he was not as well qualified as some other candidates, Thomas was a rare breed: a conservative Republican black lawyer.

KEY EVENTS

1988 Civil Rights Restoration Act In 1984 in *Grove City v. Bell*, the Supreme Court ruled that organisations which received federal funds only had to be in compliance with the area of civil rights legislation for which they had received the money. The new Act said that all aspects of civil rights legislation had to be complied with before any funds could be given. This illustrates the more liberal approach of Congress to civil rights than either President or Supreme Court in the 1980s and also the constitutional power of the legislature.

KEY PEOPLE

George H.W. Bush (b. 1924) Born into a politically active family, he was decorated for bravery in the Second World War. Represented Texas in the House of Representatives 1966–70 and was US Ambassador to the United Nations 1971–74. He was selected as Vice Presidential running mate to Ronald Reagan in 1979 after his own unsuccessful Presidential campaign. On civil rights issues he came to the Presidency with a liberal record, for instance voting for the Fair Housing Act of 1968. He was less keen on what he saw as 'artificial' civil rights such as bussing and affirmative action. He vetoed the Civil Rights Bill of 1990 seeing it as 'a quota bill', that is a purely statistical exercise to increase the employment opportunities of African Americans by affirmative action.

Appointment of Clarence Thomas The Senate only approved Thomas by 52 votes to 48. This was partly because of Democrat opposition to a strong Republican, but also because Judge Thomas was accused of sexual harassment by Anita Hill, who was one of his legal advisers, on the eve of his appointment. Thomas strongly denied the charges and no case was ever brought against him.

Election of African Americans Increasing numbers of African Americans were elected to public office, some even in the previously racist Deep South: in Alabama, John Hurlett was elected Sheriff in 1970 in Lownes County; in Atlanta, Andrew Young was elected to Congress in 1972 and Maynard Jackson became the town's Mayor in 1973; Richard Arrington was elected Mayor of Birmingham in 1979.

Blacks holding public office In 1964 just 100 blacks had held public office: by 1992 it was over 8,000. 36 were elected to the House of Representatives in that year. African Americans were about 11 per cent of the population and had provided over 8 per cent of the House.

POLITICAL AND ECONOMIC PROGRESS IN THE BLACK COMMUNITIES

Did the Voting Rights Act have as much impact as the Civil Rights Act?

After 1965 there was an immediate and dramatic increase in the black vote especially in the south. The NAACP concentrated on getting the black voters registered in states like Mississippi (see table below) where registration had been poor before.

Percentage of black adults registered to vote by state

Year	Alabama	Georgia	Louisiana	Mississippi
1964	19.3	27.4	31.6	6.7
1968	61.3	60.4	60.8	67.5

However, after this rapid increase, the figures settled down and by the elections of 1976 under 60 per cent of eligible blacks had registered to vote and fewer than 50 per cent actually voted.

How far was there a growth in black representatives?

Black representatives soon followed black voting as **African Americans were elected** in increasing numbers to public office in federal and state positions in the south. Most supported the Democrats. The party that had formerly favoured white supremacy now became heavily dependent on the votes of black Americans. The Voting Rights Act meant that blacks could control their own localities, sometimes in the most racist areas. It was only a few years after Bull Connor had left office but a world away in attitude.

As the percentage of black people was smaller in the north, getting elected there could be an even bigger challenge but Harold Washington became Mayor of Chicago in 1983. This reflected economic as well as social and political change. 100,000 black voters had been registered for voting with a campaign financed by black businessmen. An increasing number of **African Americans held public office**.

Did electing African Americans make a difference?

Political involvement did not necessarily produce greatly improved conditions for African Americans, except for a minority of wealthy blacks who benefited from the general economic prosperity. **Mayors in large cities** had to avoid alienating their white liberal coalition partners. The prevailing mood was not a money-spending one and the support of wealthier blacks for the Democrats was uncertain. The advantage of greater access to public office was partly cancelled by financial and political constraints. One problem was the low turnout of black voters. This suggested that poor blacks remained alienated from a political system which they felt offered them little.

How effective were the civil rights organisations?

After 1970 the changing political, social and economic scene produced alterations in the way civil rights organisations operated. Many of the more militant ones which had been influenced by Black Power, fell by the wayside.

SCLC survived, but Ralph Abernathy proved limited as a leader and left the organisation in 1977. His successor, Joseph Lowery, was a church minister from the King generation and ensured the traditions of the organisation were carried on. However, the times were less suited to its direct and confrontational style of campaigning. The legalistic traditions of the NAACP continued. However, as in the past, their leaders such as Benjamin Hooks were accused of not being sufficiently in touch with poor black America. Hooks struggled to increase membership from the 200,000 to which it had fallen when he took over in 1977.

HOW IMPORTANT WAS JESSE JACKSON TO CIVIL RIGHTS LEADERSHIP?

By the 1980s his growing reputation put **Jesse Jackson** in a position where he could aspire to leadership of the civil rights movement, tracing his line back to King and the

KEY TERMS

Black mayors in large cities like Harold Washington (Mayor of Chicago 1983–87), Tom Bradley in Los Angeles (elected 1973 and re-elected five times) and David Dinkins in New York (1990–93).

KEY PEOPLE

Jesse Jackson (b. 1941) emerged as a prominent SCLC official as a young man. Studying theology in Chicago in 1966, his knowledge of conditions of blacks in the north was used by King in his campaign. Jackson had organised Operation Breadbasket. In 1971 he founded his own organisation PUSH (People United to Serve Humanity) and was again successful in getting thousands of new jobs for African Americans making use of affirmative action regulations. Twice campaigned for the Democratic Party nomination for the Presidency.

Rainbow coalition This included poor whites, Native Americans, Hispanics, Asian and Arab Americans as well as African Americans. In both 1984 and 1988 Jackson was well supported by African Americans who disliked President Reagan's economic policies, especially welfare reduction. The use of local support, based on help from black churches for national civil rights goals with a charismatic speaker at emotional meetings, was reminiscent of King's style of campaigning. In 1984 Jackson was third out of seven candidates but in 1988 with more white support and closer links to the Democrat Party (and no links to Louis Farrakhan) he did even better, winning 7 million votes (twice as many as in 1984) and finishing second to Michael Dukakis.

Bifurcation The splitting of the black community in two. All African Americans had suffered together when faced with continued racial discrimination after Emancipation but by the 1980s the wealthier black middle class was becoming increasingly prosperous while the very poorest African Americans were becoming relatively poorer and poorer in comparison with the rest of the nation. So they developed correspondingly different social and political attitudes.

SCLC. Moreover, the Christian basis to his views, his style of speaking and his overall programme (if somewhat more pro-capitalist) was reminiscent of the King era. As a Democrat, Jackson had two serious attempts to become the Party nominee for the Presidency in 1984 and 1988 as part of a newly formed **Rainbow coalition**. His strategy was to persuade disillusioned African Americans to have more faith in the existing political system. He hoped to attract both the previously apathetic blacks and those of a more revolutionary Black Power persuasion to support him. Jackson also hoped to unite a variety of races into a winning coalition with liberal-minded Democrat whites who had also become disillusioned with the political system.

What was the significance of Jackson's candidacy?

Jackson had highlighted the importance of the black vote, first apparent even in small numbers with President Truman forty years before. Blacks were now over 12 per cent of the American electorate and would tend to vote for an African American – colour-blindness had not arrived.

Some civil rights figures saw Jackson as an old-fashioned throwback to the past when black ministers told their flock how to behave and what to believe. This approach to civil rights was considered unnecessary because now they could elect their own candidates to represent them. Power could move from bottom to top. It was argued that the demand of the integrationists in the 1960s had been achieved: '*a black face in a high place*'. Now there was a desire to move from individual successes to a proportional representation of blacks in political life as a whole. Many white politicians now accepted this. When campaigning for the Presidency in 1992, Bill Clinton said he wanted to make his administration '*look like America*'.

WHAT WAS THE SOCIAL AND ECONOMIC POSITION OF AFRICAN AMERICANS BY 1992?

What was Bifurcation?

Many African Americans were now taking economic and

political advantage of the opportunities they had as a result of civil rights changes, becoming civil servants, bankers and publishers as well as the more traditional lawyers, teachers and ministers of religion.

This meant that the gap between the continuingly high proportion of poor African Americans and the increasing numbers of the upwardly mobile black middle class widened between 1960 and 1992. Some well-off black Americans became socially detached from their fellow blacks. By the mid 1980s, almost 40 per cent of black families had succeeded in acquiring a middle class lifestyle but another 30 per cent declined into deeper poverty. Cutbacks in welfare provision in the 1980s and the growth of the illegal drug market were changing the social environment for those African Americans still living in inner cities. No longer was there shared suffering and group identity.

One result was that they moved away from inner city ghetto-like areas, leaving behind a substantial black underclass, poorly educated with nobody to articulate their problems. Better off blacks had avoided crime, unemployment and urban chaos but their departure deprived the areas of leadership and a stable presence.

Class and race issues became linked.

What does the Rodney King Affair tell us about the state of black civil rights in 1992?

When African American Rodney King was stopped for drunken driving in Los Angeles in April 1991 he resisted arrest and was very severely beaten repeatedly by police. The horrific incident was caught on video camera. Despite the very clear evidence seen by the whole world, in March 1992 an all-white jury acquitted the policemen who were accused of serious assault. A stream of protest erupted in the form of race riots in the city. Over 50 people were killed and over 2,000 injured. The jury appeared to be in denial regarding racist police, and the way the protestors behaved clearly rejected the King philosophy and shows that the threat to law and order through rioting caused by racial grievance was still high. These events illustrate that the traditional debates surrounding black civil rights were still very much alive as the twentieth century neared its end.

OVERALL CONCLUSION

Life had frequently been transformed for the better for many African Americans between 1960 and 1992: much of this could be linked to civil rights campaigns and policies.

- Segregation in public places had disappeared.
- Blacks were voting on an equal basis to whites and increasingly being elected to public office.
- All political figures within the main parties accepted the principle of racial equality and condemned discrimination.
- Middle-class blacks had increased their numbers and were prominent in American business life.
- Opposition (especially violent opposition) to civil rights legislation had largely disappeared. The KKK remained as a fringe group with little support.

However:

- Unemployment remained high: in 1992, the figures for blacks were 14.2 per cent, nearly twice the national average (7.8 per cent). The unemployment rate for black male teenagers was 50 per cent.
- The economic gap between blacks continued to widen. One in seven black households in 1990 had an annual gross income exceeding $50,000 but, overall, improvement was at best patchy and at worst non-existent. In 1978, female-headed black families earned a median income of under $6,000.
- By 1992 blacks and whites often continued to live apart from one another, save for a few integrated upper middle class areas like Philadelphia's Mount Airy. Poor black ghettos were still prevalent in inner cities.
- 23 per cent of young African-American men were in prison, on parole or on probation. Although police forces were often less discriminatory and regularly

recruited blacks, the Rodney King affair showed that racist feelings were not always far from the surface.

- Black attainment in schools had vastly improved since the 1960s. By 1992 76 per cent of blacks graduated from high school, just 6 per cent lower than whites. However, there were signs that some schools were starting to re-segregate, for example the Supreme Court was still ruling on educational segregation questions in 1992. Moreover, in *Freeman* v. *Pitts* in the same year, relating to schools in Atlanta, Georgia, the Court confirmed they could do no more to aid desegregation which had started to re-appear because of house ownership patterns among black and white.

The problems remaining centred on traditional questions such as unemployment, housing, health care and family problems but there were also newer ones such as business closure and drugs. Feelings of hopelessness among poorer blacks were unchanged from the 1960s: memories of great black leaders were starting to dim. Unlike the '**we shall overcome**' generation, the 'hip hop generation' had lost faith in the system to produce reform. The economic crisis was of both a structural (moving out of the city) and fiscal (less government spending) kind. The most acute problems remained among the young, as they had 30 years before. King's 'dream' had only partly been fulfilled.

KEY TERMS

We shall overcome A song with gospel roots from around 1900, adapted to become the unofficial anthem of the civil rights movement in the 1960s. President Johnson's use of the phrase in speaking to Congress early in 1965 indicated his degree of commitment to the civil rights movement at this time.

'In the 1980s and 1990s…many racial problems continued to be unresolved, and even worsened, yet there were also some advances…Legal or de jure segregation may have passed away but de facto economic and residential segregation remained.'

Kevern Verney, *Black Civil Rights in America*

QUESTIONS TO CONSIDER

1. Was Black Power's overall contribution to civil rights positive or negative?

2. Compare the contributions to civil rights in this period of Congress, the Presidency and the Supreme Court.

3. How far and why was there less progress on civil rights in employment, education and housing than on questions of voting and representation?

EXAM STYLE QUESTIONS

1. Assess the view that the Supreme Court was the most important branch of the federal government in assisting African Americans achieve their civil rights in the period 1865–1992?

2. To what extent were the activities of white racist groups the most important reason for the continued discrimination against African Americans from 1865 to 1992?

3. Assess the view that the federal government was more of a hindrance than a help to the attainment of African American civil rights in the period 1865 to 1992.

Section 2: Trade Union And Labour Rights 1865–1992

WHAT WERE TRADE UNION AND LABOUR RIGHTS?

The rights pursued by trade unions were different from the civil rights for which African Americans struggled throughout the period between 1865 and 1992. Although racial, ethnic and gender discrimination in the workplace was present for much of this period, a significant proportion of the workforce already possessed the fundamental rights of citizenship that continued to be denied to many African Americans for so long. Much of the struggle for trade union and labour rights was focused on the right of trade unions to exist at all, to be recognised as representing their membership and to do so in negotiations with employers for improvements in pay and working conditions. They campaigned for appropriate structures to be put in place that obliged employers to bargain with the representatives of the workforce and that established systems for mediation, conciliation and arbitration. Labour rights included also the freedom of workers to withdraw their labour by going on strike without fear of losing their jobs or being subject to intimidation by employers.

Progress to the achievement of these rights was dependent on a number of factors that at various points served to promote or impede success. Throughout much of this period, employers were at best, reluctant and for the most part, resistant to the unionisation of their employees. Their suspicion was frequently shared by the federal and state authorities. Changes and fluctuations in the economy and in the structure of the workforce impacted both positively and negatively. Of critical importance was the workforce itself, divided by race, ethnicity and gender, sometimes tainted by militancy and fickle in its support for the unions that were attempting to serve its interests.

CHAPTER 6

1865–1914 'Your huddled masses'

Was the new immigration an obstacle to the development of workers' solidarity before 1914?

Hypothesis:

- Racial and ethnic divisions were the most significant barrier to the achievement of trade union rights before 1914.

WHAT WAS THE EXTENT OF UNION AND LABOUR RIGHTS IN 1865?

In 1865, union and labour rights were limited to what workers could negotiate with their employers in their own workplace. Such unions as did exist were small and exclusively for skilled workers. Employers were under no legal obligation to recognise the existence of labour unions let alone their right to negotiate on behalf of their members to improve working and living conditions. However, between 1860 and 1900, as US industrialisation accelerated, the number of industrial workers jumped from 885,000 to 3.2 million. Production moved into factories and manufacturing processes became a series of repetitive and monotonous tasks.

The small craft unions that existed in 1865, opposed employers' attempts to reduce wages and to provide sickness benefits for their members. Their strength came from the fact that they were a **closed shop** – they only admitted craftsmen (skilled tradesmen). The concept that union strength could come from numbers did not yet exist. Yet, by 1865, industrialisation was well underway and was generating a large workforce of semi and unskilled workers who were excluded from the craft unions. This fast growing workforce, therefore, had no representation or protection from exploitation by employers. This situation did, however, prompt some labour leaders to recognise that there was a need to organise labour on a larger scale if the worst evils of industrialisation were to be avoided and the rights of workers were to be established and recognised.

William H. Sylvis was one such leader who was one of the first to promote the idea of working-class solidarity from his position as president of the Iron Moulders' International Union. To this end, he called a convention of workers' leaders in 1866 and out of this came the National Labor Union. This was an attempt to form a single association that would cross craft lines and draw a mass membership. The new organisation campaigned for an eight-hour day, currency and banking reform, the ending of convict labour (see page 35), a federal labour department and immigration restrictions, particularly of Chinese. The NLU also promoted the cause of working women. Sylvis encouraged African-American workers to form unions but these were to be separate from the NLU.

The NLU was short-lived. Between 1866 and 1867, a strike by the Iron Founders failed. This weakened its position but did not deter the membership. By 1868, the union had 300,000 members across the USA. After the strike, Sylvis recognised that the only way that labour rights could be established was through political reform. However, his sudden death in 1869 prevented further change and marked the demise of the NLU.

WHAT WAS THE IMPACT OF INDUSTRIALISATION ON THE POSITION OF WORKERS?

By the 1880s, traditional skills were disappearing and both men and women workers were becoming increasingly unskilled and low paid. By 1890, unskilled women made up 35 per cent of the workforce. The expansion of the factory system created an unprecedented demand for unskilled labour. By the 1880s, nearly one-third of the workers in the railroad and steel industries were common labourers. In construction, machine tool industries and garment manufacturing, industrialists used the **contract system** to hire unskilled labourers. Unskilled workers moved from city to city and from industry to industry looking for work and

William H. Sylvis (1829–69) was born in Armaugh, Pennsylvania. Taught by his father, he started work as a wagon maker and at the age of 18 began an apprenticeship as an iron maker. After completing his training, he joined the Journeyman Stove and Hollow-Ware Moulders' Union of Philadelphia. Soon after becoming secretary of the union, he began to contact other iron moulder unions with a view to establishing a national union. Progress on this was interrupted by the outbreak of the Civil War. In 1863, he brought together 21 local branches to form the Iron Moulders' International Union. He promoted the dignity of the working man and urged that the membership should not be divided along religious or racial lines.

Contract system involved the employment of workers that could be laid off in slack periods.

earned about a third of the wages of skilled artisans. In the late 1870s, bricklayers earned $3.00 per day but unskilled labourers a mere $1.30. Only southern millworkers, averaging 84 cents per day, earned less.

At this time, millions of workers had few rights and could do little to improve their working conditions. Both skilled and unskilled workers worked 12 hour shifts, often under hazardous and harmful conditions. In steel mills, inexperience with complicated, heavy machinery and lack of safety precautions led to high accident rates. Children as young as eight worked in coal mines and cotton mills and were vulnerable to accidents, often resulting from lax supervision. In coal mines, lung diseases often resulted from excessive dust levels, and injuries to women and children were common.

On the railroads, there were also safety problems. In 1889, 2,000 railway workers were killed as a result of accidents. Employers resisted the introduction of health and safety standards on the grounds of cost. Workers disabled following industrial accidents and those widowed as a result, received minimal aid from employers. Sickness clubs were formed but compensation was inadequate. Until the 1890s, the courts considered employer negligence one of the normal risks borne by the employee. Workers were forced to join self-help schemes such as fraternal organisations and ethnic clubs for sickness and accident benefits. However, the amounts paid out were usually too small to give much relief. When workers were killed or maimed, their families were forced to depend on relatives or neighbours for help.

THE GROWTH OF TRADE UNIONS BEFORE 1914

The Knights of Labor
The Knights of Labor (KOL) was founded in 1869 by **Uriah Smith Stephens** and achieved some initial success particularly after it attracted the membership of the National Labor Union following its demise. However, it gained real momentum after 1879, when **Terence V. Powderly** became its leader. His intention was to unite skilled and unskilled labour, and to remove the barriers of

racial and cultural origin imposed by existing local labour associations. Women were also welcomed into the KOL. The union demanded an eight-hour day, equal pay for women and the abolition of child labour. Powderly rejected strikes as a means of achieving its ends, preferring to seek reforming legislation to establish workers' rights and improve conditions. By 1881, its membership had grown to 20,000, however, not all of the rank and file membership necessarily supported Powderly's anti-strike position. In 1885, he was obliged himself to abandon his principles when action against members of the KOL working at the Wabash Railroad by its owner, Jay Gould, clearly presented a threat to the existence of the union. The ensuing strike brought the Wabash Railroad to a standstill and effectively forced Gould to halt his anti-union campaign. This success boosted the membership of the KOL which rose to 700,000 in 1886. This number included 10,000 women and 50,000 African Americans.

By this time, the KOL leadership felt strong enough to extend its activities to politics by influencing elections at local and national level. The idea of labour unions with the capacity to influence policy decisions alarmed some politicians. Their nervousness was exacerbated by the industrial unrest that characterised the 1880s and early 1900s largely as a result of a **slump in the economy** that impacted negatively on wage levels, prices and levels of production.

After the violence of the Haymarket Affair in 1886 (see page 104), the KOL's reputation was destroyed and its influence and support dwindled. At that point in time, however, it was the nearest that workers came to establishing some kind of solidarity. By the 1890s its membership had dwindled to 100,000. At this time, internal divisions led many of the unions to break away from the KOL and join the Industrial Workers of the World. Others joined the American Federation of Labor.

The American Federation of Labor
The most significant development in this period was the American Federation of Labor (AFL) that effectively replaced the KOL after its foundation in December 1886.

1886 Puck Cartoon, 'Arbitration is the true balance of power' Library.

This was one of the first successful national labour federations seeking to link all unions and became the largest. Its leader, **Samuel Gompers,** argued that to stand up to large corporations, labour had to harness the bargaining power of skilled workers, who were not easily replaced, and concentrate on practical goals of raising wages and reducing hours. Whilst seeking reform through legislation, Gompers also supported the use of strikes and boycotts. Nevertheless, some of the USA's most influential businessmen, including **Marcus A. Hanna** and **J. P. Morgan**, were prepared to work with him in an attempt to establish the machinery for giving workers the right to **mediation** and **conciliation**. By 1914, the Federation had over two million members although they still represented only a small percentage of the national industrial workforce. Moreover, some unions, even within the AFL, were sufficiently powerful to retain a degree of independence. One of these was the **Teamsters Union.** By 1924, the AFL was the only remaining major national federation of trade unions and continued to play a significant part in labour relations through the period of this study. Its activities will be discussed in subsequent chapters.

The Industrial Workers of the World

Less effective was a union set up in Chicago in 1905 calling itself The Industrial Workers of the World ('Wobblies'). It was a more militant organisation with a reputation for violence. Employers therefore regarded it with suspicion. However, it stood out at the time for its defence of the rights of the poor and of illiterate workers such as immigrants. Its membership peaked at around 100,000 members in 1923 who were mainly western miners, lumbermen, fruit pickers and itinerant workers. The 'Wobblies' use of violence and sabotage meant they faced constant harassment through arrests and prosecutions by government officials. By 1924, divisions were occurring within the leadership of the union and, as a result, its strength was broken.

WHY WAS THERE SUCH LITTLE PROGRESS IN THE DEVELOPMENT OF LABOUR AND UNION RIGHTS IN THE LATE NINETEENTH AND EARLY TWENTIETH CENTURY?

The Haymarket Affair 1886

In May 1886, violence broke out between police and striking workers at the McCormick Harvester Plant in Chicago. Four workers were killed when the police opened fire. The following evening, a protest rally took place in Haymarket Square in the city. During the rally, a bomb was thrown, killing seven policemen. The police retaliated by opening fire on the crowd. A further four workers were killed. This violence was blamed on German anarchists led by Johann Most and August Spies and eight were arrested. No evidence connected them to the bomb throwing but all were convicted and five executed. Illinois governor John Altgeld pardoned the three survivors in 1893. Americans became convinced that a foreign conspiracy gripped the nation and animosity towards labour unions intensified.

Old immigrants This refers to the first wave of immigrants to the US who arrived from the early part of the nineteenth century, coming largely from England, Scotland, Germany, Scandinavia and Holland. Many came in search of cheap land on which to farm and joined the westwards internal migration that was underway from the middle of the nineteenth century. After 1848, poor Irish people began to arrive in the US escaping from the Potato Famine and poverty. With the exception of the Irish, these immigrants were predominantly Protestant and although treated with suspicion initially, they became largely accepted.

This incident is indicative of the extent of suspicion and animosity generated by the new immigration of the late nineteenth and early twentieth centuries. It particularly manifested itself in the workplace and created deep divisions between the existing white, Protestant and, usually, skilled workers. These formed the almost exclusive membership of existing unions at local and national levels. For these workers, the arrival of immigrant labour exacerbated the existing tension that was caused by the influx of African-American workers in the closing decades of the nineteenth century (see page 107). In examining the reasons for the slow progress in establishing workers solidarity, the extent to which the workforce was divided along racial and ethnic lines is a crucial factor.

The divided workforce
Old versus new immigration
The arrival of the **old immigrants** in the middle and late nineteenth centuries met the growing demand for labour as industrialisation gathered pace. In mines and factories, some were willing to take on dangerous and dirty jobs. Poor, immigrant women, in particular, were prepared to accept high levels of exploitation because they needed the money. They worked over 16 hours per day in 'sweatshop' conditions without complaint, for fear of dismissal. Their apparent acceptance of bad working conditions angered

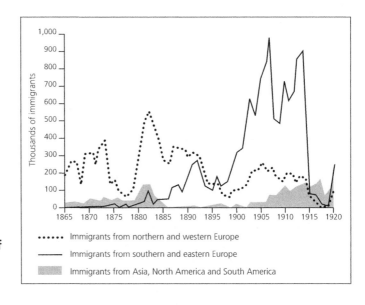

Changing patterns of immigration to the USA, 1865–1920.

many native-born Americans, who believed that immigrant workers kept wages low and reduced their own bargaining power.

The situation worsened in the late nineteenth century with new immigrants arriving from Southern and Eastern Europe and China and Japan. By 1900, over 70 per cent of immigrants came from such countries as Italy, Russia, Greece and the **Austro-Hungarian Empire** and many were Catholic or Jewish. By 1910, immigrants accounted for three quarters of the population of many cities. Between 1900 and 1930, nearly 19 million people entered the United States. As the nineteenth century ended, the greatest threat to social order came from millions of poorer foreigners pouring into American cities and from the growing industrial working class. Woodrow Wilson was fearful of admitting into American society *'multitudes of men of the lowest class'*, fearing that *'a miscellaneous immigrant was creating social chaos'*. Chinese immigration was stopped in 1882 and Japanese immigration in 1907.

Trade unions struggling to gain recognition and increase their influence saw millions of African Americans and immigrants as a serious threat and so discriminated against them by refusing them admittance to their union organisations. As the semi and unskilled workforce came to be dominated by immigrant labour, this refusal was a serious barrier to solidarity and weakened the position of the union leaders as they struggled to gain recognition for labour rights.

There were suspicions in some political circles and amongst some sections of the native, white population, that some immigrant groups, especially, though not exclusively, Italians, brought with them from their mother countries traditions of radicalism, violence and anarchy and stirred up unrest amongst other workers. This seemed to be confirmed by the levels of violence that accompanied strikes involving immigrant labour. Between 1881 and 1905, seven million workers participated in 37,000 strikes, some of which involved damage to property and looting. The activities of **the Molly Maguires (1873)** in the anthracite mining districts of Pennsylvania, the violence

KEY PLACES

Austro-Hungarian Empire A large empire in Central and South-Eastern Europe which existed before the First World War and was ruled over by the Hapsburg family. It contained territories known today as Austria, Hungary, Bosnia, the Czech Republic, Slovakia and Romania.

Country	Total
Germany	5,500,000
Ireland	4,400,000
Italy	4,190,000
Austria-Hungary	3,700,000
Russia	3,250,000
England	2,500,000
Sweden	1,000,000
Norway	730,000
Scotland	570,000
France	530,000
Greece	350,000
Turkey	320,000
Denmark	300,000
Switzerland	258,000
Portugal	210,000
Holland	200,000
Belgium	140,000
Spain	130,000
Romania	80,000
Wales	75,000
Bulgaria	60,000

European Immigration to the USA 1820–1920.

KEY PEOPLE

The Molly Maguires were a group of Irish immigrant miners who formed a secret association to fight for better conditions in the anthracite mines of north-eastern Pennsylvania. During a series of strikes in 1873 resulting from wage cuts, railroad cars were derailed, coal tips set on fire and a superintendent murdered. Pinkerton detectives infiltrated the organisation and 19 men were arrested, convicted and hanged.

and bloodshed that characterised the Haymarket Affair (1886) in Chicago and the Homestead Strike (1892) (see page 111 for further discussion of this strike) are some of the most notorious examples of protests that went badly wrong during this period, although the latter did not involve immigrant labour. This produced reactionary attitudes not only on the part of employers and the general public but also among the labouring classes themselves. The mass of workers were reluctant to join unions, either from a sense of disapproval of their methods or as a result of employer intimidation.

African-American labour

Following the end of slavery in 1863, African Americans began to enter the industrial workforce in increasing numbers, at first in urban areas in the south and, after 1877, increasingly in the north (see also pages 27–29). This multicultural mix in the workforce is crucial in explaining why labourers were not more united at this point. Immigrants from Europe were divided by language and religion and were treated with hostility and suspicion by white, native-born Americans. Both the immigrant and white American workforce refused to work with African Americans. For example, The National Labor Union, formed in 1866, urged African Americans to organise but in racially separate unions (see page 100 for further discussion).

Divisions such as these impeded the development of the kind of unity and solidarity that labour needed in order to assert its rights and be recognised. Instead, employers were able not only to reject any concept of labour rights but also to exploit the divisions. Hence, in times of unrest, white Americans and immigrant workers were laid off and replaced by black labour. The ability of the workforce to protest was also fundamentally weakened by poverty and the need to survive. Troublemakers were dismissed and labelled as such, making it hard for them to find other employment. This did much to impede the emergence of the kind of assertive leadership necessary to unite the labour force and win change and reform.

To reach a balanced assessment of the impact of the divided workforce on the slow progress towards union organisation and the acquisition of labour rights, it is essential to consider other powerful factors that were at work in the USA before the outbreak of the First World War.

Laissez-faire capitalism and big business

It could be argued that a significant factor in explaining the weakness of organised labour was the power of the employers. One source of their strength was the **laissez-faire** policy pursued by the government. This effectively empowered capitalists to form powerful business corporations and to make huge fortunes. This made it possible for a small number of highly successful capitalists to control several key industries and, in the process, come to monopolise them; for example, **Andrew Carnegie** (steel) and **John D. Rockefeller** (oil). Although there were moves by the end of the century to curtail monopolies, for example the **Sherman Anti-Trust Act (1890),** unfettered by restrictive legislation, manufacturers could and did cut wages without warning, lay off workers and change working hours. In these circumstances, the workers themselves had no right of redress and certainly no mechanism for expressing their dissatisfaction. Strikes and protests were organised from time to time but employers resisted any kind of union organisation in their businesses. In some cases, they employed labour spies to operate under cover among the workforce and root out potential disruptive elements. The use of armed force in the event of attempted strikes, as in the Pullman strike (discussed in Chapter 6), was not unusual, although strike breaking was carried out by local rather than federal militia.

The Supreme Court and the partiality of the law

The fact that not only the authorities, but also the courts, supported the employers further limited the development of labour representation after court injunctions were used to break strikes after 1894. In the first decade of the twentieth century, a series of Supreme Court decisions further impeded attempts to give workers their rights. The judgement in the case of *Lochner* v. *New York (1905)* actually invoked the Fourteenth Amendment to declare as

KEY TERMS

Laissez-faire The belief that there should be no government interference in the organisation and operation of business and commercial concerns.

KEY PEOPLE

Andrew Carnegie (1835–1919) Moved from Scotland to the USA in 1848. In 1899, he founded the Carnegie Steel Company and controlled 25 per cent of the nation's iron and steel production. He retired in 1901, having sold his company for $250 million. During his lifetime, he gave over $350 million to educational, cultural and peace organisations.

John D. Rockefeller (1839–1937) controlled 90 per cent of US oil refineries. He formed The Standard Oil Trust in 1882 which was replaced by the Standard Oil Company of New Jersey in 1899. He amassed a personal fortune of $1billion and gave $550 million away to philanthropic projects.

KEY EVENTS

The Sherman Anti-Trust Act (1890) outlawed business trusts. These were huge companies that came to monopolise trade in a particular product or commodity. The Act also declared illegal any contract or combination that attempted to stop trade.

unconstitutional a law imposing a ten-hour day, claiming that it violated the rights of workers to determine their hours of work. However, others placed federal injunctions on unions that organised strikes and attempted to boycott unfair employers or encouraged others to do so.

CASE STUDY (1): AFRICAN AMERICANS AND THE RIGHTS OF LABOUR

The development of union membership and representation for black workers represents a landmark in the movement for civil rights for African Americans. It was slow to come but the struggle for labour rights contributed to the wider struggle in two significant ways:

- The rejection of black workers by white unions forced them into forming their own labour associations. This contributed to their emerging self-awareness and solidarity. It also enabled some to develop leadership skills and abilities.
- African-American historians such as John Hope Franklin and Alfred A. Moss Jr. (*From Slavery to Freedom*, 1994) saw the final admittance of black people to national unions as significant. It helped to create a sense of belonging among African Americans and of national identity. This provided further impetus to the demand for equal rights in every aspect of their lives. Ultimately, trade unions would become a powerful pressure group. In the meantime, membership gained political significance for some, particularly for the black leadership that emerged.

The situation of freedmen in the south, bound by sharecropping and the crop lien system has been discussed earlier in this book (see Chapter 1, page 19). Many enslaved African Americans had acquired skills. Hence, blacksmiths, carpenters and other craftsmen, wishing to throw off plantation life, went in search of work in urban areas. Inspired by Booker T. Washington (see pages 35–39), many established their own businesses despite experiencing discrimination and violent intimidation.

Rejection by the union movement

Initially, the mass of black labour, both skilled and unskilled, was treated with hostility and remained excluded from the union movement in the late nineteenth and early twentieth century. Apart from the inherent racial prejudice, black workers were perceived as a threat. Not only were they used as 'scab' labour to thwart strike action but they were also seen as being responsible for keeping wages low. They did, however, represent a significant section of the workforce, particularly during and after the First World War when thousands moved to the heavily industrialised north in response to the wartime demand for labour (see also Chapter 3, pages 44–45).

It could only be a matter of time before white-union leadership recognised and accepted that the movement for labour rights could only succeed if labour was totally united. This would mean admitting African Americans and other rejected minorities into the unions. This latter point was not entirely lost on those attempting to establish a national labour movement in the late nineteenth century. The Knights of Labor had certainly wanted to admit African Americans as well as members from other ethnic groups and around 60,000 black workers joined. The American Federation of Labor similarly rejected discrimination. Unions were allowed to affiliate only if they admitted all workers as members. However, many circumvented this rule by establishing separate branches of the same union at local level. The Federation tolerated this when its white membership began to dwindle as a result of its inclusive policy. As white unions operated a closed shop in many firms, African American workers were effectively excluded from entering those industries and this further polarised the total workforce.

Black unions

As early as 1869, African Americans had begun to form their own unions. The National Negro Labor Union was founded in that year and attempted, unsuccessfully, to affiliate with white skilled unions. Ongoing discussions about unity with the American Federation of Labor during the First World War produced nothing. Later, in 1925, when Philip Randolph formed the Brotherhood of

Sleeping Car Porters and Maids (BSCP), the Pullman Company refused to work with it. Randolph himself held radical views and even many black workers regarded the 'Brotherhood' as suspicious. Nevertheless, it gained the support of the American Federation of Labor as well as the National Association for the Advancement of Colored People and was finally recognised by the Pullman Company in 1935 (see Chapter 7, pages 122–25 for further discussion of the BSCP campaign).

CASE STUDY (2): THE HOMESTEAD AND PULLMAN STRIKES OF THE 1890S – TO WHAT EXTENT CAN THESE BE SEEN AS TURNING POINTS IN THE DEVELOPMENT OF TRADE UNION AND LABOUR RIGHTS?

The Homestead Strike (1892)

This dispute took place at the Homestead steel works and involved a labour lockout and strike beginning on 30 June 1892 which lasted 143 days. It is claimed to have been the most serious industrial dispute in American labour history. It ended in a battle between strikers and the Pinkerton National Detective Agency (private security agents) on 6 July 1892 and in occupation of the plant by the state militia. The dispute occurred in the Pittsburgh-area town of Homestead, Pennsylvania, between the **Amalgamated Association of Iron and Steel Workers (the AA)** and the Carnegie Steel Company. It exemplifies very well the extent to which violence and intimidation could escalate at this time in response to the actions of ruthless, anti-union employers and equally determined unions fighting for workers' rights.

The AA had already led a bitter strike on 1 January 1882 to prevent management forcing contracts on all workers. Violence occurred on both sides but the strike ended on 20 March in complete victory. The AA brought out the workers again on 1 July, 1889 when negotiations for a new three-year collective bargaining agreement failed. Although victorious, the union was forced to accept significant wage cuts. Carnegie officials conceded that the AA essentially ran the Homestead plant after the 1889 strike. Its membership doubled and the local union treasury had a balance of $146,000. The union grew more belligerent and relationships between workers and managers worsened.

However, the AA strike at the Homestead steel mill in 1892 was a landmark in the history of union strike action. It differed from earlier large-scale strikes which had failed as a result of poor organisation and lack of effective leadership. This strike was organised and purposeful and set the pattern for future industrial disputes involving strike action. Andrew Carnegie had placed industrialist **Henry Clay Frick** in charge of his company operations in 1881. Frick was determined to break the union at Homestead, a stand that Carnegie supported. In preparation, Frick ordered the plant to manufacture large amounts of steel so

'Homestead troubles' (Front page of Frank Leslie's Illustrated Weekly.) A drawing showing the attack of the strikers and their sympathisers on the Pinkerton men.

that the plant could weather any subsequent strike. He then withdrew union recognition.

The lock-out

With the collective bargaining agreement due to expire on 30 June 1892, Frick and AA leaders began negotiations in February. As the steel industry was prospering, the AA asked for a wage increase. Frick countered with a 22 per cent wage decrease affecting nearly half the union membership. On 30 April, he announced that he would bargain for 29 more days. If no contract was reached, Carnegie Steel would cease to recognise the union. On 28 June, Frick locked workers out of the plate mill and one of the open hearth furnaces. On 29 June when no collective bargaining agreement was reached, Frick locked the union out of the rest of the plant. A high barbed wire fence was erected and the plant sealed to the workers.

On 30 June, AA leaders announced that the company had broken the contract by locking out workers before the contract expired. The Knights of Labor, who also had workers at the plant, agreed to walk out with the skilled AA workers. Workers at Carnegie plants in Pittsburgh, Duquesne, Union Mills and Beaver Falls went on strike in sympathy and were determined to keep the plant closed. Using a steam-powered river launch and several rowboats, they patrolled the Monongahela River alongside the plant in order to blockade any attempt by the management to bring in scab labour. Men also divided themselves into units along military lines. The plant and the town were surrounded by picket lines and 24 hour shifts established. Ferries and trains were watched. Strangers were challenged for explanations of their presence in town and escorted away if one was not forthcoming.

Management responses

The company sought replacement workers in newspapers as far away as Boston and St Louis. Early on 6 July, Frick implemented plans to place Pinkerton detective agents in the mill. At 10.30 a.m., 300 agents assembled on the Davis Island Dam on the Ohio River, five miles below Pittsburgh. Pinkerton agents fired on the crowd killing two and wounding eleven. The crowd responded in kind killing two and wounding twelve. Although the violence had subsided by the late afternoon, the general tension remained and on 12 July, the Pennsylvania State militia arrived. Its occupation of the plant lasted for 95 days. On 18 July, sixteen of the strike leaders were arrested and charged with conspiracy, riot and murder. Each man was jailed for one night and forced to put up a $10,000 bond, a guarantee of future good conduct.

The end of the strike

On 23 July, Alexander Berkman, an anarchist, shot Frick twice in the neck and then stabbed him with a knife. He was convicted of attempted murder and received 22 years in prison. The incident prompted the final collapse of the strike. Hugh O'Donnell offered what was effectively unconditional surrender and on 12 August the company announced that 1,700 men were working at the site and that production had resumed at full capacity. In autumn, 33 members of the strike committee were accused of treason under the state's Crimes Act of 1860. Most went to jail while awaiting trial; a few went into hiding. Support for the strikers evaporated. The AFL refused to call for a boycott of Carnegie products in September 1892. Wholesale crossing of the picket line occurred, first by eastern European immigrant workers and then by all workers. The strike collapsed and the state militia withdrew on 13 October.

What were the results of the strike?

- The action almost bankrupted the union. Nearly 1,600 men were receiving a total of $10,000 in weekly relief from union coffers. With only 192 out of more than 3,800 strikers in attendance, the Homestead AA members voted 101 to 91 to return to work on 20 November 1892.
- The striking AA affiliate in Beaver Falls gave in on the same day as the Homestead members. The affiliate at Union Mills held out until 14 August 1893. By then the union had only 53 members – it was broken.
- The strike broke the AA as a force in the American labour movement. Many employers refused to sign contracts with their AA unions while the strike lasted.
- A union recruiting drive in 1896 was crushed by Frick. In May 1899, 300 Homestead workers formed an AA union branch but Frick ordered the Homestead works to

close and the effort failed. Carnegie Steel remained non-union for 40 years.

- By 1900, not a single steel plant in Pennsylvania remained unionised. Many branches disbanded and others were easily broken.
- AA membership fell to 10,000 in 1894 from its peak of over 24,000 in 1891. A year later, it was 8,000. By 1909, AA membership had sunk to 6,300. A nationwide steel strike of 1919 was unsuccessful.

To this extent, the strike adversely affected the progress of securing rights for workers. Moreover, its impact was not restricted to the steel industry. Employers in other industries became nervous of accepting the unionisation of their workers.

The Pullman Strike (1894)

On 10 May 1894, workers at the Pullman Palace Car Company went on strike. The company, owned by George Pullman, made sleeping and 'parlour' cars leased to virtually all the railway companies in the USA. Pullman prided himself on being a 'model' employer. His workers lived in a company-owned town, where the manufacturing plants were situated, on the outskirts of Chicago. Pullman always claimed that his workers were well-paid and contented. However, in 1893, when the USA was in the grip of an economic depression, he suddenly cut wages by 25 per cent and laid-off over a third of his workforce. The reduction in wages was not matched by a reduction in living costs in his supposedly ideal industrial town and, consequently, the workforce was angry. An attempt to negotiate at least a reduction in rents was rejected by management. The three representatives of the workers at the meeting were subsequently sacked. The sackings precipitated the strike. On 11 May, the Pullman works closed.

Two years earlier, the American Railway Union (ARU) had been formed by **Eugene Debs** to unite railway workers all over the country. This was a militant organisation that quickly seized on the case of the Pullman workers. The workers joined the union and Debs took over the leadership of the strike. After the company refused to

Eugene Debs (1855–1926) was born in Alsace, France and emigrated to the US where his family settled in Indiana. In 1875, he was a founder member of the Brotherhood of Locomotive Firemen, becoming grand secretary in 1880. The Brotherhood was mainly focused on providing services and support to its members rather than collective bargaining. In 1893, Debs left the Brotherhood and formed the American Railway Union (ARU) which was more militant. Whilst serving his prison sentence for his part in the Pullman Strike, he became a socialist. He was imprisoned for his political beliefs and for his opposition to America's involvement in the First World War but this did not prevent him from standing as the Socialist Party candidate for the presidency on five occasions.

discuss **arbitration** procedures, all ARU members were asked to refuse to operate trains using the Pullman carriages. The action soon brought much of the railroad network to a standstill, especially trains leaving Chicago. The union told railroad companies that they would operate their services without the Pullman cars, but the companies claimed that they were unable to do this because their contract with the Pullman Company required them to haul the sleeping cars on all journeys. Company managers agreed that they would resist union action. The strike was broken. Passenger trains also pulled the mail cars and, as the conflict deepened, this proved to be a crucial factor.

When the railroad companies appealed to the federal government for help, claiming that violence was being used to stop the movement of trains, the Attorney-General responded by issuing an order restraining anyone from interfering with the movement of the mail or inciting other railroad workers to do so. Strikers agreed to operate trains pulling the mail carriages, but the railroad bosses refused to allow their trains to move without the Pullman sleepers. Finally, on 3 July 1894, President Grover Cleveland sent in federal troops, ostensibly to ensure the movement of the mail, but actually to break the strike. Debs and the ARU officers were arrested and later imprisoned for breaking the order. The ARU offered to end the strike at the Pullman works, provided that the workers were all reinstated. However, when the company resumed production on 2 August 1894, leaders of the strike from within the company were not given back their jobs.

The significance of the Pullman strike

Of the many late-nineteenth century examples of labour protest, the Pullman strike is particularly interesting. Its several strands reveal much about labour rights in the USA at the end of the nineteenth century, and the lengths to which employers and the authorities were prepared to go in order to curtail or deny them:

- The strike arose as a result of the refusal of the management to recognise the right of the workers to engage in **collective bargaining** to protect their standard of living or to improve their working conditions. The reaction of management in this case is typical of the

KEY TERMS

Arbitration The legal process of settling disputes between labour and management in hearings conducted by an impartial 'referee' in order to arrive at a settlement acceptable to both parties.

Collective bargaining is when employees' representatives join together to discuss issues, such as wages or working conditions.

anti-union attitude of the owners of major companies at the time. Any attempt to exert these rights was regarded as potentially subversive and was consequently resisted, often violently.

- It reveals how far federal authorities were prepared to go to suppress any assertion of the rights of labour. In this instance, it superseded that of the state, whose duty it was to restore and maintain order. Federal intervention of this kind was resented, particularly by state officials. For example, John Altgeld, the State Governor of Illinois, was sympathetic towards the workers and wished to use the state militia to resolve the situation rather than invoke federal authority.
- This was the first time that the law had been invoked to break a strike. When the Supreme Court legalised the use of injunctions, employers gained a powerful weapon against labour unions. Aggressive employer associations and conservative federal, state and local officials thwarted efforts to build a strong working-class movement. Employers continued to use court injunctions against strikers until 1932 when their use was prohibited by federal legislation.

CONCLUSION – WHAT HAD BEEN ACHIEVED BY 1914?

Organised labour had made some progress,

- At the end of the nineteenth century there were 500,000 trade union members. By 1910, there were over two million and by 1920 there were five million members. However, these represented only 20 per cent of the non-agricultural workforce. There were still a significant number of industries which were non-unionised, particularly the newer, mass production industries such as steel, textiles and automobiles. The acquisition of rights for workers still rested on the outcomes of negotiations and agreements which were negotiated by unrecognised unions with employers. Too many of these employers were focussed on profit margins and either suspicious of, or hostile to unions, largely as a result of the frequency of disruptive strikes during this period.
- The progress towards workers' solidarity was clearly hampered throughout this period and beyond as a result

Trade Union Membership 1900–15 (in thousands)

1900	791
1905	1,918
1909	2,116
1915	2,560

(Source: *Bureau of Labor Statistics*)

A rise in union membership is indicative of poor wages and working conditions and job insecurity.

of divisions between the skilled and unskilled, native born white workers and immigrant and black labour.

- Where unions existed, most were affiliated to the American Federation of Labor which sought to influence public policy on labour issues by pressurising candidates in local and national elections as a means of gaining some political support for the establishment of workers' rights in law. Increased employer attacks on labour such as those manifested in the Homestead Strike pushed the AFL towards political action. Trade union leaders and their membership became more actively involved in Congressional as well as local elections. Gompers urged support for **Woodrow Wilson's** presidential campaign of 1912 and achieved some success as, after Wilson was elected, a new Department of Labor was created with a former trade union official as its head. Also, the Clayton Antitrust Act passed in 1914, limited the use of court injunctions against striking workers, provided that there was no damaging of property, and allowed peaceful picketing.
- Whilst some progress had been made in the campaign to extend workers' rights, by 1914 many of these rights were limited to white, male workers and were surrounded with uncertainty about their permanence. Much still depended on the fluctuations of the economy and on the ongoing struggle with powerful employers.

QUESTIONS TO CONSIDER

1. Assess the relative importance of each of the following factors in limiting the progress of labour union rights before 1914:

   - Divisions between skilled and unskilled workers.
   - Leadership.
   - The actions of businessmen and employers.
   - Immigration, racial and ethnic diversity.
   - Militancy within the labour unions.
   - State and federal authorities.

2. To what extent do the Pullman and Homestead Strikes illustrate the obstacles to the recognition of labour rights before 1914?

CHAPTER 7

1915–45 War, boom and bust

The heyday of workers' rights?

Hypothesis:

- Trade unionism and the establishment of labour rights made some progress as a result of New Deal policies and wartime necessity.

WHAT WAS THE IMPACT OF THE FIRST WORLD WAR?

The First World War saw some improvement in the position of trade unions. In spite of the racial tensions caused by the influx of immigrant and African-American labour into northern industrial areas, the needs of war and the opportunities it offered to industrialists to increase their profits encouraged a more conciliatory policy towards unions. Between 1914 and 1918 factory production increased by 35 per cent. Whilst prices rose, real wages increased by 20 per cent so workers were generally content. For the first time, the federal government recognised the unions as organisations representing labour and negotiated with them, through the National War Labor Board, to ensure the maintenance of high levels of uninterrupted production. In return for their co-operation with a no-strike policy, the Board agreed to guarantee the rights of workers to join unions and to collective bargaining. Employers also agreed to safeguard working conditions by responding positively to the request of the War Labor Board to implement an eight hour working day. In response to these measures, Gompers and the AFL ordered their workers to refrain from strike action for the duration of the war. Union membership increased during the war years from 2.7 million in 1916 to 5 million by 1920.

The aftermath of the War 1919–20

The immediate aftermath of the war saw an upsurge of unrest that, in 1919, was accompanied by outbreaks of extreme violence that resulted in death, injury and the wanton destruction of property, particularly in Chicago. Whilst these riots were racially motivated (see Chapter 3 page 45), the unrest was also fuelled by the influx into the labour market of returning soldiers and the irrational fear of communist infiltration that reached fever pitch between 1919 and 1920. Known as the 'Red Scare', this manifested itself in extreme reactions by employers to any kind of industrial protest which was viewed as subversive even when labour unions were exerting their recognised rights. A **spate of strikes broke out in 1919** that exacerbated these feelings. For example, labour unions in Seattle organised a general work stoppage. Although this was an orderly protest, the Mayor of Seattle accused union leaders of attempting to cause anarchy and called for federal troops to deal with the strike.

What gains were made by trade unions during the 1920s?

Between 1920 and 1929, Americans enjoyed an unprecedented level of economic prosperity. During these years, wage levels rose steadily and a whole range of consumer goods became available, largely due to the new techniques of mass production. These, together with the availability of credit, led to a huge increase in demand for such things as cars, refrigerators, washing machines, vacuum cleaners and cookers. High tariffs protected US industry from foreign competition. There was a widely held belief, especially in political circles, that this economic progress was unstoppable.

In the midst of this affluence, however, the 20s were characterised by an upsurge of **nativism**, together with the continued obsessive fear of Communist infiltration that rendered union leaders and any kind of industrial action open to suspicion and accusation of subversion. Massively increased output from manufacturing industry as a result of the assembly line methods of production, increased the wealth and power of employers. This was further increased during the 1920s by the formation of **giant corporations**, through mergers of smaller concerns. These employers, keen to keep the wheels of manufacturing industry turning, adopted their own methods of satisfying the work force.

KEY EVENTS

Spate of strikes Strikes 1916–1920

Year	Number of Strikes	Number of workers involved in strike action
1916	3,789	1,599,917
1917	4,450	1,227,259
1918	3,353	1,239,989
1919	3,630	4,160,348
1920	3,411	1,463,054

Source: *US Bureau of Labor Statistics*

KEY TERMS

Nativism Means the hostile response of one cultural group seeking to preserve its inherent characteristics in the face of increasing ethnic diversity. In this context, it refers to the reaction of native white Americans and the 'old' immigrants to the massive influx of 'new' immigrants in this period.

KEY IDEAS

Giant corporations The most powerful included Ford, GM and Chrysler (automobiles), General Electrics and Westinghouse (electricity production) and US Steel in the steel industry.

Real wages The term describes what wages can actually buy or pay for in any given economic situation. When the economy is buoyant and prices are stable or even falling, the purchasing power of earned income will be greater.

'Yellow dog contracts' The derisory term used by a trade union leader to describe the contracts signed by workers that prevented them from joining a union. Although this practice had been common since the end of the nineteenth century, the term itself wasn't used before 1921.

Welfare capitalism – an alternative to workers' rights?

The rise in **real wages** and the dramatic fall in unemployment during the 1920s reduced many of the causes of the industrial unrest. Moreover, what appeared on the surface to be conciliatory action by employers – improved working conditions, a reduction in working hours, benefits including insurance and pension plans, profit-sharing schemes and recreational facilities – were, in effect, a ruse on their part to avert strikes and industrial unrest that might disrupt production. This 'welfare capitalism', as it came to be called, included the setting up of 'company unions'. Representatives could meet with employers to discuss such things as grievances, production levels and plant safety. However, they were not allowed to call strikes and did not have the power to negotiate wages. Behind the scenes, management spies and private police continued to work for employers to suppress any attempt at unionisation. Workers were also obliged to sign '**yellow dog contracts**' if they wanted employment in big business enterprises.

> '*This agreement has been well named. It is yellow dog for sure. It reduces to the level of a yellow dog any man that signs it, for he signs away every right he possesses under the Constitution and the laws of the land...*'

> From an article by the editor of the *United Mine Workers' Journal*, 1921

Henry Ford is a good example of 'welfare capitalism' at work. Ford owned the biggest factory complex in the world at River Rouge, his birthplace in Dearborn, Michigan. Here he employed 80,000 workers who endured the monotony of the car production line. In 1914 he had reduced the length of the working day to eight hours, doubled the daily wage to $5 and introduced a scheme of profit sharing. By 1927, when the new factory opened, the workforce remained tightly controlled and closely supervised. Ford's Protection Department employed strong-armed security men who watched over potential union organisers, intimidating and assaulting them. It was not until 1941 that any labour union was recognised by the Ford Company for the purposes of collective bargaining.

Strikes 1921–29.

Year	Number of strikes	Number of workers involved in strikes
1921	2,385	1,099,247
1922	1,112	1,612,562
1923	1,553	756,584
1924	1,249	654,641
1925	1,301	428,416
1926	1,035	329,592
1927	707	329,939
1928	604	314,210
1929	921	288,572

Source: *US Bureau of Labor Statistics*

Workers on the outdoor Ford Assembly line c.1914.

CASE STUDY – A. PHILIP RANDOLPH AND THE BROTHERHOOD OF SLEEPING CAR PORTERS AND MAIDS: THE PROGRESS OF AFRICAN-AMERICAN UNIONS

This campaign for the recognition of the **BSCP** as a Company union was a lengthy one since it was opposed, not only by the Pullman Company, but also by many African Americans themselves. The Pullman Company was one of the largest employers of African Americans in the

1920s and 1930s. On the surface, it appeared that many porters were well-paid and able to enjoy a comfortable lifestyle. However, in practice, working for the Pullman Company was less lucrative than it appeared to onlookers. What was not obvious was that the porters relied on tips for much of their income. This was humiliating in that it made them dependent on the condescension of white passengers who referred to them all as 'George', after the first name of George Pullman the company founder. In addition, porters spent roughly ten per cent of their time in unpaid setting-up and cleaning-up duties at the beginning and end of every journey. They also had to pay for their food, lodging and uniforms, which could account for half of their wages. If their passengers stole a towel or water pitcher they had to stand the cost. As privileges, they could ride at half fare on their days off but could not ride in **Pullman coaches**. The job offered no career structure or promotion prospects for the black porters as the next rung on the ladder (the position of conductor) was a job reserved for whites.

The company quashed all efforts to organise a union during the first decades of the twentieth century by isolating or sacking union leaders. It also employed a large number of employee spies who informed the company of employees' activities; in extreme cases Company agents assaulted union organisers. When 500 porters met in Harlem on 25 August 1925, they decided to make another effort to organise. They launched their campaign in secret but chose an outsider, **A. Philip Randolph** to lead it, under the dramatic motto, 'Fight or Be Slaves'.

At this time, the African-American community was still estranged from organised labour. While the AFL officially did not exclude black workers, many of its affiliates did. At the same time, the notion of economic separation promoted by Booker T. Washington (see pages 35–39) led many black leaders to look with distrust on joining with white union leaders on issues of common concern. Some even denied that blacks and whites had any common interests at all. Some were inclined to trust their white employers rather than fellow black workers. However, in the 1920s, this view was beginning to change as some elements within the AFL began to lower these barriers whilst groups such as the **Socialist Party of America** and the **Communist Party** began to focus on the rights of black workers. Randolph himself was a prominent member of the Socialist Party (for Randolph's political views see also page 52).

A. Philip Randolph with railroad employees c.1925.

Resistance from the Employers

The Pullman Company response was to denounce the new union as an outside agency prompted by foreign ideologies. At the same time, it sponsored its own company union, sometimes known as the Employee Representation Plan or, on other occasions, the Pullman Porters and Maids Protective Association, to represent those loyal employees who were not drawn to the BSCP Union. The Company had support from some local authorities in banning meetings of the BSCP. Undeterred, the BSCP continued fighting for several years against the Pullman Company and its allies in the black community who remained opposed to the action.

Progress?

While it had organised roughly half the porters within the Company, by 1928, the union was no closer to gaining

KEY TERMS

The Socialist Party of America was a political party formed in 1901. It gained support from some immigrant communities especially German and Jewish. It also attracted particular groups of workers, for example, coal miners, some agricultural workers and African-American workers .It splintered during the First World War as some of the membership was opposed to the involvement of the USA whilst others supported it. This stand also resulted in a fall off in membership.

The Communist Party of the USA played an important part in the labour movement in the USA. In the early days, it did much to help trade unions to become organised; the Party also promoted the equality of African Americans, particularly within organised labour. The Communist Party was also a strong supporter of civil rights (see pages 51–52).

recognition than it had been in 1925. The BSCP leaders decided that the only way to force the issue was to take strike action. However, the leadership was divided on what a strike could accomplish. Some leaders wanted to use it as a show of strength. Randolph was more cautious, hoping to use a strike threat as a lever to get the Pullman Company to negotiate. However, changes to the law regarding labour relations within the railway industry meant that, by 1934, the BSCP was in a position to claim that it was the only legitimate union to represent the porters in negotiations with the Pullman Company. Consequently, Randolph demanded that the **National Mediation Board** should certify it as the representative of these porters. The BSCP defeated the company union in the election held by the NMB and was certified on 1 June 1935. Two years later, the union signed its first collective bargaining agreement with the Pullman Company.

WAS PROGRESS TOWARDS THE ACQUISITION OF LABOUR RIGHTS HALTED BY THE GREAT DEPRESSION?

The prosperity bubble soon burst. On 24 October 1929, share prices on the New York Stock Exchange on Wall Street fell faster and lower than ever before. Millions of dollars were lost as the Wall Street Crash brought the American golden age of prosperity to an abrupt end. The total collapse of the economy that ensued led to factory closures and bankruptcy for large numbers of businesses. More disastrously for the labour force, unemployment soared from 3 per cent in 1929 to 25 per cent by 1933. In terms of numbers, these figures represent a daily increase of 12,000, reaching a total of 13 million by 1933. Unemployment made individuals and families destitute. African Americans were particularly badly affected since unemployment among them was double that of white Americans. Industrial cities such as Chicago were also badly affected and voluntary relief organisations were unable to cope with the huge tide of destitution.

In these circumstances, people who were in work were pleased to have a job at all. However, there was greater conflict between employers and workers. Incidences of strikes, sit-ins and the occupation of factories by desperate workers increased (see table on page 130). Employers called in the police or, in some cases, employed their own strike-breakers. Consequently, by 1933, only ten per cent of the workforce was unionised because although workers had the right to join unions, they did not have the right to take strike action. However, employers had the right to sack them if they went on strike. Sackings of striking workers were common.

THE NEW DEAL – A TURNING POINT IN THE DEVELOPMENT OF UNION RIGHTS?

In among all of the misery, the Republican President, **Herbert Hoover,** lost the confidence of the people when he failed to respond positively to the effects of the Depression. In 1932, therefore, US voters elected a new President, **Franklin D. Roosevelt**, a Democrat. Roosevelt was given unprecedented powers by Congress, for 100 days, to implement a programme of reform that would get the American people back to work. A further challenge was to settle the industrial unrest that existed when he took office.

Franklin D. Roosevelt.

National Industry Recovery Act (1933)

On 16 June 1933, Congress passed the National Industry Recovery Act (NIRA), which established the National Recovery Administration (NRA). The aim of the NRA was to foster co-operation between the different sides of industry by developing agreed codes of practice about issues such as production levels, wage rates, working hours, prices and trade union rights. Of these, perhaps the most significant was a law giving workers the right to organise trade unions and take part in collective bargaining. Companies who joined the NRA were allowed to display a blue eagle symbol. By 1934, 557 codes had been agreed by joining companies, covering 23 million workers.

However, its positive effects were limited. Employers such as Henry Ford refused to sign the NRA code and those codes that were agreed, generally favoured employers more than employees. The NIRA also came under the scrutiny of the Supreme Court, which once again raised the issue of states' rights over those of the federal government when it declared the NRA unconstitutional in 1935.

Was the National Labor Relations (Wagner) Act of 1935 a turning point?

In 1935 the cause of trade unionism was taken a step further by the passage of the National Labor Relations Act. This is also known as the Wagner Act after **Robert Wagner**. Roosevelt, himself, was very nervous of empowering organised labour. While it had potential political advantages in increasing Democrat support, it also involved an implicit reduction in the control of industrialists over their workforce. This was not Wagner's intention. His aim was to regulate and reduce labour disputes by providing a structure for collective bargaining. This would reduce picket line violence and avoid the disruption to production that was caused by strikes. He believed that only legislation would reduce the ability of powerful industrialists to subvert attempts to give any rights to their workers.

Why was the Act significant?

- The Act was the first piece of national legislation that recognised the right of workers to elect their own representatives to take part in collective bargaining with employers and therefore was a landmark in the development of US labour rights. The Supreme Court declared the Act constitutional in 1937.

- It gave workers the right to join trade unions and to bargain collectively through their own chosen representatives. It also permitted 'closed shops'. The dubious practice of employers in organising spies on the shop floor and blacklisting alleged 'agitators' was also banned.
- It also set up a five-man **National Labor Relations Board (NLRB)** that had the power to bargain on behalf of the workers and to stop companies from using blacklists and company unions. The NLRB also had the power to re-instate unfairly dismissed workers.
- Having established and protected the rights of labour, the Act facilitated the expansion of trade union membership. This rose from 3.7 million members in 1933 to 9 million in 1938. Although major employers, especially in automobiles and steel, initially resisted the pressure from their workers for the unionisation of the industry, they eventually capitulated. In 1937, General Motors and Chrysler recognised the Union of Auto Workers. By the end of that year the union could boast 400,000 members. US Steel accepted The Steelworkers Organizing Committee also in 1937.
- **The Fair Labor Standards Act of 1938** created a $25 minimum weekly wage for industrial workers and a payment of time and a half for hours worked in excess of 40 per week. It also prohibited the employment of children under 16 years.

How effective was the National Labor Relations Act in extending labour rights to all workers?

The rise in union membership is clearly an indication of some success. However, disputes between employers and their employees continued to be acrimonious. Moreover, divisions within the trade union movement itself continued to deprive the mass of unskilled workers of their rights. This was especially true of labour in mass-production industries such as automobiles and textiles. The American Federation of Labor was predominantly interested in amalgamating craft unions to the exclusion of unskilled

**John L. Lewis
(1880–1969)** Lewis was a
veteran labour leader who was
President of the United
Mineworkers from 1920 until
1960. In 1935, he organised
the Committee for Industrial
Organizations (CIO) and was
its President between 1938
and 1942 after its expulsion
from the AFL.

**Congress of Industrial
Organizations (CIO)**
Originally the Committee for
Industrial Organizations, this
was formed in 1935 by eight
unions from within the AFL.
At the time, it remained part
of the AFL in an attempt to
promote the organisation of
unskilled workers in mass
production industries at a
time when the AFL supported
largely craft organisations. The
CIO's efforts failed to change
policy, partly in response to
the aggressive style of its
leadership, some of whom
were later suspected of having
communist sympathies. In
1936, the AFL expelled the
CIO unions within its ranks.
It subsequently broke away
and formed a rival union
organisation. This split
weakened the labour
movement until 1955 when
the AFL and the CIO
amalgamated.

labour. Consequently in 1935 a breakaway group led by
John Lewis, formed the Committee on Industrial
Organisation, which, by 1937, was known as the **Congress
of Industrial Organizations (CIO).**

The CIO set about the task of organising labour in the
mass-production industries (steel, automobile and glass, for
example) gathering 3.7 million members in the process.
Employers resisted with every means at their disposal the
closed shop that the CIO established. By the end of the
1930s, strikers were using a new form of protest – the 'sit-
in' or 'sit-down' strikes. This was used effectively in 1937 to
gain recognition from car manufacturers of the right of
their workers to join a union. Only Henry Ford held out
until 1941. Black workers and other ethnic groups
benefited from the opportunity to join the CIO, as did
many women's unions. The CIO's consistent support for
equality of labour gave African Americans the confidence
to take part in strikes.

What did the New Deal do for disadvantaged workers?

New Deal legislation certainly made a significant impact
on the unionisation of workers, thereby extending their
rights in the workplace. However, these were largely skilled
workers. In spite of the work of the CIO, there remained a
significant number of unskilled workers, including
agricultural domestic workers and all those generally at the
lower end of the wage scales, who still had no leadership or
organisation to give them a powerful voice. Other groups
of workers also remained powerless:

• African Americans and Mexican Americans continued to
  face discrimination in the workplace (see also Chapter
  3). This was exacerbated by the agricultural policies of
  the New Deal which resulted in the eviction of large
  numbers of black and Hispanic Americans who had
  migrated to the cities in search of work. There were no
  new employment opportunities for Native Americans
  (see Chapter 11). Roosevelt's Fair Employment Practices
  Commission in 1941 was, however, an attempt to
  eliminate racial and ethnic discrimination in war-time
  industries.

- The position of women in the workplace was not improved. Although a number of women's unions had been formed and even though the NIRA and the Fair Labor Standards Act (1938) had established a minimum wage, it upheld differentials in pay between men and women (see pages 128–29 and Section 4, Chapter 15, pages 234–35).
- As described earlier, welfare reforms helped some of the poorer paid. However, attempts by federal government to help those in need were constantly thwarted by the conflict between states' rights and federal government. Discrimination was particularly experienced by African-American women.

Therefore, the extension of the rights of labour to all workers was by no means complete when the USA entered the Second World War in 1941.

Strikes and Union Membership 1931–46.

Year	Number of Strikes	Number of Workers involved	Union Membership	% of workforce
1930	637	182,975	3,401,000	11.6
1935	2,014	1,117,213	3,584,000	13.2
1937	4,470	1,860,621	-	-
1940	-	-	8,717,000	26.9
1945	-	-	14,322,000	35.5
1946	4,985	4,600,000	-	-

Source: *US Bureau of Labor Statistics*

WAS THE SECOND WORLD WAR A SETBACK FOR ORGANISED LABOUR?

During the period of US involvement in the Second World War, control of industry was effectively taken away from manufacturers and owners. This weakening of employers, albeit temporarily, tipped the balance in favour of the workers since their effort was essential to the war effort. Levels of production in agriculture and industry increased massively. These **levels of production** were achieved by centralisation of planning and direction. In particular, the

Levels of production
Food production rose by nearly a third and manufacturing output doubled. The production of iron, steel, magnesium and aluminium doubled and that of copper trebled. Aircraft production increased from 2,000 in 1939 to 96,000 in 1944; in all, the United States turned out 300,000 aircraft during the war, 275,000 of them military. American shipyards produced 55 million tons of merchant shipping.

Office of War Mobilization set up in May 1943 established priorities and set production targets.

The **National War Labor Board (NWLB)** was established to adjudicate in wage disputes. In July, facing pressure for wage increases, the Board adopted a formula for dealing with wage disputes that permitted a 15 per cent cost of living increase. As a result, wage rises and increases in overtime pay boosted average industrial earnings by 70 per cent during the war.

Trade unions grew rapidly in size during the war years from 8.9 million in 1940 to 14.8 million in 1945. The NWLB looked favourably on labour unions. In response to demands for a 'closed shop', it worked out a 'maintenance of membership' arrangement which proved to be to the union's advantage. At the same time, action was taken to exert control over union action. In 1943, the President was empowered to seize any plant where strike action threatened to interfere with war production. It also made it illegal to instigate such strikes and required unions to give thirty days notice of all strikes. In addition a number of states, especially in the south, passed 'right to work' laws prohibiting the closed shop. In 1941, the Ford Motor company finally recognised the Auto Workers Union.

The increase in wartime production, the expansion of the armed forces and the halting of overseas immigration led to a fall in unemployment from 9 million in June 1940 to 783,000 in September 1943. In fact, there were labour shortages which provided employment opportunities for young people, the handicapped, women and African Americans. The number of women at work increased by 50 per cent during the war and, by 1943, they made up a third of the total workforce. They represented 40 per cent of the workers on aircraft assembly lines. They were generally paid less than men for the same work and both the unions and management opposed the principle of equal pay.

The impact on black labour

In the war years, more than one million black Americans found jobs in the industrial centres of the north and west (for migration figures see page 44). Black factory workers remained restricted to the more menial jobs. To object to this, A. Philip Randolph, the leader of the Pullman Porters Union, threatened a march of 50,000 on Washington in June 1941. The President responded with an order forbidding racial discrimination in all defence projects and creating a Fair Employment Practices Committee, although it lacked enforcement powers. Black migration led to riots in several northern cities, the worst being in Detroit in June 1943 when 25 blacks and 9 whites were killed. The presence of over one million blacks in the armed forces was a further source of racial strife.

POST-WAR LABOUR – A BACKWARD STEP?

The potentially tenuous nature of any gains made during this period became apparent almost immediately after the war. The end of wartime controls unleashed a massive wave of strikes. In political circles, there was a growing belief that the unions were becoming too powerful. The anti-Communist focus of US foreign policy after 1945 produced an obsessive suspicion of the activities of the Communist Party of America, many of whose members were active in the trade union movement. When the Republicans won both Houses of Congress in the elections of 1946 they resolved to restrain union activity. They steered through Congress **the Taft-Hartley Act (The Labor Management Relations Act) of 1947** which restrained the powers of trade unions and sought to purge organised labour of Communists. This weakened the CIO in particular, whose origins were based on some support from the Communist Party. Divisions between non-Communist and Communist led unions certainly weakened the CIO. This was compounded when the CIO expelled ten Communist-led unions in 1949, depriving the organisation of one-third of its members and also some of its most capable leaders. This weakened the claim of the CIO to represent the interests of the unskilled working classes and contributed to the amalgamation of the CIO with the AFL in 1955.

In passing this Act, the Republicans made it clear that they had no desire to court the support of the unions and their

KEY EVENTS

The Taft-Hartley Act (Labor Management Relations Act 1947) This act made it illegal for unions to operate a 'closed shop' and affirmed the right of states to pass 'right to work' laws. Under this Act, the President could order a sixty day 'cooling-off' period prior to strike action. It also strictly regulated the conduct of unions in their dealings with employers. Union leaders were required to make a sworn statement of non-Communist allegiance before they could vote for members of the National Labor Relations Board.

membership. This became very apparent when **President Truman** attempted to veto the Taft-Hartley Act in order to retain the labour vote and he was overruled by Congress.

By 1950, however, there had been two more positive outcomes of the long running struggle between employees and General Motors when, in 1948, a pay code linked to standard of living costs was introduced. In 1950, this package was extended to include a five-year contract giving pensions and cost of living increases to employees. Such agreements on the part of employers were, of course, part of a strategy to avert strike action.

CONCLUSION

The period between the two world wars was one of economic extremes that inevitably impacted on workers. It is clear that significant progress was made in recognising the rights of labour, establishing this in law and putting in place the systems and mechanisms to ensure that these laws could operate effectively. Much of this was the result of New Deal legislation, particularly the National Labor Relations Act (1935) which represented a turning point in the establishment in law of workers' rights.

Measured in terms of union membership, the 1930s must be seen as a high point. Union membership trebled between 1932 and 1939 from just under two million to nine million. Previously semi-skilled and unskilled workers unionised themselves. The increasing membership also meant that the unions became a political force, the Democrats being particularly keen to attract the vote of organised labour.

It could also be argued that, to some extent, the uneasy balance between workers and employers had swung in favour of the workers and their unions. To some degree this was a combination of the post-Depression imperative to reduce unemployment and to stimulate the economy and then the necessity for the government to be in control of wartime production. This was, however, an uneasy balance that was not readily accepted by employers and one that depended heavily on the continued political support for organised labour. When peace came in 1945, many of the old tensions between employer and employee reappeared with the federal government playing an often controversial role.

The divisions between skilled and unskilled workers as well as the inequality determined by racial and ethnic differences remained as a barrier to effective solidarity. The growing influx of female labour into the workforce, both during the war and in the immediate post war period, provided a further source of potential division and conflict within the labour movement.

QUESTIONS TO CONSIDER

1. Was the period between the two world wars (1914–45) one of change or continuity in the struggle for labour rights?

2. Reconsider each of the potential agents or inhibitors of change identified at the end of Chapter 6 (pages 117–18). Discuss the extent to which they remained key factors by 1945. Had the relative importance of each changed in the period from 1915 until 1945?

3. What had the formation of the CIO contributed to the advancement of the rights of labour by 1945?

GNP (Gross National Product) is the total value of goods and services produced by all US citizens, calculated over a fixed period of time, usually annually.

J.K Galbraith (1908–2006) and *The Affluent Society* (1958)

Galbraith was an influential Canadian-American economist whose books were best sellers in the 1950s and 1960s. He taught at Harvard and served as an adviser in the administrations of four Presidents – Roosevelt, Truman, Kennedy and Johnson. In *The Affluent Society* he called for a new economic thinking in order to eliminate poverty and create affluence. He argued that America needed to invest money from taxation in building highways and in education.

His ideas influenced the 'war on poverty' policies of Kennedy and Johnson. Federal spending doubled in the 1950s to $180 billions. The money was used to build roads and airports, provide education, support the financing of home mortgages and maintain farm prices.

CHAPTER 8

1950–69 Reaction and reform

Did the actions of the federal government after 1950 promote the consolidation of trade union rights?

Hypothesis:

- Organised labour enjoyed the rights it had gained but economic prosperity and changing political priorities were weakening its power and influence by 1969.

POST-WAR AMERICA – WAS THE US IN THE 1950S REALLY AN 'AFFLUENT SOCIETY'?

Introduction

During the 1950s, the United States passed through a period of unrivalled prosperity and economic expansion. Between 1950 and 1960, the **GNP** rose from $318 billion to $488 billion. By the end of the 1950s,

- 60 per cent of American families owned their own homes,
- 75 per cent owned cars,
- 87 per cent owned at least one television,
- the average worker's income, adjusted for inflation, was 35 per cent higher than in 1945 and 200 per cent higher than in the 1920s.

The prosperity enjoyed by millions of Americans was underpinned by scientific developments and new technology. Between 1945 and 1960,

- the number of hours and workers needed to produce a car fell by 50 per cent,
- the first nuclear power plant opened in 1957,
- the chemical industry became the fourth largest US industry and electronics the fifth,

- in 1944, International Business Machines (IBM) produced the Mark 1 calculator. By the mid-1960s, more than 30,000 main frame computers were being used by banks and insurance companies. Computers enabled fewer workers to produce more goods in less time than ever before.

Labour rights in danger?

Rapid economic change brought about by the new technology, coupled with new working practices, completely transformed the labour movement. Particularly significant was the decrease in the number of **blue-collar workers** as a result of automation replacing more and more workers in the steel, coal and automobile industries. In the 1950s, trade union membership in these industries dropped by more than 50 per cent, reflecting the reduction in the size of the workforce resulting from this new technology. Newly created jobs were concentrated in the **white-collar** and **service sectors** of the economy and in public employment. White-collar workers were often heavily concentrated in federal, state or local government occupations. They signed no-strike agreements and were often barred from joining trade unions. These restraints made them difficult to unionise. Women represented an increasing proportion of the labour force but, at this time, many of them thought of trade unions as being something for men. Consequently, organised labour saw its proportion of the labour force drop from 36 per cent in 1953 to 31 per cent in 1960.

By 1950, it could be argued that there was a sense of complacency amongst a proportion of the trade union membership, partly as a result of the benefits which had previously been hard earned at the negotiating table in the 1930s and during the war years but also as a result of post-war economic growth. Millions of American workers now enjoyed higher wage levels than ever before with an average working week of less than 40 hours. Many received additional benefits such as paid vacations, healthcare provision and automatic wage increases tied to the cost of living. By 1955, when the merger of the American Federation of Labor and the Congress of Industrial Organizations brought 85 per cent of union members into a single unit (AFL-CIO), the old militancy of the labour

KEY TERMS

Blue-collar workers are wage earners in manual, industrial jobs.

White-collar workers in this context describe men and women in professional, technological, clerical and sales occupations.

Service sectors Examples of the service sectors are the leisure industry, retail outlets, eating places, real estate, secretarial and professional services.

Teamsters Union members holding picket signs supporting higher raises and pensions.

movement had disappeared. The decision to merge these two labour organisations, that had supported the different sectors of the workforce, was born from a growing awareness that, given the impact of economic change and the structural changes within the workforce, there was an increasing need for greater solidarity within the labour movement.

Strikes and Union Membership 1950–70.

Year	Number of strikes	Number of workers	Union membership	% of workforce
1950	3,606	3,030,000	14,267,000	31.5
1955	4,320	2,650,000	16,802,000	33.2
1960	3,333	1,320,000	17,049,000	31.4
1965	4,511	1,545,200	17,299,000	28.4

Source: *US Bureau of Labor Statistics*

Poverty

However, whilst many Americans were participants in the 'affluent society', amongst millions of others the need for strong labour unions was never greater. As late as 1960, around 35 million Americans (20 per cent of the population) lived below the **poverty line.** One-third of the poor lived in depressed rural areas where two million **migrant farm workers** lived in extreme poverty. As the more affluent residents and successful businesses moved from the inner cities to the suburbs, the poor flooded in and urban problems intensified. Half of the housing in New York's heavily black Harlem district pre-dated 1900 and was in a poor state. A dozen people might share a small apartment with broken windows, defective plumbing and gaping holes in the walls. Harlem's rates of illiteracy, infant deaths, incidences of illnesses such as tuberculosis, narcotics use and crime were significantly above both those of the city and national averages.

As the decade of the 1950s drew to a close, improving the lives of millions of poor Americans represented the biggest challenge, both to labour unions and a host of other agencies, not least the two main political parties.

DID THE POLICIES OF SUCCESSIVE FEDERAL ADMINISTRATIONS IN THE 1960S SUPPORT THE FURTHER DEVELOPMENT OF LABOUR RIGHTS?

Kennedy's 'New Frontier' (1960–63)

At the 1960 Democrat Convention, **John Kennedy** announced the theme of 'The New Frontier' – reform at home and victory abroad. Although Kennedy achieved only a narrow victory over his Republican rival Richard Nixon, his inauguration in 1961 did symbolise the beginning of a new era, the crossing of a 'new frontier'.

However, the ambitious programme of social reform with which his presidency began was only partly successful. His lack of support in Congress meant that his reform agenda was frequently opposed by a coalition of Republicans and southern Democrats. In 1961, the bill to increase the minimum wage was rejected by Congress, although those workers already subject to the Act saw their hourly rate marginally increased from $1.15 in September 1961 to $1.25 in September 1963. In his attempts to redress the problems of inflation, Kennedy succeeded in persuading the Steelworkers' Union to accept a non-inflationary contract with employers that included acceptance of minimal rises in wages. However, the employers failed to keep their agreement not to raise steel prices so the workers

'For the problems are not all solved and the battles are not all won and we stand today on the edge of a New Frontier. The frontier of the 1960s. A frontier of unknown opportunities and perils, a frontier of unfulfilled hopes and threats.'

John F. Kennedy speaking at the 1960 Democratic Convention

KEY PEOPLE

President John F. Kennedy (1917–63) was elected a Congressman in 1945 and a Senator in 1952. In 1961, he became President of the USA, the youngest ever elected. His 'New Frontier' programme of social reforms was only partially successful. However he was prevented from future initiatives by his assassination in Dallas, Texas, on 22 November 1963.

lost out since they were not able to benefit from the increased profit levels.

The Equal Pay Act of 1963 (see page 259) made wage discrimination on the basis of gender illegal and established the principle of 'equal pay for equal work'. The act was an amendment to The Fair Labor Standards Act (1938). In the judgement of the Bureau of Labour Statistics, the salaries of women compared with those of men rose dramatically following the Equal Pay Act. By 1970, the earnings were equal to 62 per cent of male earnings in 1970 rising to 80 per cent in 2004.

Lyndon B. Johnson (1908–73) was born in central Texas. His own experience of rural poverty in his early life made him sympathetic to the plight of the poor when he later entered politics. He was elected to the House of Representatives in 1937 and became a Senator in 1948. He became John F. Kennedy's running mate in the 1960 presidential election and was sworn in as Vice President in 1961. After he was sworn in as President following the assassination of Kennedy in 1963 and following his election as president in his own right in 1964, he was determined to press on with the extension of civil rights and his programme of social reform to improve conditions for the poor and especially for the elderly.

Johnson's 'Great Society' (1963–68)

Lyndon Johnson succeeded to the presidency on the assassination of John Kennedy in 1963 and quickly launched his vision of a 'Great Society'. With the support of the labour unions, he won a landslide victory over his Republican opponent in 1964 with 61.1 per cent of the popular vote. His first priority in creating a 'Great Society' was to reduce the number of people living below the poverty line. This was achieved by the creation of millions of new jobs and increased spending on social security benefits.

With the focus overwhelmingly on the war on poverty, advancing the rights of organised labour seems to have assumed less importance. However, some aspects of his reforming policy did impact on labour rights and on the workforce:

- **The Civil Rights Act of July 1964** prohibited discrimination on the grounds of race, colour, religion, sex or national origin. This benefited African Americans, Hispanics and other ethnic groups who had faced discrimination in jobs and in the workplace.
- **The Economic Opportunity Act 1964** established the Office of Economic Opportunity to fund and co-ordinate a job corps to attract and train young people in vocational skills or, alternatively, to provide education that would prepare them for further education in order to increase their employability.

- **The Age Discrimination in Employment Act of 1968**
  prohibited employment discrimination in hiring and
  firing against persons of between 40 and 65 years old in
  the United States. As well as covering hiring and firing,
  the Act covered promotions, wage levels and lay-offs. It
  also became illegal to include a statement of age
  preferences in job notices and advertisements and the
  denial of benefits to older employees.

Union gains in the 1960s

Following the creation of the AFL-CIO in 1955 with a
combined membership of 16 million workers, American
unions began to bargain over wages and working
conditions. Established unions were able to bargain
successfully with leading firms in such industries as autos,
steel, trucking and chemicals. Contracts were periodically
negotiated covering workplace relations and regulations for
promotion and layoffs as well as procedures giving workers
opportunities to voice grievances before neutral arbitrators.
Wages rose steadily, by over two per cent per year and
union workers earned around 20 per cent more than non-
union workers of similar age, experience and education.
Unions also won a growing list of benefits including
medical and dental insurance, paid holidays and vacations,
unemployment insurance and pensions. Competition for
workers forced many non-union employers to match the
benefit packages won by unions but unionised employers
provided benefits worth 60 per cent more than were given
to non-union workers.

The impact of civil rights action and legislation on the rights and opportunities of African Americans in the workplace

The campaign for black civil rights that came to dominate
the domestic scene in the two decades that followed the
Second World War, presented a particular challenge to union
organisations in the US. On the one hand, they were
fundamentally concerned with the acquisition and
preservation of rights and, therefore, were instinctively
supportive of the movement. On the other hand, in the case
of the majority of major unions, their practices had been
fundamentally racist. Nevertheless, in the 1950s and 1960s,
the AFL-CIO strongly supported the civil rights movement

by funding civil rights organisations and lobbying politicians for civil rights legislation. The AFL-CIO encouraged unions to abandon policies that discriminated, especially against African-American workers, even though it meant losing affiliated unions in the southern states such as Mississippi. Within this climate created by the civil rights movement, some unions were able to recruit members among non-white Americans. However, the key concern for unskilled workers in the 1950s and 60s, was the introduction of new technology into industry. This not only reduced the size of the workforce but also demanded new skills and higher levels of education. This exposed the poor standard of education available to black people and remained an issue to be addressed by state and federal government.

However, in practice, the trade unions were unhelpful when it came to promoting equal opportunities for the mass of black unskilled workers. Whilst the AFL-CIO pursued a non-racial policy, black workers were poorly represented on the leadership body. Moreover, the smaller affiliated unions did not necessarily follow the policy. Inadequate levels of education or lack of relevant experience could easily be used legitimately to exclude black applicants for jobs. Racism was particularly evident in the very big companies such as Ford Motors, where out of a total workforce of 7,665 workers, only 74 were black. Discrimination was also rife in the building trade which was booming in the 1960s. Although **Richard Nixon's** policy of affirmative action (see page 86) created some opportunities at the end of this period, it was difficult for young blacks to obtain craft apprenticeships or to be accepted into craft unions. By 1969, black people held only about three per cent of apprenticeships in skilled trades. Plumbers, electricians and carpenters were traditionally exclusively white.

CONCLUSION: GAINS AND LOSSES BY 1969. WAS UNIONISM ALREADY IN DECLINE BY THE END OF THE 1960s?

Clearly, in the post-war era, a framework of entitlement to rights in the workplace was securely in place identifying the

KEY PEOPLE

Richard Nixon (1913-94) took a law degree at Duke University, North Carolina, and practised as a lawyer before joining the US navy in 1942. He was a Congressman between 1946 and 1950, and a Senator from 1950 to 1952. He was Eisenhower's running mate in 1952 and became Vice President, taking a strong stand against Communism. In 1960, he was the Republican presidential candidate, but was defeated by John F. Kennedy. In 1968 he was elected President. His first administration was occupied mainly with foreign affairs. Re-elected in 1972, his second term was overshadowed by the Watergate scandal surrounding a break-in to the Democratic Party headquarters. He eventually admitted covering up the crime, and resigned on 9 August 1974.

criteria within which negotiation and collective bargaining could take place. The right to join a trade union was accepted and established in law. Consequently, unions were able to work collaboratively with employers, where necessary, to improve earnings and working conditions for their members. Strike action was reduced in consequence. Employers were adopting more cunning approaches to deal with the workforce, seeking to gain the upper hand through generous packages of fringe benefits which reduced the propensity of their employees to support militant action should this be proposed by their unions. Nevertheless, the progress made by organised labour in reaching agreements with General Motors was significant.

During the 1960s it became increasingly obvious that changes were underway that threatened to weaken the power and influence of labour unions.

- The relative comfort and prosperity enjoyed by a significant number of mainly skilled workers made them less likely to have recourse to union-led action. Employers were able to exploit this with the introduction of no-strike and non-union clauses in workers' contracts.
- Union membership began to decline in the private sector in the United States immediately after the Second World War although, after 1960, public sector workers won new opportunities to form unions.
- From the late 1960s, trade union membership reduced further, largely as a result of technological change that resulted in a shrinking of the workforce and an expansion of a more highly skilled workforce.
- More significantly, organised labour was vulnerable to political swings and fortunes as well as economic change. There were signs that the close association between organised labour and the Democrat Party was weakening whilst the Republicans demonstrated open hostility. As government priorities changed, so the prominent position that industrial relations had occupied, was taken over by the war on poverty and by foreign policy (particularly the war in Vietnam).

The merger that created the AFL-CIO ensured that organised labour remained a force to be reckoned with by the end of this period as the organisation increasingly became occupied with the position of semi and unskilled labour. Many facets of discrimination were also confronted in the context of the civil rights legislation of the 1960s. However, discrimination remained an issue for African-American labour and for other ethnic groups who still struggled to gain effective recognition of, and support for, their rights from trade unions.

QUESTIONS TO CONSIDER

1. Did the post war prosperity and economic change effectively undermine the power of organised labour before 1969? How significant was the merger of the AFL and CIO by 1969?

2. Discuss the impact of scientific and technological changes in the workplace on the power of the labour unions. By the 1960s was scientific and technological change more important than those factors already identified as impacting on progress?

3. Do you agree that fluctuation in the economy was the most significant factor in explaining the erratic progress made by labour unions in achieving and exercising their rights?

4. How important were the actions of the federal government in promoting the rights of labour? Answer this question with reference to the period from 1920 until 1969.

CHAPTER 9

1970–92 The wheel has turned full circle

Labour unions in decline?

Hypothesis:

- By 1992, organised labour had ceased to be a powerful force in asserting and protecting the rights of workers.

INTRODUCTION: THE 1981 AIR TRAFFIC CONTROLLERS' STRIKE

On 3 August, 1981, the Professional Air Traffic Controllers Organization (PATCO) called a strike with the intention of bringing air traffic to a standstill all over the US. The controllers wanted a $10,000 dollar wage rise, a shorter working week (32 hours instead of 40 hours because of the stressful nature of the work) and better retirement benefits. Of its 17,500 members, 13,000 obeyed the call and walked out. Negotiations had begun in February 1981 with the Federal Aviation Administration (FAA) but the idea that workers should be paid more for working fewer hours was unacceptable to the federal government. In spite of the fact that a potential settlement was on the table, the strike went ahead, deliberately planned to coincide with the summer vacations – the busiest time of the year. In addition, such action was likely to have a devastating impact on commercial air traffic and, therefore, to potentially damage the national economy. By going on strike the controllers had contravened a law passed in 1955 that banned government workers from taking strike action.

President Reagan responded swiftly and decisively. On the same day, he publicly announced that if the strikers did not return to work within 48 hours, their contracts of employment would be terminated. Reagan, a former union leader himself, was a man of his word. Believing that they were indispensable, the striking controllers were shocked to receive, not only the termination of their employment, but also a lifelong employment ban. The non-striking

KEY PEOPLE

Ronald Reagan (1911–2004) was born in Tampico, Illinois. He studied economics and sociology at Eureka College, Illinois and subsequently became a Hollywood actor (after 1937). He entered politics in 1966 when he was elected Governor of California and served two terms in this office. In 1980, he won the Republican nomination for the presidency and was sworn in as President in January 1981. The focus of his first term in office was to obtain legislation from Congress to stimulate the economy and restore national prosperity. He is judged to have been largely successful by the end of his second term of office in 1989. Reagan's right-wing politics along with his single-mindedness in pursuing economic improvement undoubtedly influenced his attitude towards, and treatment of, the trade unions.

Ronald Reagan.

controllers were augmented by 3,000 supervisors and 900 military air traffic controllers to minimise the disruption and keep the majority of America's air traffic moving. Meanwhile, training programmes for air traffic controllers were accelerated to provide permanent replacements for this temporary emergency arrangement.

The strikers received little sympathy from the general public, who saw the actions of these already well-paid workers as being against the public interest. Whilst leaders of the AFL-CIO condemned Reagan as a 'union buster', other unions were angry because the illegal action of PATCO had brought them all into disrepute. PATCO leaders were sent to prison for ignoring court injunctions banning the strike and huge fines were subsequently levied against them. The union was destroyed.

The Air Traffic Controllers' strike can be seen, to some extent, as a turning point in the history of organised labour in the US. It can be argued that the response of the federal government and that of the FAA led to a re-definition of labour relations in the US, evidence for this being in part that the incidences of strike action subsequently plummeted. It certainly is indicative that changes were taking place in attitudes towards organised labour and that the power and influence of the unions in the closing decades of the twentieth century were diminishing. The key indicators of note are,

- the apparent hostility of the Republican Government to organised labour in the person of the President, Ronald Reagan
- the change of tactics by employers in dealing with industrial disputes, in this case, the blatant deployment of 'scab' labour. (Employers had always had the right to do this but had rarely used it.)
- the lack of any expression of solidarity from other workers, to some extent attributable to the fact that the controllers were seen to be already well paid in comparison to a significant proportion of the workforce
- the negativity of public opinion towards striking workers who were perceived to be holding the country to ransom.

By 1992, membership of industrial unions in the US had fallen dramatically from 27 per cent in 1970 to 12 per cent by 1990. Incidences of major stoppages due to strikes also fell from 381 in 1970, to 187 by 1980 and to 31 between 1980 and 1995. These figures alone are indicative of the decline of workers' organisations that performed a crucial role in ensuring the rights of workers besides exerting considerable political influence. But was this entirely the result of the Air Traffic Controllers' Strike or were other factors at work that contributed to this apparent demise?

Strikes involving 1,000+ workers only 1970–92.

Year	Number of strikes	Number of workers taking strike action
1970	381	2,468,000
1975	235	965,000
1980	187	795,000
1985	54	324,000
1990	44	185,000
1992	35	362,000

Source: *US Bureau of Labor Statistics*

Trade Union membership 1970–90.

Year	Number of Members	% of workforce
1970	19,381,000	27.3
1975	19,611,000	25.5
1980	19,843,000	21.9
1985	16,996,000	18.0
1990	16,740,000	16.1

Source: *US Bureau of Labor Statistics*

WHY WAS THERE A MARKED DECLINE IN ORGANISED LABOUR FROM THE LATE 1970s?

The weakening of organised labour can be explained by closer examination of four main areas of change in the last three decades of the twentieth century, all of which are connected:

1. The changing economy and structure of American industry.

2. The changing composition of the workforce.

3. The shift in the 'balance of power' between employers and the labour unions.

4. The changing political attitudes and policies.

The changing economy and organisation of American industry

By the mid-1970s, economic growth in the US was slowing down. To some extent, this can be explained by the increase in foreign competition in manufacturing industries that reduced the demand for home produced goods and therefore profits. This situation was not helped by rising **inflation** that increased production costs as well as consumer prices, reducing further the competitive capability of American industries. By 1979, prices had risen by 13 per cent. The knock-on effect was a reduction in productivity that, combined with the impact of inflation, resulted in a fall in the real wages of 80 per cent of semi-skilled and unskilled workers and a rise in unemployment.

On the other hand, although the further expansion of high-tech industry had shrunk the workforce and reduced the demand for unskilled labour, it had created an increasing need for skilled workers. The wage levels of these workers rose significantly. Between the mid-1970s and 1992, the gap between poorer paid workers and the better off widened. At the top end of the scale, the salaries of chief executives rose by an estimated 340 per cent. In other words, a minority got richer whilst the majority got poorer. Such a division, however, did not lead to industrial unrest, in part because the critical mass in the middle appears to have settled for, and made the best of, what they had rather than risk losing it by demanding more. This is evidenced by the reduction in strike action. Also, increasing opportunities for married women in the workplace provided a second income that enabled families to maintain a reasonable standard of living (see also pages 255–56). Poorer people were also affected by reductions in welfare benefits during the Reagan administration (1981–89) which increased their need to hold on to whatever work they could get. All of these factors impacted on the membership of labour unions and account for the significant drop in the number of strikes between 1980 and 1995.

Increased competition and the reduction in productivity had significant outcomes for American industry. This resulted in the rationalisation of large manufacturing industries into smaller concerns in order to reduce unit costs so making them more competitive. They relocated into more rural areas outside the major urban conurbations marking the end of the massive industrial enterprises that had been the norm in the early and middle years of the century. Many of these smaller firms were established in the south and south-west, a traditionally anti-unionist area. Relocation inevitably involved a reduction in the size of the enterprise and of its workforce. Unionisation was further adversely affected by the increasing trend for some of the larger industrial concerns to establish subsidiaries in the developing countries and for a sizeable proportion of the annual GNP to be provided increasingly by an ever expanding service economy with a sizeable but less easily organised workforce (see below for further explanation).

The changing composition of the workforce

Economic change resulted in the greater dispersal and fragmentation of the workforce which was not conducive to the promotion of solidarity. The movement and relocation of industry meant that the concentration of large numbers of workers in one place of work generally became a thing of the past. This made trade union organisation and recruitment more difficult. The outcome of reductions in productivity resulted in larger numbers of unskilled workers being employed either as casual or part-time labour. The service economy employed increasing numbers of female workers who were generally low paid, part-time and for the most part (though not exclusively) uninterested in union membership.

The unskilled workforce was also divided culturally and ethnically. Existing immigrants, Hispanic and African-American workers were augmented by a **new wave of immigrants from Asia** in the closing decades of the century, the majority of whom were unskilled and prepared to work for low wages. This only served to exacerbate long established divisions in the labour movement, especially within previously exclusively white trade unions. Given that these workers were either not interested in union membership, or were prepared to work for employers

New wave of immigrants from Asia

Asian immigrants before 1965 were relatively small in number and so comprised a small proportion of the population. In 1965, the Hart-Celler Act removed the barriers that existed from earlier legislation that limited the number of immigrants from Asia. Some of those who entered the US after this date, were professional and skilled workers but the largest proportion were unskilled. Initially, the largest numbers of Asian immigrants were escaping from communist regimes (such as Korea, China, Cambodia and Vietnam). However, as time passed, others followed to join their families already established in the US. This accounts for the rapidly increasing numbers. Other immigrants arrived at this time from the West Indies and from Europe.

Asian Immigration since 1979 (numbers in 000s)

	1971–80	1981–90
Cambodia	8.4	116.6
China	202.5	388.8
India	176.8	261.9
Korea	272.0	338.8
Laos	22.6	145.6
Vietnam	179.7	401.4

From the World Almanac, 1995

who operated non-unionised business concerns, the influence of the trade unions was clearly limited.

The marked change in the composition of the workforce by the 1980s was the continuing growth in the number of white-collar workers to meet the needs of high tech industry and the reduction of blue-collar workers effectively made redundant by increased automation. This accelerated the trend that had begun in the 1960s so that, by 1980, there were 50.5 million white-collar workers compared with 30.5 million in 1960. Unlike blue-collar workers, white-collar workers were less well disposed to trade union membership. Many benefited from generous welfare schemes provided by their employers and so were more inclined towards supporting them rather than embarking on union action.

The shift in the 'balance of power' between employers and the labour unions

The propensity on the part of employers to keep their businesses buoyant as they faced competition and the reduction of profits, inevitably increased their determination to gain the upper hand in their dealings with the unions. The fact that some businesses were unionised and others not, was in itself an issue for them in a competitive arena. Non-unionised firms had greater flexibility when it came to the negotiation of wage levels. This kept production costs lower, potentially increased profit margins and enabled them to be more competitive. These circumstances put them at an advantage in comparison to owners of unionised firms. There was, therefore, an increasing tendency for employers to flout the law in their dealings with workers by denying them their rights, particularly in relation to wage agreements as well as working hours and conditions.

This trend was encouraged when it became clear that employers could get away with it. Whilst there were increasingly isolated examples of industrial action, workers generally failed to protest. Complaints that were made about unfair practices to the National Labor Relations Board (see page 128) were processed so slowly that this gave a clear signal to employers that they could risk pushing at the boundaries of the laws that were intended to protect workers rights. By the late 1970s, the elected membership of the NLRB had fewer union leaders in its ranks than in earlier times, itself indicative of their waning influence. Consequently, it showed itself less well disposed to meet union demands. Moreover, in this new climate that accommodated the interests of employers before those of workers, employment lawyers and advisers emerged to help employers circumvent the law, which they frequently did without challenge. By the 1980s, there was no doubt that the 'balance of power' had swung away from the labour unions and in favour of the employers. There can be little doubt that the outcome of the Air Traffic Controllers' Strike in 1981 must have provided further encouragement to other employers.

Changing political attitudes and policies

In the closing decades of the century, organised labour could no longer rely on the same level of support from politicians as they had done previously. They had been traditional supporters of the Democrats who had appreciated this close association since, when union membership was high, it usually guaranteed them the working-class vote. However, by the late 1970s, as membership declined and the unions could no longer claim to represent the masses, their value to the Democrats diminished. Without political support, the power of organised labour was significantly reduced.

This is not to say that the period was devoid of labour-related legislation. In 1970, for example, Richard Nixon's policy of Affirmative Action (see page 86) did benefit black and immigrant workers as well as those from other ethnic groups by challenging discrimination in employment. In addition, the **Occupational Safety and Health Act of 1970** did establish health and safety regulations in the workplace. This was an achievement, as the labour unions were successful in ensuring that the responsibility for setting standards for health and safety rested with the Department of Labor not an independent board that might be swayed by employers. In 1977, **President Jimmy Carter** (Democrat) and Congress established the hourly minimum wage at $2.65. However, by 1978, the attempts by the

(see page 86)

KEY EVENTS

Occupational Safety and Health Act of 1970 This was the primary federal law governing occupational health and safety in the private sector and federal government. It aimed to ensure that employers provided employees with an environment free from hazards such as exposure to toxic chemicals, excessive noise levels, mechanical dangers, heat or cold stress and insanitary conditions. Until this Act, legislative efforts to ensure the health and safety of workers were minimal.

KEY PEOPLE

President Jimmy Carter (b. 1924) was born in Plains, Georgia. He graduated from the Naval Academy in Annapolis, Maryland in 1946 and served for seven years as a naval officer. He entered state politics in 1962, becoming Governor of Georgia in 1970. He became a candidate for the presidency in 1974, won the election in 1976 and was sworn in as president in 1977. Carter was a devout Baptist by religion which influenced his life in politics. As President, he worked hard to address unemployment and inflation and to improve the environment. He was keen to improve the quality of life of the poorest people. Although he reduced unemployment, he was less successful in bringing down inflation.

AFL-CIO to persuade Carter to introduce reforms to the National Labor Relations Act (1935) failed – a reflection of the extent to which the Democrats were more interested in gaining the support of employers rather than the workers.

However, it was Ronald Reagan who, from the offset of his presidency, clearly set out to curb the power of the unions. This was one aspect of a policy designed to revitalise American industry by lifting restrictive regulations imposed by the federal government on businesses and giving greater autonomy to employers. Another fundamental principle of his economic policy was the privatisation of publicly owned businesses and services. None of these measures was in the best interests of workers. Reagan's ruthless response to the PATCO dispute should be seen in the context of this policy since it sent a clear message to employers on how they should proceed in their relations with the unions. He supported them further by ensuring that, as the members of Labor Relations Board were presidential appointments, it was dominated by officials who were in agreement with his radical position. This increased the likelihood that judgements made in disputes between employers and employees were more likely to be decided in favour of the employer.

WHAT REMAINED OF TRADE UNIONISM BETWEEN THE 1970s AND 1992?

Trade union membership overall may have declined significantly by 1992 but the unions did not expire. Certainly, their power and influence was significantly reduced. This was as a result of the combination of factors that have been discussed above. On the other hand, the 1970s did see an upsurge in the membership of trade unions amongst public sector workers, including teachers, bank employees and **municipal** workers. In response to this, the AFL-CIO created a public service department within its organisation. 1970 saw the first nationwide strike of public employees when the US Postal Workers took industrial action. In 1972, teachers went on strike in response to the reduction in real wages. In 1975, the American Federation of State, County and Municipal

KEY TERMS

Municipal the equivalent of local council workers in the UK.

Employees organised a strike involving 80,000 members. This was the first legal strike of public sector employees.

Unfortunately, this kind of industrial action by those directly serving the public (especially that by teachers), alienated public opinion because of its immediately negative impact on their lives. However, of the strikes that took place from the mid 70s until 1992, the majority were localised and small scale.

Further development also took place within black trade unionism. In 1972, black union officials and black labour leaders met rank and file members in Chicago and formed the Coalition of Black Trade Unions (CBTU). These represented 37 national unions. The assembly of 1,200 black trade unionists was the first and largest of its kind. Its purpose was to consider where the trade unions should place their support in the forthcoming presidential elections but it also sought to establish the position of black trade unions within the labour movement since there was a strong belief that the AFL-CIO was not sufficiently committed to supporting black unions and, through them, black workers. The CBTU showed particular interest in the position of black women workers. A number of African-American women attended the Chicago conference and five became members of the executive committee of this new organisation.

CASE STUDY: WOMEN IN THE TRADE UNION MOVEMENT BEFORE 1992

Background
From the mid-nineteenth century until the end of the twentieth and beyond, American women, either as individuals, in groups or organisations, demonstrated their ability to be outspoken critics, activists, lobbyists and protesters on a range of issues relating to many aspects of American life about which they felt strongly. The fundamental quest of many for recognition of women's rights inevitably took them into the workplace where women throughout this period faced varying degrees of discrimination, most notably in pay and, in some

National Women's Trade Union League rally in St Louis, 1913.

circumstances (for example married women), for their right to work at all. African-American, Hispanic and immigrant women experienced the worst levels of exploitation being paid the lowest wages, as well as working long hours in poor and often dangerous conditions. Certainly in the period from 1865 until 1920, pressure for reform of the treatment of women in the workplace was, for many female activists, inextricably bound up with the campaign for the franchise (see Section 4, beginning on page 224 for further expansion of these points).

Trade union organisation before 1970

The Women's Trade Union League (WTUL) was the earliest formal women's trade union organisation established in 1903. Under the leadership of **Mary Kenny O'Sullivan** and **Rose Schneiderman**, the League's work was predominantly focused on encouraging and supporting women in organising themselves into unions and also on opposing sweatshop working conditions. The latter was spurred on by the fire at the **Triangle Shirtwaist Factory in 1911** that killed 145 workers.

The aims of the League also incorporated pressure for the franchise, recognising that women needed political influence to bring about the legislation that would provide protection at work. The WTUL wanted laws establishing an eight-hour day and a minimum wage. This put it at odds with male trade union organisations and especially the AFL who opposed the idea of legislation which they saw as usurping the role of trade union negotiation. The WTUL continued its pursuit of legislation into the New

Deal era of the 1930s, supported by **Eleanor Roosevelt**, the wife of the President, Franklin D. Roosevelt and a member, herself, of the WTUL.

The failure of the New Deal legislation (The National Industrial Recovery Act 1933 and the Fair Labor Standards Act 1938) to deliver equal pay meant that women continued their protest. Some male unions, for example, the United Auto Workers, supported equal pay for women if only to ensure that employers would not be tempted to replace them with cheaper female labour. However, it was the influx of women into the workplace during the Second World War that led to their more direct action in pursuit of equality. Between 1940 and 1944, there was a dramatic increase in the number of women joining unions (800,000 in 1940 to 3 million by 1944). Many of these new union members were directly recruited into existing male unions (for example the Electrical Workers' Union) or were organised in women's sections within the larger unions, from which they pursued their own issues. For example, the Women's Bureau within the United Automobile Union campaigned for equal rights in the workplace. There was also an increase in the number of women in paid work as union officials.

By the 1960s, the increasing number of women entering the workforce and the aspirations of many for a career and improved prospects, resulted in trade-union women becoming more directly involved in union and strike action, often successfully. For example, in 1962, women were active in the New York Hospital Workers strike. Female pressure contributed to the agreement by the State Governor to recognise the right of hospital workers to collective bargaining. As a result, in 1968, the union was able to secure a minimum wage of $100 per week for all workers, male and female. Meanwhile, women at the Levi-Strauss Blue Ridge jeans plant in North Georgia staged a **wild cat strike** in 1967. When the employers brought in scab labour in an attempt to break the strike, the female strikers set up their own factory, supported by union men in the Copper Company, which operated on the basis of equality.

KEY EVENTS

The Triangle Shirtwaist Factory Fire, March 1911
This was New York City's worst industrial disaster. The factory employed 500 workers – mainly young immigrant women. It occupied the top three stories of a ten-storey building. Some of the workers were very young girls (aged 12 and 13 years) who worked fourteen hour shifts for very low wages. It proved to be a turning point in the campaign to improve the working conditions of immigrant workers. The fire claimed the lives of 146 women who were trapped on the ninth floor by the smoke and flames coming up the stairwell. There were no effective fire exits. The fire roused the needle workers to go on strike and raised public awareness of the exploitation of female workers. As a result, the airless sweatshops with their few exits and rickety stairways, were abolished by New York State law.

KEY PEOPLE

Eleanor Roosevelt (1884–1962) wife of President Franklin D. Roosevelt and a mother of six children. She was determined to pursue her own career and interests after marriage. She actively supported organisations attempting to improve the position of women, such as the WTUL. She also supported groups opposed to discrimination and racism.

KEY TERMS

Wild cat strike A strike undertaken by workers without the agreement of their union leaders.

Coalition of Labor Union Women 1974 had four main areas of focus:

1. The promotion of affirmative action in the workplace.
2. Strengthening the role of women in the workplace.
3. Organising more women into trade unions.
4. Increasing the participation of women in the democratic processes.

Olga Madar (1915–96) was born in the coal mining town of Sykesville, Pennsylvania. She first experienced gender discrimination when working at the Chrysler plant in 1933. There was no union at the time. She paid for a degree course and graduated in 1938 with a degree in physical education. She joined the United Auto Workers Union (UAW) in 1941 and organised their community recreation programmes. From this position, she worked to eliminate gender and racial discrimination in the workplace. In 1974, she was elected as UAW's first female vice president and was a driving force in the establishment of the CLUW.

How influential were women in the trade union movement after 1970?

By the 1970s, the US was well in the grip of radical feminist activism and the anti-feminist backlash (see Chapter 17) and, to some extent, this probably affected the propensity of working women to join unions. In many respects, issues that affected women in the trade union movement were also incorporated into feminist demands. As more married women entered the workforce, for example, the provision of child care facilities and paid maternity leave were common causes. Generally speaking, however, working class women did not identify with the feminist movement since they did not see them as fighting for equality for all women. Instead, they turned to union action in pursuit of their rights. What emerged has been described as 'trade union feminism'. Increasing numbers of women joined unions in the 1970s. This was obviously also a reflection of the increasing number of women entering the workforce, many of them immigrants or from ethnic minorities.

This process was boosted in 1974 by the formation of the **Coalition of Labor Union Women (CLUW)** affiliated to the AFL-CIO. The CLUW was the result of a conference organised by **Olga Madar** and **Addie Wyatt** held in Chicago to explore ways in which women in the trade union movement could have a stronger voice and, therefore, more influence. It was a response to the apparent reluctance of the AFL-CIO leadership to recognise the growing presence of female trade unions and the causes for which they fought. The 3,200 delegates were keen to show that they meant business. Olga Madar became its first president.

'You can call Mr. Meany (President of the AFL-CIO) and tell him there are 3,000 women in Chicago and they didn't come here to swap recipes!'

Myra Wolfgang (see page 157) speaking at the Chicago conference in March 1974.

At a time in the 70s when strike action was generally abating, there were some notable examples of militant union action taken by women. In 1972, for example, Mexican-American women at the Farah Manufacturing Company went on strike demanding the right to belong to a union. The striking women campaigned across the US, calling for a boycott of Farah goods. The call must have had some effect as two years later, the owner, Willie Farah, reinstated the workers and agreed to recognise their union. In 1975, Navajo women working in the electronics industry occupied their factory as a protest against the refusal of their employers to allow them to form a union. Between 1977 and 1979, female bank workers in Willmar, Minnesota staged the longest bank strike in US history demanding equal pay and promotion prospects. Their action attracted support from many women's organisations outside the union movement who encouraged the withdrawal of savings from accounts in the bank to increase pressure on the employers to settle.

> 'I don't believe in burning your bra, but I do believe in our having our rights...it has changed a lot of things for me.'

A striker in the Farah Manufacturing Company strike. (Quoted by Mary Cohen in *The Sisterhood: The True Story of Women Who Changed the World*, 1988)

During the 1970s, women in the same industries and also in agriculture networked around the US to establish solidarity in achieving similar opportunities. For example, women coalminers in Tennessee linked up with women in Wyoming, New Mexico, West Virginia and Illinois to put pressure on coal companies to employ women. The trade union movement also began to address wider issues affecting women in the workplace, for example **sexual harassment** and safety issues, particularly in the newer industries such as electronics and atomic energy.

In spite of this fervent activity in the 1970s, the closing decades of the century, economic change and employment patterns impacted on the female workforce as well as the male. The dramatic fall in union membership must also have reflected the apathy of women workers for the reasons that have been discussed earlier. But union activity by

KEY PEOPLE

Addie L. Wyatt (b. 1924)
was a civil rights' campaigner, trade union activist, a leader of women. In the early 1980s, she was considered to be one of the most influential African Americans. She was born in Mississippi and, on entering the workforce, immediately experienced discrimination. Having failed to gain a white-collar job, she became a meat packer in 1941 and a union activist. She was elected vice president of the United Packinghouse Food and Alliance Workers Union. She worked closely with Martin Luther King during his civil rights campaigns as his labour adviser. She worked to achieve equal rights for women in the workplace. In 1976, she became the first black woman to lead an international union when she became international vice president of the United Food and Commercial Workers Union, a post she held until 1984. She was the first chair of the National Women's Committee of the Coalition of Black Trade Unionists.

KEY CONCEPTS

Sexual harassment
Awareness of this as a problem for women in the workplace led to the involvement of women's groups in helping women workers; for example, the Working Women's Institute in New York and the Coalition Against Sexual Harassment in Minneapolis.

Myra Wolfgang (1914–76) was born in Montreal, Canada and moved to Detroit in 1917. In 1932, she began work as a receptionist at what was to become the Hotel, Motel and Restaurant Employees Union and subsequently became a union organiser. In the 1930s, she organised soup kitchens for striking auto workers and led a sit-down strike lasting eight days at the F.W. Woolworth Company. She continued her trade union activity throughout her working life. She campaigned for the minimum wage, for child care centres for working women and job training schemes for mothers. She served on President Kennedy's Commission on the Status of Women in 1962 and testified against the Equal Rights Amendment because she believed it would risk those labour laws and standards that protected women in the workplace.

women had clearly gone some way to gaining recognition for the rights of women in the workplace, to narrowing the gap in wages and securing better prospects for at least some sections of the female workforce. (See Chapter 17 for further discussion of changes in the position of women by 1992.)

CONCLUSION

It can be argued that, by 1992, organised labour had retained most of the rights that successive governments had established. However, some had been eroded by the growing weakness of the trade union movement brought about by the changing political and economic climate.

- The right to join a trade union remained in law but the increasingly stronger position of employers had facilitated the creation of non-union enterprises which falling wage values forced workers to accept.
- The right to collective bargaining remained even in non-unionised firms but, without union representation, the workers remained in a weak position. Even in unionised firms, the workers' need for a job made them less inclined to attempt to dictate the terms.
- The right to strike remained, with some exceptions (such as government workers) although many employers felt sufficiently secure to introduce no-strike clauses into terms of employment.
- There had been a shift in public opinion that ensured strikes were viewed less sympathetically than in earlier times, especially when these inconvenienced the general population.
- The hostility of the Republican administration in the early 1980s and the lack of commitment on the part of the Democrats made it possible for politicians and employers to chip away at the earlier legislation to free industry and commerce from the potential barriers to economic progress that organised labour could create.
- The changing economic organisation and structure and the falling numbers of workers joining unions further weakened the labour movement. It seemed that many sectors of employees either no longer recognised the

need for trade union representation or were encouraged to reject it.

The wheel had almost, though not completely, turned full circle. Women had made some advances towards equal opportunity and status. Moreover, many areas of discrimination had been removed by the civil rights legislation of the 1960s. There remained, however, significant numbers of the population who had never really experienced protection or equality in the workplace. These were predominantly African-American and Hispanic workers who remained in low paid, service occupations and who were most vulnerable to unemployment. These formed the majority of the 11 per cent of Americans who existed below the poverty line by 1992 and who had no-one to represent them in the workplace (see also Chapter 5).

QUESTIONS TO CONSIDER

1. Was the Air Traffic Controllers' strike a symptom or a cause of the weakening of trade unions in the closing decades of the twentieth century?

2. In the period from 1865 until 1992, the following can be identified as factors promoting or inhibiting progress towards the acquisition of rights for workers:

   - The economy and the structure of the workforce
   - Politicians and policy
   - The divided workforce
   - The organisation of labour
   - Employers
   - The impact of war.

   Track each of these from 1865 to 1992 and discuss the extent to which their significance changed at key points across the period.

3. Identify the turning points across the period and consider which were the most significant.

4. Were trade union and labour rights won by their leaders and members or were they given?

EXAM STYLE QUESTIONS

1. To what extent were the 1920s and 1930s the most important period of progress for organised labour in the USA from 1865 to 1992?

2. Assess the view that the formation of the American Federation of Labor was the most significant development in the successful acquisition of trade union and labour rights between 1865 and 1992.

3. Assess the view that the most important obstacle to the extension of trade union and labour rights between 1865 and 1992 was the resistance of the employers.

4. The 1960s have been described as the 'golden age' for trade unions and their membership. How far do you agree with this view in the context of the period from 1865 until 1992?

Section 3: Native Americans 1865–1992

'They made us many promises, more than I can remember, but they never kept but one; they promised to take our land, and they took it.'

Red Cloud of the Pawnee tribe

In the closing decades of the nineteenth century, the Native American (American Indian) 'nations' lost thousands of acres of the land that had been granted to them by treaties. On their diminished reservation land, they were cut off from their natural means of subsistence and became increasingly dependent on the meagre supplies provided by the government. Poverty, starvation and disease resulted in a substantial decline in the Indian population. Largely as a result of government policy, their culture and way of life was destroyed as they became exposed to the government's policy of 'Americanisation'. In the context of the struggle for civil rights, its meaning for Native Americans was the recovery of the land that was rightfully theirs and recognition of their right to self-determination – to be governed by their own tribal councils and to live according to their own laws, religious beliefs and customs.

For much of the period from 1865 until the 1960s, successive governments clung to the vision of a totally assimilated people. This was partly because they were not prepared to recognise the concept of 'nations within' implied by self-determination and because it was considered essential to reduce the financial dependency of the Indians tribes on the state. Policies designed to limit, and ultimately destroy, tribal loyalties and end the reservation system continued through the period as different pathways were devised to achieve total assimilation. By these policies, they were to be absorbed into American society, become independent and self-supporting. It was anticipated that they would finally cast off their tribal inheritance. For much of this period, the Indians were limited in the extent to which they could resist.

These policies caused misery and great hardship as Indian peoples were separated from their natural environment and way of life. Whilst government strategies met with some success, legislators failed to appreciate that the power of the spiritual and cultural legacy could not be easily destroyed. Native Americans were not united in their opposition to assimilation and for the most part, they were dependent on others to take up their cause until, inspired by the black civil rights movement, they took up the cause of independence and self-determination in the closing decades of the twentieth century. By 1992, they had gone some way to achieving success.

CHAPTER 10

1865–1900 'They made us many promises...'

The last days of a proud people?

Hypothesis:

- In the closing decades of the nineteenth century, American Indians were deprived of their rights and freedom.

NATIVE AMERICANS IN 1865

Who were the Native Americans?

The **Native American** tribes (named 'Indians' by Christopher Columbus in 1492) inhabited the North American continent for thousands of years before the white man arrived. At the beginning of the nineteenth century, 86 independent tribes, some of them large enough to be called 'nations', had been identified across the US. By the mid-nineteenth century, they continued to live according to their own tribal customs, religion and laws under the jurisdiction of their tribal chieftains. However, by 1865, the process was already underway to break down their traditional culture and lifestyle. From the end of the nineteenth to the end of the twentieth centuries, **American Indians** made the least progress of any ethnic group in the

Groups of Indians in traditional dress.

USA in improving their status and, consequently, their quality of life. Whilst the policy of the federal government towards the Native Americans can be blamed for their condition, it must also be acknowledged that they resisted assimilation and wanted only independence and their own lands.

The largest population of Native Americans, occupied the vast area of the USA known as the Great Plains. Early in the nineteenth century, explorers, hunters and traders had reported that this area, in the heart of the continent, was a desert, incapable of sustaining civilised life. It was, therefore, happily left to the Native Americans. The tribes here were almost entirely **nomadic**. They roamed the Plains freely, following the huge herds of buffalo that provided them with everything that they needed to survive. This determined their lifestyle, living conditions, laws, government and religious beliefs. Tribes existed independently of each other and inter-tribal rivalry and hostility was common. Collectively, the lifestyle of Native Americans was totally alien to that of the white settlers who encountered them. They lived in tepees, worshipped nature and the elements, lived under their own laws and tribal government, spoke their own tribal languages and indulged in ceremonies and rituals that Christian, white Americans saw as pagan and uncivilised.

KEY TERMS

Nomadic The Plains Indians did not inhabit permanent settlements. They followed the buffalo herds, living in tepee villages that could be quickly assembled or demolished in response according to the sighting of the herds. They were totally dependent on the buffalo in order to survive.

What factors had changed the lives of the Native Americans by 1865?

1. The impact of westwards expansion

The government of the US was content to let the American Indians live freely on those areas of the continent that white Americans did not want. By 1865, this was mainly the vast area in the centre of the continent known as the Great Plains. From the mid-nineteenth century, it became government policy to attract settlers to populate these wide open spaces in the West. The westwards expansion of the US frontier from the early decades of the nineteenth century onwards was a significant factor in radically changing the way of life of the Indians. As white settlers pushed westwards beyond the natural frontier of the Appalachian Mountains, the Indians were gradually removed from their traditional lands. A large, forced

1865–1900 'They made us many promises ...' The last days of a proud people?

163

The Native
American tribes of
the Great Plains and
battle locations.

migration of the tribes native to Georgia, Alabama,
Mississippi, Virginia, Tennessee and Florida (approximately
70,000 Indians) had been the outcome of the Indian
Removal Act of 1830. These tribes were given land in
Oklahoma (designated 'Indian Territory'), on the Plains, to
create space for white American families to settle on their
original homelands. In the late 1840s, trails across America
to the west coastal plain encouraged wagon trains of settlers
to head west to the fertile farmlands of Oregon. In 1849,
gold was discovered in California. Both of these
developments resulted in increasing numbers of white
Americans moving west. This new settlement in turn,
displaced many of the tribes who lived in California and
Oregon and for whom fishing was their natural means of
subsistence. Those who remained, lost their right to fish
freely. Many of those who were forcibly re-located onto
lands on the Plains perished because, cut off from their
natural means of subsistence, they did not have the skills to
hunt for food.

2. The impact of the Civil War

The outbreak of the Civil War in 1861 resulted in a number of developments that had profoundly affected the tribal life of the Plains Indians by 1865 and, ultimately, radically changed their lifestyle. How and why did this happen?

US Government Treaties with the Indians A series of treaties made between the federal government and the Indian tribes. In each case, the Indians relinquished more of their land. In some, land was offered in exchange for that being taken, usually less desirable for white settlement. Government promises were subsequently broken.

1851 Fort Laramie Treaty (Sioux, Arapaho, Cheyenne)

1861 Fort Wise Treaty (Cheyenne and Arapaho)

1867 Medicine Lodge Treaty (Kiowa, Comanche, Plains Apache)

1868 Fort Laramie Treaty (Lakota, Sioux, Arapaho)

From 1869 the government refused to make separate treaties with individual tribes.

The Sand Creek Massacre 1864 A troop of cavalry attacked an undefended Cheyenne camp killing and mutilating elderly men, women and children.

The Plains Wars 1862–67 These were a series of clashes rather than wars between the Indian tribes and units of the US Army:

Little Crow's War 1862 (Sioux)

Cheyenne Uprising 1863

Red Cloud's War 1867 (Sioux)

Winter Campaign 1868 (against the Cheyenne).

By 1865 several tribes, but most notably the Sioux and Cheyenne, were hostile to the encroachments of white settlers on the Plains and also to the presence of the army on their lands. Units of the regular army were stationed on the Plains in a series of forts across the West. Their remit was initially to offer protection to wagon trains and settlers in areas where the Indians were known to be hostile. In some instances, there were positive relationships between the army and the Indians. Indians traded both at the fort and at trading stations. There were also a number of violent skirmishes and atrocities were committed on both sides.

The Indians had already begun, in 1851, to hand over vast areas of their lands for settlement via **a series of treaties** made with the government, as they had begun to realise that they were powerless to resist indefinitely the power and strength of the US government and its army. Some tribes, the Sioux for example, signed several treaties and each time handed over more and more of their land to open up land for settlement by ever increasing numbers of white farmers. However, this restricted their freedom to follow the herds of buffalo and, therefore, potentially cut off their sole food supply. This, in turn, threatened their whole way of life. Treaties addressed this on paper with promises of government aid to ensure that the people were fed. Sadly, this was not always forthcoming. During the Civil War, when federal government funding was stretched, essential aid did not reach the Indians. In some cases, government-appointed Indian Agents were corrupt and sold the food destined for the Indians for their own profit. Consequently, the tribes starved. Hunger drove them to hostility that resulted in a series of Indian uprisings.

As there was no fighting during the Civil War west of the Mississippi, regular soldiers were withdrawn from the

1865–1900 'They made us many promises …' The last days of a proud people?

165

Plains to fight in the East. They were replaced by volunteers who were untrained and ill-disciplined. Many despised the Indians. The outcome was a number of brutal atrocities that resulted in a serious deterioration in relationships with the Indians. The most notorious of these was the **Sand Creek Massacre in 1864**. This and other similar incidents led to **warfare on the Plains** spasmodically between 1862 and 1868. By 1868, several of the older chiefs had come to appreciate that against the white man's army the Indians had little hope of final victory and reluctantly made peace by signing treaties.

During the Civil War the federal government was determined to secure control of the lands west of the Mississippi. This was done by the creation of **federal territories** governed by officials appointed by the federal government in Washington, by populating these vast open spaces with settlers. The vision of the federal government was one of the mid-west populated by homesteaders (small-scale farmers) and to this end the Homesteads Act was passed in 1862. This released land in 160 acre plots, available to farmers for free on the basis that they would farm the land for five years. By 1865, 20,000 homesteaders had settled on the Plains. A small number of these were Native Americans. But the expansion of homesteading could only be achieved at great cost to the Indian tribes. In 1864, for example, the Navajo and Apache had been moved onto **reservation** land to fulfil the **government's ideal of Indians as farmers,** their children receiving the white man's education and all of them converted to Christianity. In the case of the Navajo the move to their allocated reservation land involved a journey on foot of almost 300 miles.

By 1865, the construction of the Union Pacific Railway was underway, the result of the federal government's determination to develop and expand the existing railway network in the east so that it stretched from coast to coast. It was part of the policy of firmly establishing government law and order in the new territories in the west but also to that of encouraging settlement there. The completion of the first trans-continental railway in 1869 was a triumph of engineering and sheer human effort but it only further

Federal territories were the new lands opened up for settlement in the mid and far-west. As territories they became subject to the laws of the US and were administered by officials appointed in Washington DC. When the population of the territories reached 60,000, they could apply to become a state. This gave them the right of some degree of self-determination. They had their own elected state assembly and governor and were given authority to make their own laws.

Reservations were the lands designated by the US government for occupation by the Native American tribes. The process began in the 1850s but accelerated in the 1860s. Usually, there were the lands that the Native Americans were allowed to retain when treaties had been signed handing over former Indian land for white settlement. The boundaries of these lands were clearly delineated in the terms of the treaty. After 1871, the establishment of reservations or alterations to the previously agreed boundaries were decided by Congress.

The government's ideal of Indian farmers. There was a belief in government circles that the Indian tribes could be 'civilised' if they could be transformed from their nomadic existence based on hunting to a settled way of life based on farming. (This is discussed further on pages 175–76 in relation to the Dawes Severalty Act.)

weakened the position of the Indians. The railroad companies, allocated land by the government to cover the cost of the enterprise, unashamedly lured settlers onto the Plains with 'buy now, pay later' schemes. For the Indians, the trains disturbed the buffalo herds and also brought even more land hungry settlers to the Plains.

HOW EFFECTIVE WERE THE ATTEMPTS MADE TO ASSIMILATE NATIVE AMERICANS BEFORE 1900?

Reservation policy

The Native Americans clearly presented the US government with a problem. Apart from the fact that more and more of their land was in demand by white settlers, they had no rights of citizenship and were not under the total jurisdiction of the law of the United States because they remained subject to their tribal laws. In addition, the fact that their independent existence gave them a degree of self-determination was unacceptable to the US government. Moreover, significant numbers were hostile and belligerent. Differences of opinion existed, particularly between politicians with no experience of the reality of life in the mid-west and the army whose officers had first-hand experience of the Plains Wars (see page 165).

Government policy, however, was to 'Americanise' the Indians, who were considered to be savages. Before this could properly be achieved, tribal bonds and the communal, tribal lifestyle had to be destroyed. This would be achieved by a process of education, by conversion to Christianity and by training the Indians to become farmers. Separated from their dependence on hunting the buffalo, their tribal way of life would be destroyed. To achieve this, the Indians were to be located on government controlled reservations and no longer allowed to roam freely and hunt the buffalo. On the reservations, every hint of tribal beliefs, customs and skills would be eradicated. The braves would no longer be allowed to show their skill and courage as hunters. The medicine men would no longer be allowed to mix their herbal remedies. Parents would be forced to send their children to school; the men would have to give up **polygamy.** The laws of the United

KEY CONCEPTS

Polygamy means the practice of having more than one wife and was common in Native American tribes. It was the means by which all the women of the tribe were cared for by the male braves, who hunted and provided food for their families. It was a custom closely linked to many others that ensured the survival of all.

1865–1900 'They made us many promises ...' The last days of a proud people?

167

Reservations in 1890:

- contained 133,417 reservation Indians
- were located in 20 states
- occupied 78,500,000 acres of land, much of it desert
- were run largely by federal agents who were supported by an Indian police force (770 officers); some were run by the US army
- had their own 'court of offences', where minor crimes were tried and the judges were Indians
- rations were given to poor and destitute Indians and those on arid land. These varied from reservation to reservation. In 1890, of the total number of 133,417 Indians, 34,785 received rations in all cases as a result of age or the poor quality of the land.

Figures extracted from a report published by the US Bureau of the Census in 1890.

States would replace **tribal laws** and Native Americans would become individual, Christian, farming families inhabiting their own designated space. Communal living would not be allowed. The power of the tribal chiefs was to be replaced, on each reservation, by an Indian Agent appointed by the Indian Bureau (or Indian Office, as it was sometimes called), an agency of the federal government set up to be responsible for all matters relating to the Indians but especially for the reservations. Native Americans were subject to the Department of the Interior and the Army.

Until 1871, reservations were set up either as the outcome of a treaty with the tribes as part of the process of re-defining the extent of tribal lands or imposed on defeated people. In 1868, for example, the Fort Laramie Treaty signed by the Sioux with the government established the 'Great Sioux Reserve'. This provided ample land for the various tribes that comprised the Great Sioux Nation. On signature, it was agreed that this could not be changed without the agreement of three-quarters of the male population of the tribes. To this extent, the rights of the Indians to determine what should happen to their land were recognised. However, after 1871, they lost this right

KEY CONCEPTS

Tribal laws had been formulated over many centuries and were closely interwoven with their need to survive. Braves committing murder, for example, would not be executed as they were needed for hunting and protection. Any Indian harming another would make recompense as decided by the tribal council and typically involved the handing over of horses or other goods as compensation. This was totally at odds with the operation of US law.

and decisions on the setting up of reservations, relocation of the tribes or re-designation of reservation boundaries were decided by Congress without consultation. The army was used to ensure that they stayed within these boundaries and had the responsibility of rounding up any who strayed.

Undoubtedly, this change of policy reflects the attitude of white Americans towards the tribes and was probably influenced to some degree by the strongly held belief in **'Manifest Destiny'**, therefore, if the land was required for farming, stock rearing, timber cutting or railroad building or any other use by white Americans then they should not have to be beholden to the Indian chiefs for their agreement. It was a view clearly expressed by Edward McCook, governor of territory of Colorado at this time:

'God gave us the earth and the fullness thereof...I do not believe in donating to these indolent savages the best part of my territory, and I do not believe in placing Indians on an equality with the white man as landholder.'

There was an overwhelming view that the Native Americans must adapt to and adopt the American lifestyle if they were to have any hope of survival. Otherwise, they would become,

'...vagabonds in the midst of civilisation...[and] *festering sores on the communities near which they were located.'*

Indian Commissioner Francis A. Walker in 1872

Further erosion of reservation lands followed the defeat of George Custer and the Ninth Cavalry at the **Battle of the Little Bighorn** in 1876; the lands of the Great Sioux Reservation were massively reduced so that by 1889, six small reservations had been created and the Lakota Sioux, who had fought Custer, reduced to starvation. These changes were forced upon the Indians without regard for the majority clause in the Fort Laramie Treaty. This was to become an important factor almost a century later when the Lakotas campaigned to recover their land. The massacre shocked the nation but some white Americans recognised that it was the culmination of the oppression and denial of the rights of Native Americans. On the reservations, they

1865–1900 'They made us many promises ...' The last days of a proud people?

169

were not only denied their civil but also their human rights.

> 'Who shall be held responsible for this event so dark and sorrowful? The history of our dealings with these Indian tribes from the very beginning is a record of fraud, and perjury, and uninterrupted injustice. ... We have driven them each year further from their original homes and hunting-grounds... We have treated them as having absolutely no rights at all... We have made beggars of them.'
>
> Reverend D.J. Burrell, sermon on the battle of the Little Bighorn, Chicago August 1876

What was life like in the reservations?

It is difficult to argue that the forced changes in the lifestyle of the Indians in the later decades of the nineteenth century were anything but destructive. Certainly, in principle, the ideal of settled, independent Native American farming communities might appear preferable to the precarious existence that accompanied nomadic life on the Plains. However, the traditional, tribal life meant that the Indians could retain their pride, dignity and independence. In theory, 'Americanisation' could have brought improvement – better homes, jobs, healthcare, for example. The reality was that freedom was lost and nothing was gained. Reservation Indians, in the care of the Government, were denied civil rights because they were classified as dependent 'wards of the state' and were not tax payers.

By locating the tribes on reservations, the government had effectively segregated them from the rest of American society. But, in spite of the intentions of the Government, reservation life ensured that tribal life was sustained. This was double-edged. Indians may have retained a sense of belonging and a pride in their shared heritage. They may have retained at least some of their tribal culture and customs. However, they also retained their traditional tribal rivalries which ensured that they could not present a united front against what they perceived to be the theft of their lands and white injustice. More importantly, whilst they clung to their tribal way of life, they were denied their rights of citizenship.

General George Crook, who had led the campaign that ended at the Little Bighorn, described conditions for Indians on the reservations in 1878.

> *'In regard to the Bannocks, I was up there last spring and found them in a desperate condition. I telegraphed and the agent telegraphed for supplies, but word came that no appropriation had been made. They have never been half supplied... The buffalo is all gone, and an Indian can't catch enough jack rabbits to subsist himself and his family, and then, there aren't enough jack rabbits to catch. What are they to do? Starvation is staring them in the face, and if they wait much longer, they will not be able to fight...All the tribes tell the same story. They are surrounded on all sides, the game is destroyed or driven away; they are left to starve, and there remains but one thing for them to do – fight while they can.'*

From Crook's Army and Navy Journal, 29 July 1878

Reservation life for many was extremely harsh. The ideal to transform Native Americans into farmers was not realised. Much of the land allocated to the Indians proved impossible to cultivate. Dependent on the food supplied by the government, they starved. Some Indian Agents were corrupt and used government resources for their own ends. Worse still, the total dependence on the white man for food, clothing and shelter was humiliating. The situation worsened in the 1880s when drought affected crops on the reservations and disease wiped out the cattle that Indians kept now they were deprived of hunting the buffalo. In any case, a wholesale massacre of the buffalo, almost rendering them extinct, ensured that Native Americans had no other source of food. Government meat subsidies to the Sioux reservations were cut at times when there were other demands on federal funding. Thousands of Indians starved. Others died as a result of epidemics of measles, influenza and whooping cough. By 1900, only about 100,000 of the estimated 240,000 Native Americans who had inhabited the Plains in 1860 remained. Add to this the debilitating effects on the reservation Indians of the availability of quantities of whisky, and the picture becomes particularly

1865–1900 'They made us many promises ...' The last days of a proud people?

171

bleak.

The final tragedy for the Indians and triumph for the army occurred in 1890 when a desperate band of two hundred starving and unarmed Sioux Indians who had left the reservation were cornered by the army at **Wounded Knee** in South Dakota and gunned down. The tragedy of Wounded Knee and its true significance was summed up by Black Elk, a Sioux Indian, reflecting on the massacre,

'I did not know then how much was ended. When I look back now from this high hill of my old age, I can still see the butchered women and children lying heaped and scattered all along the crooked gulch as plain as when I saw them with eyes still young. And I can see that something else died there in the bloody mud, and was buried in the blizzard. A people's dream died there. It was a beautiful dream…the nation's hoop is broken and scattered. There is no centre any longer, and the sacred tree is dead.'

Christian missionaries working on the reservations to convert the Indians were largely unsuccessful. Whilst going through the motions of adopting Christianity, they continued to practise their tribal religious rituals in secret.

One of the few examples of successful reservation life was

KEY EVENTS

Massacre at Wounded Knee (1890) Wounded Knee is the site in South Dakota where the Sioux Indians were finally rounded up by the US army in 1890. This was the result of the growing popularity throughout the reservation lands of a religious ritual called the 'Ghost Dance' – an attempt by desperate people living in misery on the reservations to regain their lost way of life. This frightened white settlers in the vicinity of the reservations who believed that a mass Indian uprising was imminent. The reservation police believed that Chief Sitting Bull was responsible and shot him as they were in the process of arresting him on the reservation. His frightened followers fled to the camp of Chief Big Foot near Wounded Knee Creek. There they were surrounded by the army who opened fire killing all of the 200 unarmed men, women and children.

Bodies being buried at Wounded Knee, 1890.

that of the Navajo tribe. Having undertaken a 300 mile journey in 1868, to be relocated on four million acres of reservation lands bordered by Arizona and New Mexico, they adapted quickly to farming, planting a range of crops. They also carefully tended and conserved the flock of 15,000 sheep and goats provided by the government, so that by 1892 it had grown to 1.7 million. Contrary to the experience of other tribes, between 1878 and the 1930s, Navajo lands had been increased by the Government to 10.5 million acres as a reward for their success and to enable them to further increase their yields. By 1900, the population had grown from 8,000 in 1868 to 22,000.

The impact of education

Education for Native American children was not seen as a right but rather as essential to the process of 'Americanisation' and the destruction of tribal culture and loyalties. Reservation schools provided by government funding were certainly of dubious educational value. Assuming that the Indian Agents used the funding as intended, provision was of poor quality. The curriculum was limited and clearly designed to determine the future role of Native Americans. Children were taught English, reading, writing and basic arithmetic. Later, the development of vocational skills was included. Teachers brought from the east were often unable to cope with the harsh conditions and returned home. Language also proved to be a huge barrier. Poor communication meant that pupils became bored and frustrated. On some reservations, it was considered that to have the required level of impact, children should be taken away from their parents and placed in reservation boarding schools. However, many ran away from these and went back to their families.

In the late 1870s, two off-reservation boarding schools were established in Virginia (Hampton Normal and Agricultural Institute) and Pennsylvania (Carlisle Indian Industrial School) and became recognised as models of vocational training. Native American children (boys and girls) transferred there after completing six years in reservation schools. While boys learnt trades such as

1865–1900 'They made us many promises ...' The last days of a proud people?

173

carpentry, masonry, harness-making and tailoring, the girls were taught to cook, sew, preserve food and take care of the home, presumably in preparation for domestic service. But the overwhelming intention was clearly to break the tribal ties of young American Indians. Their hair was cut short, they wore uncomfortable uniforms and were harshly disciplined. Beatings, solitary confinement and diets of bread and water were inflicted for breaking the rules. These included speaking in their tribal languages. During the eight years that they spent at these schools, they spent the equivalent of three years living with white farming families where the boys laboured and the girls became servants. The clear intention of the whole regime was to purge young people of their tribal ways.

Carlisle Indian School.

Opportunities for graduates from Carlisle and Hampton were limited. In the early years, young American Indian graduates were employed in the Indian agency offices and schools when they returned to their reservations. However, as time went by, these opportunities were in short supply. Later graduates were employed to administer discipline in the schools. Some worked as interpreters to Indian Agents. Others became Indian scouts to units of the army located near their reservations. The vast majority, however, simply returned to reservation life. Here, they were to some extent, alienated from their families and reservation communities. Having been schooled to be models to their tribes of 'Americanised' Indians, they were regarded as untrustworthy. Therefore, they found themselves trapped between two cultures.

Philanthropic organisations

In addition to the efforts of the government to civilise Native Americans, white philanthropic organisations proliferated in the closing decades of the nineteenth century, although many were short-lived. One of the most influential was the **Indian Rights Association.** The membership of these organisations was largely motivated by their religious beliefs and included Quakers, Catholics and Protestants and missionary societies. Their common purpose was reform. They viewed the Indians as existing at an earlier stage of civilisation to their own. These groups were generally agreed that the tribes should be assimilated into American society and achieve equality with all Americans. They did not all agree as to how this would be achieved. Not surprisingly, they focused on the lifestyle, religious beliefs and rituals of Native Americans as key indicators of their primitive state and worked to persuade them to abandon their traditional ways, although they were frequently critical of government organisations such as the Board of Indian Commissioners, set up in 1869, who they labelled as 'dishonest' and accused them of mistreating the Indians in their care and protection. Some reformers found outlets to pursue their purpose by working in education for Indian children or working for the Indian Bureau on reservations.

CASE STUDY: THE DAWES SEVERALTY ACT 1887

What did the Dawes Act seek to achieve?

By the late 1880s, it was becoming increasingly clear that, as the means of de-tribalising and assimilating the Indians into the culture of 'white America', the reservation policy had failed miserably. Consequently, the decision was made in Congress to divide up (allot) reservation lands on the plains into homesteads to be allocated to Native American

1865–1900 'They made us many promises …' The last days of a proud people?

175

families. This was achieved by the **General Allotment Act 1887** which became more commonly known as the **Dawes Act** after Henry Dawes, the sponsor of the bill. Dawes was convinced that the ownership of land would be a real civilising influence. It was a view shared by others who were opposed to the treatment of Native Americans on the reservations and who helped to put together the detail of the Act. It is clear that no-one respected, understood or wished to understand the deeply spiritual dimension of tribal culture or the strength of the bonds that bound American Indian peoples together.

Alice Fletcher, leader of a group called 'Friends of the Indians' and who helped to frame the Dawes Act expressed what she hoped the Act would achieve:

> 'The Indian may now become a free man; free from the thraldom of the tribe; freed from the domination of the reservation system; free to enter into the body of our citizens. This bill may therefore be considered as the Magna Carta of the Indians of our country.'

Henry Dawes claimed that:

> '...to be civilised was to wear civilised clothes...cultivate the ground, live in houses, ride in Studebaker wagons, send children to school, drink whiskey [and] own property.'

Did the Dawes Act achieve its objectives?
In so far as there was an intention within the Act to destroy the reservation system, it was largely successful. Although some reservations remained, the Navajo reservation, for example (see pages 172–73), most were significantly reduced in size or disappeared almost completely. By 1900, of the 150 million acres of reservation land recognised by the Government in 1887 as belonging to the Indians, only about 78 million acres remained.

Land-owning Indians paid taxes and, therefore, gained full rights of citizenship. From their perspective, however, this was not particularly appreciated at this point in time. Like the African Americans they faced discrimination and

The General Allotment (Dawes) Act 1887 The terms of the Act were:

Each Head of the family to receive 160 acres of farmland or 320 acres of grazing land for 25 years in trust.

Further subdivisions of land to be allotted to single persons or orphaned children.

After 25 years, Native Americans to have full ownership of the land.

All Native Americans farming allotted land to have full rights of citizenship.

Unallotted land on the reservations to be offered to white Americans for settlement.

prejudice when they attempted to assert their rights. The concept of the division and ownership of land was alien to their beliefs that the land belonged to all living creatures and could not therefore belong to individuals. Some settled to farming and were successful but much depended on the quality of the land they were allocated. Many did not adapt and their enterprises failed. Significant amounts of land allotted to the Indians were bought by white settlers when its Native American owners were unsuccessful and got into debt. Unfortunately, unused as they were to the having such large sums of money, this was quickly squandered on consumer goods and they were thrown back either on the support of other families who retained their land or forced to return to the ever decreasing reservation lands. In so far as it is possible to find evidence, it would appear that those Indians who had been educated by white society proved to be amongst the most unsuccessful. Significant amounts of land allotted to the Indians found its way into the hands of white settlers when its Native American owners were unsuccessful and got into debt.

The policy of allotment adversely affected the status and rights of some American Indian women. This was particularly the case in those tribes that were traditionally matriarchal (such as the Iroquois and the Cherokee). This meant that all family property belonged to the wives whilst the responsibility of the men was hunting and making provision for the family. Under the Dawes Act, land was allotted to the male head of the family.

Resistance to the allotment policy came from the **five civilised tribes** still located on Indian Territory in what was to become the state of Oklahoma. They had been exempted initially by the Dawes Act. However, a subsequent amendment to the Act (the **Curtis Act**) was passed by Congress in 1898. This proposed the termination of the rights of these tribes to be self-governing by 1906. Proposals were also afoot in Congress to combine Indian Territory and Oklahoma Territory into the state of Oklahoma. The tribes attempted to pre-empt this by proposing that their lands become the separate state of Sequoyah. A constitution was presented at the **Muskogee Convention in 1905**. Although there was a majority vote

1865–1900 'They made us many promises …' The last days of a proud people?

177

in support of Sequoyah at the convention, it was rejected by Congress and the two territories were combined into the State of Oklahoma in 1907. Between 1898 and 1907, 100,000 Indians from 'Oklahoma' were assigned lands. Approximately 2 million acres of the former Indian Territory were opened up for white settlement.

The extent to which the allotment of land authorised by the Dawes and Curtis Acts resulted in promoting the assimilation of Native Americans is doubtful. American Indians resisted assimilation. The loss of their tribal lands increased their determination to remain separate and to pursue the restoration of what had been, from their perspective, unlawfully taken away from them. Hence, the forecast of Thomas Jefferson Morgan (Commissioner of Indian Affairs) in 1900 that, *'The great body of Indians will become merged in the indistinguishable mass of our population'* may have been overly optimistic.

CONCLUSION

By 1865, the process of removing the rights of self-determination that Native Americans had enjoyed for centuries was already underway. Whilst the reservation policy pursued by the US government may not have achieved its objectives, it nevertheless subjected the Indians to misery, deprivation, alcohol abuse and disease. By 1900, only around 100,000 of the 240,000 Indians who had inhabited the Plains in 1865 remained. It deprived them of their freedom, their pride and their self-respect. Far from transforming them into Americans, it condemned them to become a people without a distinctive identity and living in the direst poverty. They were and remained the poorest group of people in the USA.

By 1900, the majority of Native Americans were left without the lands that had been given to them by treaty in the 1860s and denied any rights of negotiation. Education was too narrowly defined in its objectives to provide young people with any prospect of self-improvement, although by the early decades of the twentieth century, some moved into higher education and began to take advantage of opportunities to enter the professions. The civil rights of those who owned their own land were of little use to them in real terms. They faced the kind of prejudice experienced by other ethnic groups in the US, particularly African Americans, especially when it came to exercising their right to vote (see Chapter 2 for further discussion of this issue).

Key factors in the subjugation of the Indians during this period had been their tribal structure to which they had clung, their lack of unity and lack of strong leadership. The stand taken by the five tribes by the early 1900s could be seen as an exception. It was certainly an early indication of their determination to retain their identity, their culture and to resist assimilation even though, at this point in time, their protest was unsuccessful.

QUESTIONS TO CONSIDER

1. How significant was the Dawes Act (1887) in the efforts of the US government to assimilate the American Indian tribes?

2. Why was Indian resistance in the last decades of the nineteenth century unsuccessful?

3. Can government policy towards Native Americans before 1900 be justified? Was anything achieved?

CHAPTER 11

1900–45 'Into the melting pot'

How successfully were Native Americans 'Americanised' in the first half of the twentieth century?

Hypothesis:

* Government policies caused suffering to the Indians but did not succeed in breaking their tribal loyalties and resistance to assimilation.

NATIVE AMERICANS AND THE 'MELTING POT'

In 1782, a French traveller, J. Hector St John de Crèvecoeur, made reference in his *Letters from an American Farmer*, to the idea of American society emerging from a melting pot (see also page 45) in which people of different nationalities and ethnic origins became fused together into one nation. It was an image promoted by **Israel Zangwill** in his play *The Melting Pot* written in 1908. In many respects, it was a reflection of the challenge to the American government presented by the mass immigration to America of people from many different parts of the world. The challenge was how these people, speaking so many different languages, bringing with them their own cultural traditions and religious beliefs, could be assimilated to create one American nation. They joined significant numbers of African Americans and also Native Americans who already inhabited the US. Such diversity prompted government policies of naturalisation and 'Americanisation', with the purpose of creating a national identity. For African Americans, recognition of equality was a right they struggled to achieve. The vast majority of Native Americans, however, who had already demonstrated a resistance to assimilation in the closing decades of the nineteenth century, continued to resist any attempt at integration and in the decades leading up to the outbreak of the Second World War, continued to claim their right to be separate.

KEY PEOPLE

Israel Zangwill (1864– 1926) His writings give insight into Jewish life at the end of the nineteenth century. The concept of the USA as the birthplace of a new race, forged in a crucible, owes its origin to Zangwill's successful Broadway play.

'America is God's crucible, the great Melting Pot where all the races of Europe are melting and reforming!....A fig for your feuds and vendettas! German and Frenchmen, Irishman and Englishmen, Jews and Russians – into the Crucible with you all! God is making the American.'

From the play *The Melting Pot* by Israel Zangwill

RESISTANCE, PRESSURE AND PROTEST BEFORE 1933

KEY EVENTS

Lone Wolf* v. *Hitchcock
1903 Lone Wolf (1820–79) was a Kiowa Chief who, along with the Commanches, made the Medicine Lodge Treaty in 1867 that established reservation lands for the use of the tribes. It contained a clause asserting that the agreement of four-fifths of the male population would be needed to change the terms of the treaty. Subsequently, Congress allotted several millions of acres of this land, ignoring the agreement clause of the treaty. Lone Wolf began legal action against Ethan Hitchcock, Secretary of State for the Interior. The judgement was not handed down until after the death of Lone Wolf. It was a significant decision because it established the right of Congress to revoke all treaties and led to the further acquisition of Indian lands. It negated decisions made by the Court in the late nineteenth century that had been more supportive of the rights of Native Americans.

For much of the period leading up to the outbreak of the Second World War, any gains made by Native Americans were largely the result of the actions of others sympathetic to their cause. The lack of a sense of common purpose amongst Native American peoples continued to be an obstacle to resisting government policies in the first three decades of the twentieth century. However, this is not to say that actions planned to assimilate the tribes did not meet with resistance from them. This was done through cases brought before the Supreme Court. The Cherokees, one of the five civilised tribes of Oklahoma, for example, continued to challenge the right of Congress to deny them their rights to live according to their own laws and traditions (*Cherokee Nation* v. *Hitchcock* 1902). The following year, in ***Lone Wolf* v. *Hitchcock***, the Supreme Court supported the power of the US Government to revoke all treaties made with Native American tribes. In making this judgement, the Court described Native Americans as *'an ignorant and dependent race'* and *'wards of the nation'* who were not citizens of the United States and therefore had no rights.

The Society of American Indians (SAI)

In 1911, a group of fifty educated American Indian men and women joined together to form the Society of American Indians (SAI). This was the first attempt at establishing an inter-tribal pressure group with the purpose of campaigning for improvement in education and better health care. Its impact was limited, however, partly by a shortage of funds to challenge discrimination in the courts but largely because of the lack of mass support from the Indians themselves. To some degree this may have been a result of difficulties in communication given that Native Americans were spread across vast areas of the US. However, SIA members themselves were not united in their vision for the future of the Native American peoples. Some sympathised with the position of the majority of Indians who were resisting assimilation. However, the majority believed that assimilation was the only route to real improvement. Consequently, by the 1920s, the SAI had collapsed, having achieved little.

DID THE INVOLVEMENT OF NATIVE AMERICANS IN THE FIRST WORLD WAR FURTHER THE PROCESS OF ASSIMILATION?

Approximately 10,000 Native American men fought in the War and gained recognition by the government for their bravery. Unlike African-American soldiers, they were not segregated in separate units and so had the opportunity to integrate with white Americans. Meanwhile, the government sponsored some Indian families to move away from the reservations to work in defence industries. This was the first stage of the urbanisation of American Indians. Some Indian women also went to work in factories to replace male workers who had gone to war. For some, their experiences of working beyond the confines of the reservations inclined them towards assimilation. Certainly, it was the view of government agents on the reservations that, irrespective of what the Indians thought themselves, the experience of the War had had a civilising influence:

'One Cheyenne, typical, no account, reservation Indian with long hair went to France, was wounded, gassed and shell-shocked. Was returned, honourably discharged. He reported to the agency office square shouldered, level eyed, courteous, self-reliant, and talked intelligently. A wonderful transformation, and caused by contact with the outside world.'

From a report by the Indian Agent for the Southern Cheyenne after 1918

VOTES FOR NATIVE AMERICANS – THE INDIAN CITIZENSHIP ACT 1924

The timing of the Act to extend the franchise to Native Americans in 1924 may suggest that it came as a reward for veterans and, consequently, as an outcome of the First World War. However, this would be misleading. Although participation in the war may have influenced this decision, it must be seen in the context of the government's relentless drive for total assimilation. In this context, it is important to recognise that this piece of legislation did not come about as a result of any campaign on the part of Native Americans themselves to secure the right to vote. Citizenship was conferred on them whether they wanted it or not. For those Indians seeking to maintain their traditional rights and resist assimilation, US citizenship was hardly a desirable goal.

Did the Act make a difference? This is doubtful. By 1924, the number of Native Americans who already possessed the right to vote had increased to almost two-thirds of the Indian population. This had been achieved partially as a result of inter-marriage but largely as a result of the allotment system emanating from the Dawes Act of 1887. The extension of the vote to all American Indians, including those still on reservations and dependent on federal support, was not intended to empower them but rather to promote assimilation.

In the first two decades of the twentieth century, this policy forged ahead in spite of its negative effects. Pressure for assimilation came from those states in the west where reservations were located. The aim remained to complete the assimilation process by transforming Native Americans into individual property owners and US citizens, hence the Citizenship Act. The bad feeling and mistrust that had been caused by government action and the hostility of state governments in the west towards them did nothing to convince Native Americans that there was anything to gain from participation in the political process. They would much rather have been given back their sovereignty and their own nationhood.

In any case, citizenship rights did not necessarily guarantee the right to vote, certainly in state elections. Many states in the west resisted the extension of the franchise to Native Americans and were able to use legal arguments and the imposition of voting qualifications to exclude them. This was reversed to some extent by the case of **Harrison v. Laveen** brought before the **Arizona Supreme Court** in 1948. The two Native Americans in this test case claimed that their rights had been violated when they were not allowed to register their vote. Yet although the court decided in their favour, other states in the west continued to restrict the voting rights of Indians.

TO WHAT EXTENT DID ATTITUDES TOWARDS NATIVE AMERICANS BEGIN TO CHANGE IN THE 1920s?

By the 1920s, the devastating impact of the allotment policy on those Indians remaining on the reservations in the west began to be widely recognised. Reservation lands in Oklahoma, on the Plains, the Great Lakes, Minnesota and Wisconsin had been drastically reduced. In the latter two states, 80 per cent of Indian land had been lost to them. This deteriorating situation attracted new reformers ready to understand and respect Native American customs and culture as well as condemn the appalling conditions in which they lived. Unlike the earlier organisations, which were largely motivated by their Christian beliefs to civilise the Indians, these were social scientists and anthropologists interested in preserving the traditions, beliefs and culture of the Indians.

Although by no means suffering the worst levels of deprivation, attention focused initially on the Pueblo Indians of New Mexico. In 1921, they lost much of their land as a result of a Supreme Court decision in 1913 that declared the Pueblo Indians as incapable of managing their own land. This was followed up in 1921 and 1923 by what came to be known as the **'Dance Order'**. This prohibited them from performing some of their traditional, ritual dances and was perceived by some as an attack on their civil and religious rights. Consequently, in 1923, a group

KEY EVENTS

Harrison v. Laveen (1948) is regarded as one of the most important legal cases in American Indian history. Frank Harrison and Harry Austin were members of the Mohawk-Apache Indian tribe. They lived on the Fort McDowell Indian Reservation in Arizona. When they tried to register their vote, Laveen, the county recorder, refused to allow it. The test case was the collaborative action of Felix S. Cohen, a legal scholar, the National Congress of American Indians and the American Civil Liberties Union. It was claimed that the plaintiffs met all the voting qualifications set out in the constitutions of the US and the state of Arizona.

KEY TERMS

Arizona Supreme Court
Each state in the USA has its own Supreme Court which normally acts as the final court of appeal for issues arising from state legislation. Only cases that have implications for the Constitution of the US will go to the US Supreme Court and then only if the defeated party in a state hearing appeals.

KEY EVENTS

The Leavitt Bill 1926 (The 'Dance Order') threatened to remove the right of the Peublos to perform some of their traditional dances.

John Collier (1884–1968)
was a man of energy and
conviction who had a lifelong
interest in traditional
communities and their
preservation. He admired the
work of nineteenth century
writers who had been critical
of the impact of
industrialisation on
community life and came to
admire the Pueblo Indians
because they were a perfect
example of a community that
had successfully resisted
attempts at assimilation. The
cause he vigorously pursued
was the restoration of the
rights of Native Americans to
self-determination. In this
respect, he was considered to
be a dreamer. His vision was
never realised.

KEY EVENTS

The Bursum Bill 1922
authorised that acquisition of
Peublo lands.

KEY CONCEPTS

The allotment policy
begun by the Dawes Act in
1887, was accelerated by the
Burke Act 1906. By the
1930s, the lands of the Native
Americans had been reduced
so that they collectively
amounted to 50 million acres,
only one-third of its size in
1887. Native American
allotment owners also
continued to lose their land to
pay taxes or just to survive.

of writers and anthropologists formed the American Indian
Defense Association (AIDA). Its aim was to campaign for
laws protecting the rights of Indians to their lands, their
beliefs, culture, traditions and their arts and crafts. The
executive secretary was a social worker, **John Collier.**
AIDA was successful in blocking the **Bursum** and Leavitt
Bills that posed such a threat to the Pueblos.

The Meriam Report (the problem of Indian administration)

The culmination of the new reform movement of the
1920s was the publication, in 1928, of this report, by the
Brookings Institute for Government Research. It presented
a very bleak picture of the impact of forced assimilation on
Native Americans. The report was partially in response to
the further encroachment onto those reservation lands
where there were likely to be oil fields. Its findings were the
result of two years of research carried out by a group of
social scientists under the direction of Lewis Meriam. The
report condemned the **allotment policy** instigated by the
Dawes Act (1887) for depriving Native Americans of their
land and failing to provide them with additional support to
achieve economic security. It also described the dreadful
conditions in which reservation Indians lived, deprived of
their basic needs, of education and of health care by
corrupt officials who diverted government funding for their
own advantage. The report claimed that the Indians were
the most impoverished people in the US. Moreover, the
policy of forced assimilation had robbed them of their self-
esteem and destroyed their families and communities.
Overall, the report was an indictment of the 40 year-old
policy of assimilation through the allotment of land
instigated by the Dawes Act of 1887. In all of this time, it
had never before been criticised. It concluded with the
recommendation that the government's priority should be,
'*the social and economic advancement of the Indians so that
they may be absorbed into the prevailing civilisation at least in
accordance with a minimum standard of health and decency*'.

In considering whether there was a change of policy at this
time, it is important to note that these reformers were not
necessarily condemning assimilation but rather the policy
of allotment followed by the government to achieve it.

President Hoover supported the recommendations of the Meriam Report and appointed a new Indian Commissioner, **Charles Rhoads**, to put together a reform package along the lines of those suggested in the report. This included the closure of unpopular off-reservation boarding schools for Native American children, which were replaced with improved reservation schools. Improved medical facilities were provided by federal funding. Nothing was done, however, to address the matter of the allotted lands. This was a disappointment for reformers such as John Collier, who believed that Rhoads' reforms had stopped short of making the really essential changes to the allotment system that he advocated. In any case, 1929 saw the collapse of the economy which resulted in the Depression. However, in spite of the critical economic situation, Hoover continued his support for the Indians. Federal aid was increased to relieve the suffering and improve the quality of life of the reservation Indians. This was continued during the Roosevelt administration after 1933 (see below).

CASE STUDY: 1933–45 A 'NEW DEAL' FOR NATIVE AMERICANS?

Was Roosevelt's new deal a turning point for Native Americans?

In many respects, the work of John Collier and the new reform movement in the 1920s anticipated what was to follow after the inauguration of **Franklin D. Roosevelt** as President in 1933. In the lengthy saga of misery and suffering, the period from 1933 until 1945 brought some relief for Native Americans. However, it cannot entirely be seen as a turning point since improvement was not sustained as the change of administration in 1945 precipitated not only a change of attitude to the Native American population, but also of policy. It did, however, lay the foundation for further reform in the 1970s. (This will be discussed further in Chapter 13.)

Central to the 'New Deal' for Native Americans was the Indian Reorganization Act (**Wheeler-Howard Act 1934**). This was largely attributable to John Collier who was

KEY PEOPLE

Herbert Hoover (1874–1964) was a Republican and became the 31st President of the United States in 1929. Like many in his party, he believed in laissez-faire (see page 108) and held the view that individuals should succeed as a result of hard work and effort. He did not believe that the government had a duty to help people in need. His support for Native Americans may, therefore, be seen as uncharacteristic.

Charles Rhoads (1872–1956) father, James E. Rhoads, was a founder member of the Indian Rights Association and, through him, Charles became very knowledgeable about Native Americans. He was a member of the reform group founded in Philadelphia in the early 1920s. Committed to improving conditions and opportunities for Native Americans, although he remained a firm believer in assimilation. In his reform package, he refused to return allotted land.

Franklin D. Roosevelt (1882–1945) (See pages 55 and 126 for biographical information). The attempts by Hoover to address the Meriam Report were limited because they failed to confront the necessity for a fundamental review of the federal government's Indian policy. Moreover, there was a need to change the negative attitude of white Americans, especially those in Congress, to the

Indians. Roosevelt's main contribution was in being prepared to undertake this task through his appointment of John Collier as Commissioner for Indian Affairs and subsequently by urging action on Collier's Indian Reorganisation Bill when its progress was slowed down by disagreements about its terms in its committee stage.

The Wheeler-Howard Act 1934 This is name that was given to the Indian Re-organization Act after it became law and reflects the diminished influence of Collier. It is named after Senator Burton K. Wheeler, head of the Senate Committee on Indian Affairs, and Congressman Edgar Howard who chaired one of the sub-committees that examined Collier's Bill. Wheeler was responsible for the majority of the modifications that were made to the Bill so that the detail of the final Act was largely attributable to him.

Gladys Tantaquidgeon (1899–2005) was born into the Mohegan tribe in 1899. She began to study anthropology in 1919 and subsequently worked amongst the northern tribes. In 1935, Collier offered her a position as a social worker on a reservation in South Dakota. She also made a study of Indian arts and crafts and worked to preserve the traditional techniques and ways of working.

appointed by Roosevelt as Commissioner for Indian Affairs. As a supporter of the rights of the Indians, this act was intended to recognise and preserve the traditional culture of the Indian tribes. Although the terms of the original Bill had been significantly modified, it still represented a fairly radical reversal of government policy. Not only were the Indians to have more influence and involvement in the administration of the reservations, but their rights to practise their own religion and to assert their cultural identity, were also protected. For example, this Act finally overthrew a law of 1883 that banned ceremonial dances and celebrations. Most importantly, it curtailed the sale of Indian lands to individual buyers. Between 1900 and 1930, the Indians had lost more than half of their land. Unallocated land lost between 1900 and 1930, was restored to the tribes. This was used to expand the existing reservations and to create new ones.

From his position as Commissioner for Indian Affairs, Collier was able to improve the quality of life for Native Americans in a number of ways and to return to them some of their lost rights of self-determination:

- Native Americans became increasingly involved in the work of the Bureau of Indian Affairs (see page 196) although it still remained under the direction of federal officials.
- The act extended political rights to Native American women and gave them the opportunity to train for domestic work.
- Collier's work stimulated an interest in Indian arts and crafts and encouraged women's co-operatives to produce them as an economic venture.
- Native American women were encouraged to aspire to higher education. **Gladys Tantaquidgeon**, for example, studied anthropology at the University of Pennsylvania. She worked for the Indian Bureau during the 1930s promoting native arts and supporting the women's co-operatives.
- He tapped into the resources available through other New Deal agencies to build hospitals, schools and irrigation systems on the reservations to improve conditions there.

What was the impact of the 'Indian New Deal'?

As the central plank of the 'Indian New Deal', the Indian Reorganization Act that finally became law in 1934 was a compromise. Much to Collier's disappointment, the Act had been substantially modified from his own ambitious plans set out in his Bill that was presented to Congress. Fundamentally, the reason for this, rested with the different aspirations and attitudes of those responsible for drafting the Bill and those politicians who received and discussed it in the Senate committee. It also reflected the increasing influence of Wheeler, an indication of the extent to which Collier's plans to return extensive powers of self-government (e.g. the authority that was given to tribal councils and the extent of the jurisdiction of their own courts) that were incorporated into his Bill, were over-ambitious in the political climate of the time. For, whilst there was some sympathy for the plight of the Indians, generally the overwhelming conviction in political circles was that assimilation and not further separation remained the way forward. The main debate, therefore, rested on the means of achieving assimilation having recognised that the allotment policy had caused misery. Education, economic sufficiency and the support for health and well-being appeared to be a more promising route so that the well-being of Native Americans would not only be improved but that through these reforms they would come to recognise the advantages of assimilation.

Seminole Woman using a Singer sewing machine in the 1930s, an outcome of the encouragement of native crafts in the New Deal.

The outcome was that, although the allotment process was brought to an end, the commitment to assimilation remained, as did the government's paternalistic attitude towards the Indians. The original proposal to provide a separate federal court to deal with Native American issues was abandoned. Although funding was made available in the short term to buy back former reservation land and some consolidation of allotted land took place, Native Americans were given only limited powers to control their own economic affairs. The failure to abandon assimilation and to provide the structures necessary to enable the tribes to become independent and self-sufficient communities, was a huge personal disappointment for Collier.

In many respects, his vision was unrealistic and possibly unachievable at this point in time. Clearly, there were vested interests in respect of those non-Indian owners of allotted land when it came to re-purchase and consolidation plans, although this did not prove to be a major obstacle in itself. Federal funds were never sufficient to buy back huge amounts of former reservation lands. Politicians in the western states were, however, anxious about the potential intrusion of federal law into their territory that the implementation of the terms of Collier's Bill implied. Consequently, they were inclined to resist its terms when the Bill was in its committee stage.

Most disappointing of all for Collier, however, was the response of many of the Native Americans themselves. Because he had neither consulted nor involved them is his plans, he had mistakenly assumed that they all wanted self-determination. Nor had he allowed for the fact that the allotment process had been underway for forty years and that some were either already assimilated or well on the way to becoming so. Others aspired to it. Some did not want self-determination at this point in time. Those who were already successfully farming their homesteads were afraid of losing them if the land was reorganised. Moreover, many lacked understanding of the legal issues within the Act and became confused in their dealings with the federal authorities. Even when Collier met Indian delegations face-to-face, he failed to convince them all or win their support for his aspirations for them.

However, the achievements of the Act were significant. The dramatic loss of land through allotment was curtailed and the funds provided by the federal government, although in many respects inadequate, did support the economic development of Native American communities. Improvements in education and particularly in health provision did have significant benefits. By 1938, census statistics indicated that the Native American population was increasing at a faster rate than that nationally. Moreover, the tribes still living on the reservations were led again by their tribal councils so there was some reaffirmation of tribal loyalties and a resurgence of tribal culture. The involvement of Native Americans in the Indian Bureau did also give them some input into the development of Indian policy. It can be argued that it was a combination of the intrusion of the Second World War and the subsequent introduction of the policy of termination (to be discussed in Chapter 12) that limited the potential long term impact of the 'Indian New Deal'.

THE SECOND WORLD WAR – A TURNING POINT FOR NATIVE AMERICANS?

Like many other ethnic groups, Native Americans were affected in a number of ways by US involvement in the Second World War between 1941 and 1945:

Cheyenne Reservation in Montana.

Japanese Americans relocated to reservation lands Following the Japanese attack on Pearl Harbour in 1941, Japanese Americans felt the full force of anti-Japanese feeling in the US. Many had settled on land along the west coast and had always been the victims of racism. This reached hysterical proportions in 1941. All Japanese Americans were suspected of espionage. As a result Roosevelt ordered that they sell their land and possessions. They were then interned in special camps for the duration of the war with Japan. After the war, they were released and allocated land in compensation. Much of this was Indian reservation land.

- During this period, approximately 100,000 Indians left the reservations or their homesteads. 25,000 of these served with distinction in the armed forces, although there was some resistance from the Iroquois tribe who refused to be drafted into the army. 75,000 moved to the urban areas to work in the defence industry. For these, it was their first experience of living and working outside their Native American world. It was also the first time that such large numbers of Native Americans had left the reservations.

- For those who remained on the reservations, it was a time of great hardship as resources were poured into the war resulting in a reduction of money spent to support the Indians. The situation was exacerbated when **Japanese Americans were 'relocated' to their reservation lands** at the end of the war.

- When the war ended, returning Indian soldiers were effectively forced, as a result of discrimination, to return to the reservations. For example, they were not able to take advantage of the educational opportunities offered to white American war veterans and were adversely affected by competition for jobs.

- Many of the munitions factory workers remained in the cities for a while at least. Ultimately, however, the majority were driven back to the reservations by discrimination and prejudice.

The National Congress of American Indians (NCAI)

By far the most lasting and significant outcome of the wartime experience was the foundation, in 1944, of the **National Congress of American Indians (NCAI)**, significant because it represented a realisation that to bring about real improvement, Native Americans had to unite in protest. It was set up in response to moves to end the reservations and absorb Native Americans into American society where they would cease to be a drain on taxpayers. Over the next decade, the NCAI worked through the courts, like the National Association for the Advancement of Colored People (NAACP) (see Section 1) to challenge discrimination in employment, unequal education provision and the breaking of treaties. At the time, it was the view of the majority of its Native American supporters that this was the way forward. It was the beginning of the Indian protest movement and the first sign that the tribes would join together to pursue justice.

CONCLUSION

The period from 1900 until the Second World War was largely dominated by the federal government's policy of assimilation, although the methods to achieve it had changed to some degree by 1945. In the first two decades, the policy of allotment continued to further reduce the extent of Indian lands. This inflicted misery on thousands of Indians struggling to survive. Whilst there was some resistance on the part of the five tribes, Native Americans generally did little themselves to oppose the erosion of their territories and their rights. The extension of the franchise to all Native Americans in 1924, could be viewed as a positive improvement. However, not all Indians were allowed to register their votes, especially in state elections. In any case the voting Native American population was such a small percentage of the whole that their vote was not of interest to politicians.

However, by the 1920s, the devastating impact of allotment on the ever diminishing Indian reservation lands as well as the effect of attempts at 'Americanisation' did elicit critical appraisal from reforming groups within the Bureau of Indian Affairs that was influential in some government circles. This resulted in the notable reforms of the New Deal era. These certainly had the potential to restore to Native Americans almost everything they had lost, both materially and culturally. However, the more positive features of these reforms relied too heavily on the influence of John Collier whose avowed intention to re-establish tribal culture and lifestyle was not shared, even by those who framed the Indian Reorganization Act. The proposed reforms failed to help Native Americans, substantially because the government was still resolutely pursuing an assimilationist policy by whatever route seemed likely to move this forward. Financial considerations and vested interests limited the positive effects that would have come from the return of allotted lands promised under the Act. Funding to support the New Deal improvement on the reservations was quickly diverted after the outbreak of the Second World War and never really returned until the 1970s. Nevertheless, the terms of the Indian Reorganization Act were not dismantled. Rather, they were perverted by the post-war policy of termination. Consequently, the provisions of the Act and the work of John Collier were undoubtedly influential in the drafting of the Indian Self-Determination and Education Assistance Act (1975) (to be discussed further in Chapter 13).

By 1945, it must be said that not all Native Americans were opposed to assimilation. Generally, these were those Indians who had made a success of their allotments and were not keen to have to return any land. These were driven by self-interest to readily accept assimilation. The experience of the Second World War introduced another dimension that was to prove a turning point for thousands of Native Americans – urbanisation, which in the closing decades of the twentieth century was to be the most powerful force to accelerate assimilation. On the other hand, some of the returning Indian soldiers who had fought in other countries and had experienced discrimination and racism, returned with increasing perceptions of the injustice and inequality suffered by Native Americans. This began to manifest itself in the emergence of Native American pressure groups opposed to government policy and determined to fight for their rights.

QUESTIONS TO CONSIDER

1. Discuss the relative importance of each of the following as agents of change and progress in the context of Native American rights, selecting the evidence you need to use to support your view:

   - Supreme Court decisions.
   - Native American pressure groups.
   - Government policy.
   - John Collier.
   - The two World Wars.

2. Was the Indian Reorganization Act (1934) a failure?

3. Did the speed of change accelerate in the period from 1900 until 1945?

CHAPTER 12

1945–69 'Urban Indians'

Did urbanisation expand or limit opportunities for Native Americans?

Hypothesis:

• Urbanisation further impoverished and degraded the vast majority of Native Americans but did not destroy their tribal loyalties.

NATIVE AMERICANS IN THE POST WAR PERIOD

The migration of Native Americans into the towns and cities around the reservations was underway before the outbreak of the Second World War. Between 1930 and 1960, the number of urban Indians in cities such as New York and Chicago increased four fold. Many of these existed in a state of impermanence between the reservation and the city, having neither left the one nor settled in the other. Undoubtedly, the war accelerated this process to some extent. However, the wartime contribution of Native Americans who had left the reservations either to fight or to work in the defence industry did little to enhance the recognition of their rights or to increase opportunities that were available to them. Those who returned to the reservations after 1945 discovered them to be greatly impoverished. Funding that had accompanied New Deal policies had been diverted into the war effort and life there had become extremely harsh. Those who had acquired new skills as a result of their wartime work or military service, found them to be useless on the reservations. On the other hand, those who remained in the cities, found life equally challenging. Returning soldiers from the War increased the competition for jobs. Consequently, Native Americans were no longer welcome in the factory workforce.

In 1948, the Bureau of Indian Affairs tried to alleviate the inevitable suffering of significant numbers of Native Americans by setting up job placement centres in major cities in the west, such as Denver, Salt Lake City and Los Angeles, for off-reservation Indians. Changes in government policy towards Native Americans from the 1950s onwards, increased the pressure on them to become urbanised.

HOW SIGNIFICANT WERE THE CHANGES IN GOVERNMENT POLICIES BETWEEN 1953 AND 1969?

The Indian Claims Commission (ICC) 1946–78

In the immediate aftermath of the War, partly in response to pressure from the NCAI and partly in recognition of the contribution made by Native Americans to the war effort, Congress set up the Indian Claims Commission. Ostensibly, this appeared to be the means whereby they would regain the lands given to them by treaties in the nineteenth century. Within a short space of time, 370 petitions had been filed. In reality, the Commission did Native Americans few favours. It worked slowly and with little regard to evidence provided by the Indian tribes themselves. Contrary to the hopes of Native Americans, when settlements were made these were largely in the form of financial compensation rather that the return of the land that the tribes hoped for. In some instances, such as the **Sioux Indians claim to the Black Hills of Dakota,** financial compensation was refused and the tribes continued to fight for their land. Although the ICC was initially set up for five years, there were so many claims that it continued its work until 1978.

In reality, the ICC was not as altruistic as might have at first appeared but was rather part of a further drive by the federal government to complete the assimilation of the Native American population and end its responsibility for reservation Indians. These still remained technically 'wards' of the US Government. As such they were seen as a drain on financial resources. Many of the politicians who worked with John Collier to improve the condition of the Indians saw this as just another route to assimilation. In this respect, there was continuity in government policy.

KEY EVENTS

The Sioux Indians claim to the Black Hills of Dakota This land was given to the Sioux nation by the 1868 Fort Laramie Treaty. The hills were sacred to the Sioux and therefore had a value beyond price. Claims for the return of this land were filed as early as 1923. The US Court of Claims rejected the Sioux claim in 1942. The ICC eventually offered financial compensation which the Sioux refused. The struggle for the restoration of the Black Hills continued beyond the end of the century and, along with other land claims, still goes on today.

The policy of termination

The introduction of more aggressive measures to hasten total assimilation began in 1953. It might be purely coincidental that this was also the time when there was increasing interest shown by timber and mining companies in Indian lands. The process that began at this time was known as 'termination'. Under its terms, Indians were no longer 'wards' of the government. Plans were set in motion to end federal control of the **Bureau of Indian Affairs** and to make Native Americans subject to the same laws and give them the same rights as all other American citizens. In other words, termination ended the recognition of the existence of Native American tribes and the treaty rights that they still retained, and recognised Native Americans as independent, self-supporting Americans.

Proposals were put forward to end the reservation system and its support by federal services. The delights of comfortable housing complete with labour saving devices outside of the reservations were widely advertised on the reservations. A Voluntary Relocation Program was established, ostensibly to provide support for the Indians, but actually to lure them away from the reservations. This gave Indians financial support for relocation, help in securing jobs and living expenses until they found work and houses. It must have seemed an attractive package, especially to young Native Americans, easily tempted by the attractions of city life that compared favourably with the harsh reality of that on the reservations in the post war period. In 1956, this was followed up by the **Indian Vocational Training Act** intended to improve the employment prospects of Indians by providing work-related training.

The end of termination

By 1968, however, the negative effects of the policy of termination were becoming apparent. By this stage, Native Americans had the highest rates of illiteracy, of disease and unemployment in the US and lived in the poorest accommodation. In a message to Congress in March 1968 entitled 'The Forgotten Americans', **President Lyndon Johnson** set out a programme to promote Indian self-help and respect. He proposed a National Council on Indian

KEY TERMS

Bureau of Indian Affairs
The name given to the Office of Indian Affairs after 1947. In 1949, it was transferred from the Department of War to the Department of the Interior. This federal government organisation controlled the money allocated for the development of Native Americans and was responsible for their education as well as for the reservations. It was seen as too bureaucratic and slow to take action because it was bound up with complex legal rules and regulations. It also had the power to take away land from the reservations giving little compensation in return.

Indian Vocational Training Act 1956
established vocational training for American Indians, including adults, so that they could obtain a 'marketable skill'. This training was provided with federal funding for all those who applied, provided that they lived near to reservations and were under the jurisdiction of the Bureau of Indian Affairs.

Lyndon B. Johnson (1908–73) was born in central Texas. His own experience of rural poverty in his early life made him sympathetic to the plight of the poor when he later entered politics. He became John F. Kennedy's running mate in the 1960 presidential election and was sworn in as Vice President in 1961. After he was sworn in as President following the assassination of Kennedy in 1963 and following his election as president in his own right in 1964, he was determined to press on with the extension of civil rights and his programme of social reform known as the 'Great Society' to improve conditions for the poor and especially for the elderly. He was sympathetic to the plight of Native Americans.

Opportunity to administer an ambitious programme of education for children of all ages from pre-school to high school and beyond, funded by the federal government. Such a programme would also provide better quality homes with proper sanitation and include legal aid to provide Native Americans with knowledge and understanding of their rights. When Richard Nixon followed Johnson into the Whitehouse, he ordered an end to the policy of termination. (Nixon's policy will be discussed further in Chapter 13).

THE IMPACT OF URBANISATION ON NATIVE AMERICANS

Ostensibly, the economic opportunities that urban life could offer might appear to be progress. The reality was less convincing. By 1960, around 60,000 Native Americans had left the reservations and gravitated mainly to the cities nearest to their reservations – Chicago, San Francisco, Oakland and Oklahoma City. After 1960, there was an increasing tendency to relocate well away from reservation lands. For many of these, relocation was forced and was, consequently, traumatic. In the urban environment, they encountered a similar reaction to that experienced by African Americans when they migrated into the cities. This was a relatively new experience for the American Indians. White hostility had not previously manifested itself so overtly, presumably because reservation life afforded limited contact with the mass of white Americans.

A small percentage of educated Native Americans found a place amongst the urban middle class. Many Native American women married white Americans, consequently cultural assimilation for them was less challenging. Moreover, job opportunities for educated American Indian women were arguably better in the second half of the twentieth century than those for men, as women found openings in the service economy and in clerical occupations. After 1968, Indian workers benefited to some extent from the policy of Affirmative Action introduced in 1968 by Johnson and the Democrats but continued by Nixon in the 1970s. This prohibited discrimination on the

1945–69 'Urban Indians.' Did urbanisation expand or limit opportunities for Native Americans?

197

basis of ethnicity in recruitment to jobs in federally funded projects or enterprises. Although the policy was strongly focused on increasing employment opportunities for African Americans, it did also offer new opportunities to at least some American Indians.

Like their African American counterparts, the reality of urban dwelling for the majority was poverty, alcoholism and **unemployment**. By 1960, around 25 per cent were classified as 'poor' and a significant number were forced to live in sub-standard, shanty town houses that did not support the extended family units common to their traditional way of life. Elderly family members were, therefore, forced to return to what remained of the reservations. Levels of unemployment varied from place to place but could be as high as 18 per cent. Life expectancy for urban Indians (44 years) was twenty years below the national average (64 years). In the meantime, further lands were lost. The tribes in Wisconsin and Oregon, for example, lost around 500,000 acres of what just happened to be valuable timber land.

It can be argued that the enforced relocation of a significant proportion of Native Americans into urban areas did not greatly advance the process of assimilation. If anything, it had the opposite effect. Native Americans were, by culture and tradition, rural dwellers. For the many who suddenly found themselves plunged into this hostile environment, the noise and speed of city life was bewildering and alien to them. The culture shock was enormous. Language was itself a barrier, not only for adults but also for Native American children attending urban schools. City life was for them all, spiritually bereft. It was a place only to work but not to live a full and meaningful life. It is estimated that between 40 and 70 per cent of re-settled Native Americans, alienated from urban life, ultimately returned to the reservations, even though the quality of life in the cities was better. Improvements that resulted from New Deal projects were not maintained because the level of funding was reduced. Reservation housing was overcrowded, dilapidated, unsanitary and lacked clean, running water. Tuberculosis, trachoma (eye disease) and alcohol abuse were rife.

National Indian Youth Council (NIYC) was founded in 1961 in New Mexico to pursue civil rights for American Indians. In particular, it attempted to preserve Indian's fishing rights in the north west (e.g. Oregon). In 1968, they staged a 'fish in' after the Washington State Supreme Court ruled against protecting the fishing rights of the tribes in that area. In the 1970s, it filed law suits to protect Indian land from the exploitation of its mineral resources. The NIYC used litigation to protect treaty rights, ensure voting rights for Indians and to gain recognition of their right to religious freedom.

John F. Kennedy (1917–63) In spite of the pledges he made to Native Americans, there was very little evident change in policy during his presidency. In 1961, he set up a task force to investigate and report on future Indian policy and programmes. Some of the proposals were implemented later but little progress was made on ending the policy of termination as powerful forces in Congress still supported it. Kennedy did provide more funding for Native American education but new school building and improvements to provision tended to be on the fringes of reservations rather than on the reservations themselves.

Lonely and without roots in the urban situation, Native-American families tended to cluster in specific areas of towns and cities, quickly forming ghettos. Here they could speak their own languages whilst preserving and sustaining their culture and traditions. Consequently, far from destroying tribal culture, enforced relocation encouraged Indians to value what they were in danger of losing, rather than what they had found in the city. Like the African Americans, they also established self-help groups and social centres. Moreover, many returned to the reservations in the summer months to take part in the long-standing tradition of tribal gatherings.

Perhaps as a result of the urban experiment, Indians became more aware of the gap between their own economic situation and that of the more affluent white Americans. Young Indians, in particular, grew more militant as the '60s progressed. In 1961, the **National Indian Youth Council** was established to protest against the injustices experienced by Native Americans.

WHAT PROGRESS DID NATIVE AMERICANS MAKE IN PURSUING THEIR RIGHTS?

The influence of the civil rights movement on Native American protest 1960–69

The growing assertiveness of young Native Americans was the result of a combination of personal frustration but, more importantly, the inspiration of the African-American protest movement for civil rights. The significant change by the 1960s was the willingness to unite in protest. So, in 1964, hundreds of Indians gathered in Washington DC for recognition in President Johnson's 'War on Poverty'.

During the 1960s, the NCAI had some successes in its quest to achieve improvement for the Indians through the courts. It had also obtained a pledge from **President Kennedy** to develop the human and natural resources of the reservations but these had not been fulfilled by the time of his assassination. Young Indians, however, became frustrated at the slow progress made by the NCAI coupled with an increasing suspicion that this organisation was out

1945–69 'Urban Indians.' Did urbanisation expand or limit opportunities for Native Americans?

199

of touch with the mass of Native Americans, based on the fact that its membership were mostly successful and assimilated Indians. Moreover, the NCAI's insistence on working through the courts also slowed down progress. There still remained a significant proportion of the Native American population who did not want assimilation. They wanted back their lands and the right to live on them with dignity and according to their tribal laws. They wanted the right to separate development and self-determination. Instead, they were descending further and further into poverty.

Militancy and 'Red Power'

In response to the emerging, militant 'black power' (see Chapter 4) the term 'red power' came into the vocabulary. Young militants demanded, amongst other things, that the Indians be known as 'Native Americans' as they engaged in a number of high profile activities to attract media coverage:

- By 1968, protest was growing stronger, particularly among younger Native Americans. The song 'As Long as the Grass shall Grow', recorded in 1968 by Peter La Farge, was one of a number protesting at the abuse of Native Americans by white people. In 1969, **Vine Deloria Jnr.** published the book *Custer Died For Your Sins*. It was followed a year later by *Bury My Heart at Wounded Knee: An Indian History of the American West*. This book, by **Dee Brown**, raised the awareness of millions about the history of the Native Americans and their plight. Native American protest at this time gained great momentum and inspiration from other protest movements, particularly the continuing black protest movement (see Chapter 4).
- In 1968, Indians in Washington State asserted their old treaty rights to fish in the Columbia River and Puget Sound. A 'fish-in' was staged after the State Supreme Court failed to uphold their treaty rights to fish.
- In 1968, the American Indian Movement (AIM) was established. This was to prove the most militant organisation promoting improvement for the Indians. AIM took up the issue of racial discrimination against Native American youths. In response, young Native

Richard Oakes (1942–72)
was a member of the Mohawk tribe and an Indian rights activist. He believed and campaigned for the right of Native American peoples to control their own destinies, to retain their land, their culture and traditional way of life. During the siege, the occupants were well organised by Oakes to ensure a quality of life on the island. However, he left the island in January, 1972 following the death of his 13 year-old step-daughter after a fall in the prison. In September 1972, he was shot and killed following an incident in northern California, where he was alleged to have ambushed a white American male. His killer, although initially charged with murder, was subsequently released without trial. This decision by the court angered the Native American community.

Adam Fortunate Eagle Nordwell (b. 1929) was born on the Chippewa Reservation in Red Lake, Minnesota. He is a member, by heritage, of the Ojibwa tribe and a Native-American activist. He was educated in a reservation boarding school and attended the Haskell Indian Institute in Kansas. Although he was not a member of the occupying 'force', Nordwell masterminded the siege of Alcatraz and conducted all the negotiations with the authorities behind the scenes. He was the author of The Alcatraz Proclamation, in which he set out plans for the island to become a centre for Native American studies and culture.

Americans patrolled the streets wearing red berets and jackets, monitoring police activities. As a result, there was a decline in the arrest and imprisonment and in the numbers of young Indian offenders.

- During the 1960s, young Indians vigorously pursued the return of 'native sovereignty'. This term was used by Native Americans to describe the power that had rested with the tribes from time immemorial to inhabit their lands and to live according to their tribal laws, religion and customs. Thus, sovereignty was a natural right that existed until the arrival of 'foreigners', who questioned, threatened and removed it through their acquisition of Indian lands. Besides the return of their tribal lands, Indian activists campaigned for the reinstatement of their fishing rights lost either to hydro-electricity schemes, the creation of dams, or commercial, sporting fishing ventures or as a result of the loss of the land they owned. These rights formed part of their native sovereignty and were pursued, usually, through cases brought before the Supreme Court.

CASE STUDY: THE SIEGE OF ALCATRAZ 1969

Background and aims

In 1969, the quest for sovereignty reached new and defiant heights when fourteen Indian men and women, from all tribes, occupied the deserted, former prison island of Alcatraz. They were led by a young and charismatic member of the Mohawk tribe, **Richard Oakes**, although negotiations behind the scenes were carried out by **Adam Fortunate Eagle Nordwell.** Until the nineteenth century, when it was wanted for the construction of the penitentiary, the island had belonged to the Ohlone Indians. Now deserted, the Native Americans who invaded the island wanted its return.

In negotiation with the government, the 'invaders' offered the government $24 in beads and cloth (the price that had been paid to the Indians for the island of Manhattan). When this was refused, the occupation continued with 80 Indians now established on the island. The siege was carefully planned and orchestrated to raise awareness of the plight of

1945–69 'Urban Indians.' Did urbanisation expand or limit opportunities for Native Americans?

201

Native Americans in the most dramatic way possible, in full view of the world's media. The selection of the site was highly emotive. Besides being formerly Indian land, Alcatraz was synonymous with a most harsh and brutal prison regime. Now disused, it was chosen by the demonstrators as symbolic of the life imprisonment in poverty on reservations and in urban areas of the Native American people as a result of federal policies and of neglect.

It received huge media coverage until it was ended on 11 June, 1971. It excited the media because, as police and militia attempted to end the occupation, it was reminiscent of the cinema struggles with the Indians, except in this particular drama they were the heroes.

The significance of the siege

Whilst the siege did not achieve its aims, there were, nevertheless, a number of significant outcomes:

- As a result of the media coverage, it drew the attention of the nation and the rest of the world to the plight of the American Indians. It laid down a challenge to politicians and people alike to take action to remedy past injustice.
- The Alcatraz incident stirred up other young Native Americans and accelerated militant action to assert their claims to Indian land, largely under the leadership of AIM. During the occupation around 10,000 Native

Americans visited the island. As a result, many others made a stand by occupying other federal lands and disobeying federal fishing regulations. In Maine, members of the Passamaquoddy tribe actually collected tolls on busy highways crossing their land.

- As the plight of Native Americans took centre stage, it promoted a reappraisal of government policy and the initiation of fundamental change that resulted in their leaders gaining more involvement in and control over many aspects of the lives of these native peoples, including health, education and economic development (see Chapter 13 for further development).

CONCLUSION

It can be argued that urbanisation and the policy of termination had a disastrous effect on the majority of Native Americans. It was a policy from which neither side gained anything worthwhile. Native Americans were condemned to poverty and misery. The policy of assimilation failed because the traumatic experience for those forcibly removed from the reservations to the city, only served to reinforce their determination to cling to their culture and way of life and to resist assimilation. Nothing was achieved in terms of the successful assertion of their rights. Their status as native people belonging to a tribe or nation was terminated.

An important outcome, however, was the sense of unity that emerged from the experience of adversity. Tribal separation was to some degree replaced by a growing awareness, largely amongst the young, of the need for solidarity to fight for what was rightfully theirs and especially to oppose the discrimination and degradation that dispossession forced upon them. Clearly, some of the messages were reaching government circles that the levels of poverty endured by Indians were unacceptable. However, at this stage, this was perceived in the context of the war on poverty which formed the core of policy in the 1960s and not in terms of injustice and the denial of fundamental rights to Native Americans.

1945–69 'Urban Indians.' Did urbanisation expand or limit opportunities for Native Americans?

203

The increasing militancy of the united front presented by Native Americans would ensure that their struggle for justice, freedom and independence would be asserted in the closing decades of the century.

QUESTIONS TO CONSIDER

1. Did urbanisation make any significant difference to the quest for Native American rights?

2. Did the policy of termination ever have any chance of success?

3. Were the advances made by Native Americans in the 1960s largely the result of changing attitudes towards the Indians and of government policy changes or were they driven by the action of Indian pressure groups?

CHAPTER 13

1970–92 A people apart?

How much had militancy and solidarity achieved for Native Americans by 1992?

Hypothesis:

- In spite of organised protest and opposition, Native Americans remained dependent on the fluctuating priorities of government policy and on the courts for the extension of their rights.

THE NIXON PRESIDENCY – A TURNING POINT FOR NATIVE AMERICANS?

On 8 July 1970, Richard Nixon (see pages 85–87) delivered his presidential message to Congress, in which he strongly criticised the treatment of Native Americans since the mid-nineteenth century,

> 'American Indians have been oppressed and brutalised, deprived of their ancestral lands and denied the opportunity to control their own destiny.'

He went on to describe their degradation and humiliation, both as a result of the poverty of their lives and the denial of the right of Native Americans to influence and control the federal programmes intended to support them, the Bureau of Indian Affairs still being dominated by white American officials. Indian leadership, he claimed, was essential to ensuring the success of the assistance that the federal government provided for these native peoples. It followed the thoughts expressed by President Johnson in his 1968 address, *'The Forgotten American'*, so although it promoted radical solutions, it represented some degree of continuity in the re-thinking of Native American policies that had been going on during the 1960s.

Nixon particularly condemned the policy of termination and called on Congress to recognise that this policy had failed to improve opportunities for Indians and had, instead, condemned them to poverty and distress. As a result, the policy of termination was ended and a reform programme was introduced to begin the process of righting the wrongs:

- In 1969, Nixon paved the way for his reforms with the appointment of a Mohawk-Sioux, **Louis R. Bruce Jnr.,** as Commissioner for Indian Affairs.
- In 1970 the pledge to return Indian lands began with a number of laws authorising the return of tribal lands to the Makah and Taos Pueblo Indians. In 1972, land was returned to the Yakama Indians of Washington State.
- A number of Indian nations that had lost this status as a result of termination, regained their recognition and rights. This gave them access to the federal courts and, therefore, the means of seeking redress for their loss of treaty rights.
- In 1972, Native Americans were given preference in employment opportunities in the Bureau of Indian Affairs to ensure greater Indian leadership and participation in the deployment and administration of federal funding.
- Nixon placed great emphasis on the improvement of educational provision for Indian children and young people. The 1972 Indian Education Act involved a substantial increase in federal funding for Indian schools, including programmes to build reservation schools. The closure of the highly controversial boarding schools was part of this reform programme that was continued by Nixon's presidential successors, Gerald Ford (Republican President 1974–77) and Jimmy Carter (Democratic President 1977–81) and so was probably his lasting legacy to the American Indians.

Nixon's actions made him very popular in the eyes of Native Americans since he had probably done more for them, in a short space of time, than any other President. It is impossible to determine how much further Nixon would have gone, particularly in respect of the return of tribal lands, or for how long the Native American issue would

Richard Nixon.

have remained a high priority. Certainly, the return of tribal lands was likely to remain a highly contentious issue since it involved such massive tracts of land and so many powerful commercial vested interests. By the time of his resignation in 1974, Nixon had barely scratched the surface and a number of **long standing claims between the tribes themselves** as well as between tribes and the federal government remained unsettled. Nevertheless, all the measures he had taken were upheld by the Supreme Court in 1974.

AFTER NIXON – CONTINUITY OR PROGRESS?

The Indian Self-Determination and Education Assistance Act (1975), although passed by Congress during the presidency of Nixon's successor, Gerald Ford, was a crucial piece of legislation that was clearly influenced by Nixon's priorities and marked a radical change of direction in federal policy. In its recognition of the right of Native Americans to self-determination, the federal government abandoned its long-held belief in the necessity for assimilation. Consequently, although often heralded as the most significant action since the New Deal (see pages 186–90), it can be argued that it was of greater importance than Roosevelt's policy. It was, in effect, two pieces of legislation in one,

- **The Indian Self Determination Act** laid down the processes whereby the tribes could negotiate contracts with the Bureau of Indian Affairs to take responsibility for their own education, health and social service provision. It also authorised the allocation of federal funding for these programmes which moved the tribes nearer to self-sufficiency.
- **The Indian Education Assistance Act** gave American-Indian parents greater involvement in their children's education through membership of their school boards.

Whilst this legislation went a long way to improving opportunities through education for Native Americans and in promoting Indian self-determination, improvement programmes depended on the extent of federal funding.

1970–92 A people apart? How much had militancy and solidarity achieved for Native Americans by 1992?

207

Initially, this was slow to arrive, which tried the patience of the militants who continued their violent protests (see pages 209–113) which caused further delay. In the last two decades of the twentieth century, as the economic situation in the USA worsened, funding was cut back. This was especially the case during the Reagan presidency (see page 144). Reagan believed in '**native capitalism**' as the means to establish self-sufficiency.

However, progress towards self-determination was further advanced by the recognition of the right of Native Americans to live according to their tribal culture:

*   In 1975, the American Indian Policy Review Commission was set up to review the historical and legal relationship between the federal government and the American Indians, with a view to advising on future government policy. Of the eleven commissioners, five were of Indian heritage.
*   The Native American Religious Freedom Act (1978) marked an important step forward in this direction by giving to Native Americans the right *'to believe, express and exercise traditional religions including access to sites, use and possession of sacred objects and freedom to worship through ceremonials and traditional rights'*. This stimulated action to recover sacred objects as well as human remains located in museums in the west or in that allotted land that included the sacred burial grounds of the tribes (see page 211). Opposition to this came from museums, archaeologists and anthropologists but in 1990 the Native American Graves Protection Act required all federally-funded institutions to repatriate American Indian remains, grave goods and sacred objects.
*   The Indian Child Welfare Act (1978) was an attempt to determine the rights of Native American parents in relation to the continuing practice of forcibly removing Indian children from their families. This was frequently the result of the lack of understanding on the part of social workers of the cultural traditions surrounding child rearing in American Indian communities, which were interpreted erroneously as neglect.

KEY TERMS

Native capitalism was intended to reduce the burden on federal or state expenditure by the development of profit-making enterprises by Native Americans themselves. In the closing decades of the century, the Reservation Indians did attempt to stimulate their economies by creating small businesses such as restaurants, gasoline (petrol) stations, shops, bingo halls, as well as making money from farming, hunting, lumbering, fishing and from the film industry. Some built factories in the reservations and provided employment for other Indians. Others used their exemption from the federal state gaming laws to establish casinos, much to the concern of those Native Americans who believed that this was damaging to their traditional way of life.

The impact of 'Red Power' on federal reform

Government reforms in the 1970s must be set in the context of the increasingly violent and provocative protests orchestrated by AIM. As suggested above, much of the action after the Alcatraz incident, was partly the result of frustration at the slow progress of implementing federal reforms.

- **1971 – Occupation of Mount Rushmore** in the Black Hills of Dakota, was an attempt to reassert the disputed ownership of these sacred burial grounds of the Lakota Sioux Indians (see page 195). AIM protesters established a camp in this area, designated as a national memorial, just below the famous sculptures of Washington, Jefferson, Lincoln and Roosevelt, renaming it Mount Crazy Horse. Although these protesters were eventually evicted, native groups subsequently laid claim to the Black Hills by setting up camps there. Ownership of this territory is still disputed.
- **1972 – AIM took over the Bureau of Indian Affairs in Washington DC.** This followed the arrival in the city of the 'Trail of Broken Treaties Caravan'. The 'caravan' in this case was a fleet of cars, buses and vans carrying around 1,000 protesters representing several of the original tribes. It was, to some extent, an outcome of the Alcatraz siege, and left San Francisco in October 1972 to travel across the continent to Washington DC. With a presidential election imminent, its purpose was to raise awareness of the plight of Native Americans as a result of their unjust treatment since the middle of the nineteenth century. Its leaders had drawn up a paper identifying twenty points that needed to be addressed. Although it was intended as a peaceful protest, the marchers found themselves without accommodation in the city and so occupied the offices of the BIA. Violence broke out when attempts were made to evict the protesters.
- **1973 – The occupation of Wounded Knee.** This hamlet is situated near to the Pine Ridge Reservation in South Dakota. It was the site of the 1890 massacre of the Sioux (see page 172) and was, therefore, a highly evocative place for all Indians. The protest arose following allegations of the suspected financial dealings of the president of the Reservation and his maltreatment of its

1970–92 A people apart? How much had militancy and solidarity achieved for Native Americans by 1992?

209

Indian inhabitants. The violent occupation of the hamlet
of Wounded Knee lasted for 71 days and involved
resistance to federal marshals, FBI agents and military
personnel. Like the Alcatraz incident, all of this was
acted out with full media coverage from across the US
and the World. It ended with a negotiated settlement.
Two of the leaders of the protest were subsequently
arrested and charged with offences committed at
Wounded Knee but were acquitted.
- Further violence erupted around the Pine Ridge
  Reservation again in 1975. During a shooting incident
  there, two FBI agents and one of the protesters were shot
  and killed. A member of AIM was tried and found guilty
  of their murder. A US Court of Appeals Judge later
  blamed the federal authorities for the fatalities, on the
  basis that their over-reaction to the situation had caused
  the protesters to panic.

The highly publicised protests organised by AIM, raised
awareness of past injustices, of broken promises and
treaties, and were undoubtedly influential in bringing
about policy changes. In spite of the fact that Native
Americans had the right to vote, as they comprised only
one per cent of the population, they effectively had little, if
any, capacity to influence policy through the political
process. However, it must also be recognised that these
activities impacted negatively. As has already been
suggested, they contributed to the slow response to the

implementation of reforming legislation in the early 1970s as the federal authorities interpreted the actions of AIM as subversive and dangerous. The level of force used to deal with the occupations is, in itself, indicative of a lack of sympathy on the part of the authorities. Moreover, the activities of the leaders of AIM were closely monitored during the early 1970s by the FBI.

Many Native Americans themselves did not believe that AIM represented their best interests and that the violent methods employed by the protesters was not in keeping with Native American beliefs and their way of life. Divisions later emerged within the movement itself about the best way to bring about change, which limited its impact. By the late 1970s, there were fewer federal actions directly related to extending Indian rights. Pressure, therefore, to regain rights was exerted through the Supreme Court.

The Native American Rights Fund (NARF) and the Supreme Court

NARF was founded in 1970 to defend the rights of Native Americans and to preserve tribal culture and way of life, in particular their right to hunt and fish. In the early 1970s, it was especially concerned to ensure that tribes that had been terminated were re-instated, that their tribal sovereignty was restored and, above all, that they could recover their lost tribal lands including their hunting, fishing and water rights. It fought for their right to vote in those states where registration was restricted and was concerned with the protection of the human rights of Native Americans such as their right to worship freely and the **proper burial of ancestral remains**. NARF was also responsible for training young Native Americans as attorneys with a specialism in pursuing Native-American legal issues. NARF was the main organisation that pressed cases in the Supreme Court on behalf of the tribes and secured some landmark decisions,

- 1974 *Oneida* v. *Oneida and Madison Counties, New York*. This was a case brought before the Supreme Court to establish the right of the Oneida tribe to sue for the return of their lands through the Supreme Court. When

1970–92 A people apart? How much had militancy and solidarity achieved for Native Americans by 1992?

211

the court decided in their favour it opened the flood gate for land claims from other tribes, especially in the east.

- **1976 *Fisher* v. *Montana*** secured the right of tribal courts to decide on all cases relating to the adoption of Indian children. Given the earlier policy of the forced removal of children from their families in the context of 'Americanisation', this was an emotive issue in itself, besides being another step to establishing recognition of tribal courts. This was the beginning of a number of actions to secure the stability of Indian families and giving them the right to decide on all matters relating to adoption and foster care.

- **1980 *United States* v. *the Sioux Nation.*** The US Supreme Court ruled that the Sioux Indians were entitled to compensation totalling $17.5 million and an additional 5 per cent interest per year since 1877 ($106 million) for the loss of the Black Hills in contravention of the Fort Laramie Treaty. The Sioux refused to accept this money preferring instead the return of their land.

- **1982 *Seminole Tribe* v. *Butterworth.*** The Supreme Court ruled that the tribe had the right to establish gambling enterprises on their reservation lands even if gambling enterprises were banned by state laws.

- **1986** in the successful case of ***Charrier* v. *Bell*** , NARF lawyers secured the agreement of the court that remains dug from the ground in Louisiana belonged to the Native-American community. Throughout the 1980s, NARF continued to campaign on this issue. As a result, over 30 states passed laws protecting Indian burial grounds and remains, requiring them to be treated with respect. The 1990 Native American Graves Protection and Repatriation Act was the culmination of NARF's campaign.

By re-asserting their rights under treaties that were long forgotten, a number of the tribes did **regain** at least **some of their lost land** as well as receiving financial compensation. Moreover, the recognition of the right of the tribes to self-determination and the respect shown for their religious traditions contributed to greater pride in their heritage. This was, to some extent, reflected in the US census which in 1970 indicated that there were 800,000 Native Americans in the US. By 1990, this figure had

KEY EVENTS

Regain lost land Some examples of land and compensation gains made by Native Americans in the '70s and '80s:

1971 native peoples of Alaska – 40 million acres of land; $1 billion in compensation

1980 Sioux Indians received $107 million for land taken from them in South Dakota

1988 a small tribe in Washington State given $162 million to resolve a long standing land dispute.

increased to 1.7 million. Whilst the Indian population was certainly expanding, it is suggested by census analysts that this significant increase reflected increased confidence and pride.

CONCLUSION – WHAT HAD BEEN ACHIEVED BY 1992?

Between 1865 and the mid 1960s, Native American peoples lost everything – their status, their lands, their right to self-determination and their dignity. Throughout most of this period they were subject to government policies that varied significantly in approach but were nevertheless sharply focused on the same objective – detribalisation and the assimilation of the American Indians into American society. Like other foreign people entering the US in the nineteenth and early twentieth centuries, they went into the 'melting pot'. By 1992, it would appear that the Indian tribes had regained much of what had been lost. The federal government had finally abandoned its policy of assimilation and promoted self-determination for Native Americans, with federal funding to support it. Their traditional rights had been restored. It seemed that Native Americans had survived the 'melting pot' and had successfully resisted assimilation.

A significant factor in bringing this about in the closing decades of the century had been the resolve of Native Americans themselves to abandon the tribal rivalries that had divided them and unite in the quest for the recognition of their rights. Indians demonstrated more assertiveness and appeared less as the victimised. The emergence of 'Red Power' had made a major contribution to the redirection of government policy, together with the recognition by successive Republican and Democratic Presidents that the past treatment of Native Americans had been cruel and unjust.

By 1992, the tribes were making some progress, at least, through cases brought before the Supreme Court, towards the reclamation of their land lost as a result of broken treaties or were receiving substantial sums in compensation for their loss. These successes, however, were limited. The ownership of vast tracts of land remains disputed.

The right of self-determination and the legal recognition of tribal government, its courts and religious practices engendered new found pride and confidence amongst Native Americans in their traditional culture. This pride was further enhanced as they also developed the capacity for economic independence. On the other hand, the extent to which assimilation had been effectively resisted is doubtful. The experience of de-tribalisation, the allotment policy, Americanisation and, finally, termination and forced relocation into urban areas was traumatic. Urbanisation in particular ensured that the vast majority of Native Americans would not return to the traditional tribal lifestyle. By 1990, approximately two-thirds of all Native Americans were still dispersed in urban areas throughout the USA. Many who were born there knew only what had been passed down to them of their tribal heritage and culture. The percentage of Indians speaking their tribal language had declined. As a result of past government policies, the majority no longer had their tribal titles, although, increasingly, these were being incorporated into their American names. The positive sign of renewal was their willingness to identify their ethnic origins in census returns. The only contact that some urban Indians had with their heritage, by the end of the century, was the annual summer 'powwow' (tribal gathering) they attended on the reservations.

Improvements in education, and particularly of higher education, provided a relatively small percentage of Native Americans with the opportunity of a middle-class lifestyle. The increase in litigation to establish rights or claim land, for example, stimulated the need for attorneys of Native American heritage. Educated American Indians found their way into the professions, many becoming academics in universities offering Native American studies. Increased enrolment in higher education establishments is indicative of young Indians with much higher aspirations for themselves. However, in spite of increased government spending on education, improved educational standards were not reflected in employment patterns and standards of living for the mass of urban Indians. Indian median income was almost half that of the nation as a whole. Unemployment remained higher amongst American Indians than any other ethnic group and they easily formed the highest proportion of the poorest people nationally. In spite of affirmative action policies and equal opportunities legislation, they faced discrimination in the competition for jobs. Federally funded programmes delivering health care and other services improved their well-being but, as the economic situation in the US deteriorated in the last two decades of the twentieth century, grants to ethnic groups were not maintained at their original levels.

Only the one third of the Native Americans who inhabited the remaining 278 reservations and tribal villages benefited from the opportunities to re-establish the tribal way of life. Although commercial concerns and Indian enterprises increased the number of jobs available for Indians on the reservations, unemployment was also very high there. However, by 1992, it is possible to talk about a discernible American Indian movement, albeit represented by a variety of groups and organisations, which remains vibrant and assertive of the rights of a proud people.

QUESTIONS TO CONSIDER

1. Was there a marked acceleration between 1970 and 1992 in the progress made by Native Americans to achieve the right of self-determination? How do you account for this?

2. Was the impact of the achievements of NARF more significant than the influence of 'Red Power' protest?

EXAM STYLE QUESTIONS

1. To what extent were the 1970s and 1980s the most significant period in the quest for Native American rights between 1865 and 1992?

2. To what extent was the emergence of 'Red Power' the most important turning point in the struggle by Native Americans to gain their rights of self-determination between 1865 and 1992?

3. Assess the view that the Supreme Court was more effective than Congress in supporting the rights of Native Americans from 1865 until 1992.

4. Assess the view that Native Americans did little to campaign for the improvement of their civil rights in the period from 1865 to 1992.

5. Assess the view that the Indian Citizenship Act of 1924 was the most significant turning point in the quest of Native Americans for recognition of their right to self-determination between 1865 and 1992.

Section 4: Women in the USA 1865–1992

INTRODUCTION – 'SEPARATE SPHERES' AND THE 'CULT OF TRUE WOMANHOOD'

Any study of the role of women and the quest for their rights throughout the whole of this period until 1992, cannot be fully understood without the recognition of the centrality of home and family irrespective of class or ethnicity. It remained a critical factor in determining the extent and success of any campaign to secure rights for women. In the home, women were believed to occupy a crucial and irreplaceable position, ensuring the well-being of husband and children. This was not a menial or submissive position. In their own sphere, women were respected and revered. The home was a very real power base for married women. Consequently, in spite of the fact that a high proportion of young women had the advantage of educational opportunities from the later decades of the nineteenth century onwards, this was a role that absorbed and satisfied the vast majority of married American women and was the ultimate goal to which the unmarried aspired. Those who became involved in pressure groups to bring about reform were frequently motivated by the need to protect home and family rather than pursue civil rights. Inevitably, there were exceptions. Through much of this period, some women came to resent the fact that when they married, they were expected to give up their jobs. Within marriage, laws ensured that there were limits to women's rights, particularly in relation to child-bearing, to property and the custody of any children should the marriage end. By the end of the period, a larger proportion of American women had become more ready to assert their rights to equality, especially equality of opportunity, and were increasingly ambitious to enter the professions, to succeed in business and to enter politics, often combined with their traditional roles within the home and family.

CHAPTER 14

1865–1914 A woman's place

To what extent were the rights of women a live issue in this period?

Hypothesis:

- The concept of women's rights were of little interest to the majority of women in the US in this period.

Introduction

Between the end of the Civil War (1865) and the outbreak of the First World War, the most notable advance made by women was in the expansion of opportunities for unmarried women in the workplace. The pursuit of women's right to the vote, which was already underway in 1865, was continued by a core of mainly middle-class, educated women, many of whom were also actively involved in other areas of social reform, most notably the exploitation of **women and children in the workplace** and the campaign against the excessive consumption of alcohol. However, for the majority of America's married women, home and family life were both absorbing and satisfying.

WHAT OPPORTUNITIES EXISTED FOR WOMEN IN 1865?

The impact of the Civil War

The Civil War (1861–65) had briefly offered the opportunity for married women to work outside the home. In the vast rural areas of the US this was usually agricultural work, as women temporarily replaced their men folk who had gone to war. Many women also worked as nurses tending the wounded. Nursing was not, however, seen as a profession by many, but rather an extension of domestic work which was appropriate for women. Progress for women in medicine beyond the level of nursing was limited. By the late 1860s, medical colleges had strict controls on the number of women they admitted and allowed to graduate, largely as a result of opposition from

KEY CONCEPTS

Women and Children in the Workplace In 1900 there were four million children working in textiles, other manufacturing industries and in coalmines. By 1907 thirty states had abolished child labour, largely as a result of the pressure from women's groups. Legislation regulating the working hours of women also came in the first two decades of the twentieth century.

male physicians. Nevertheless, there was an increase at this time in the number of women beginning to be admitted into higher education generally.

Growth of industry

The Civil War had also acted as a catalyst speeding up the progress of the US towards becoming the world's leading industrial nation. This increased the work opportunities for women when the war ended. By 1870, 13 per cent of all unmarried women already worked in domestic occupations or increasingly in factories. This figure was to expand significantly in the remaining decades of the nineteenth century. The situation for married women, however, did not change significantly. Married women were often barred from working outside the home, either by the policies of some employers or by state legislation. In any case, the overwhelming expectation was that, once they were married, women would give up their jobs and be entirely focused on home and family. Married working-class women, however, who needed to augment the family income to escape poverty, took in laundry, mending or lodgers.

Westward expansion

Further westward expansion in the 1860s and settlement on the hostile territory of the **Great Plains** proved especially hard for women in this area. Here, living in isolation from communities and frequently at a distance from main lines of communication, married women were the cleaners, cooks, nurses, teachers, medicine makers, manufacturers of basic commodities and farm labourers. Many died in childbirth due to the lack of medical care or became seriously depressed as a result of loneliness, poverty and the sheer unrelenting struggle to survive. For these women, little was to change until well into the twentieth century although some, at least, had been given the opportunity to own land in their own right under the terms of the **Homestead Act of 1862.**

The Fifteenth Amendment 1870

This **amendment to the Constitution** established that the Federal and state governments could not withhold the right to vote on the grounds of race. In practice, states retained

1865–1914 A woman's place. To what extent were the rights of women a live issue in this period?

219

the right to impose their own voting qualifications. Campaigners for women's suffrage were angry that this right was not extended to include gender.

WOMEN AND WORK 1865–1914

Introduction

The closing decades of the nineteenth century and the decade and a half before the outbreak of the First World War were a period of change and opportunity for some sectors of female society. This was precipitated by:

- the changing economy: the continued development of the manufacturing industry, big business and urbanisation;
- the changing lifestyles of many middle-class married women: the increasing availability of consumer goods that transformed the home life;
- better education prospects.

There was, however, little change in the acceptance of 'separate spheres' and where opportunities did open up for women in the workplace, significant differentials existed in the earnings of men and women. For the majority of unmarried women, marriage, home and family remained the desirable goal even though some were prepared to wait a little longer to achieve it by marrying later.

To what extent did the changing economy of the US increase opportunities for American women?

By the turn of the century, opportunities for working-class women expanded as a result of the growth of manufacturing industry. These changes largely benefited unmarried women between 1870 and 1900. Whereas in 1870 13 per cent of all unmarried women worked outside the home, by 1900 the numbers of women workers had tripled so that they now made up 17 per cent of the total workforce. Young unmarried women left domestic service for the more lucrative work available in the textile, garment making and food processing industries that were expanding in most major cities across America.

Female shop assistants in Raike's Dept. Store, Dayton, Ohio 1893.

KEY EVENTS

Immigration The nineteenth and early twentieth centuries witnessed mass immigration to the USA, first from Ireland and northern Europe and then from southern Europe and other parts of the world. Between 1815 and 1860, 5 million immigrants arrived from Europe, 3 million of which arrived between 1845 and 1854. Another 10 million arrived in the closing decades of the nineteenth century. Although restrictions were imposed in 1921 (Quota Act) and 1924 (Johnson Reed Act) a further 18 million immigrants had entered the USA by 1929.

KEY TERMS

Hispanics These Spanish speaking Americans originated in Mexico. Initially, they crossed the border for seasonal work only. From about the turn of the century, many began to settle on the west coast of the US, later migrating to take up opportunities for work in the cities.

By the 1890s, unmarried women with a high-school education could graduate from the factory floor to the clean, safe and more salubrious offices of business enterprises. The invention and production of the typewriter and telephone transformed this area of work previously dominated by men. Here young, female, white collar, clerical workers could earn $7 a week and gain some status. This expanding trend continued, as did the increasing number of unmarried women employed in the shops and stores that began to proliferate in the later years of the nineteenth century. By 1900, there were around 949,000 women working as teachers, secretaries, librarians and telephone operators. This had risen to 3.4 million by 1920. There was, however, no career pathway for women in white collar work – men remained the managers. Almost certainly, the expectation that these young women would at some point marry and leave the workforce determined their future prospects.

But the picture was not one of progress and improvement for all women. As young white women left the factory floor, their places in the factories were increasingly taken by young **immigrant** women – European, **Hispanic** and also some African-American women (see Chapter 2) whose experience of work was very different. As cheap, unskilled workers, unprotected by legislation, their working conditions were poor, their hours long and their wages low. By the end of the nineteenth century, immigrant female factory workers had to work, on average, 70 hours to earn

1865–1914 A woman's place. To what extent were the rights of women a live issue in this period?

221

just $5. The numbers of young immigrant women continued to increase during the first two decades of the twentieth century. By the early 1900s, they not only worked in factories but also filled other menial occupations in domestic service, laundries and bakeries abandoned by white women. Poor and immigrant married women were often forced by extreme poverty to take factory work.

The number of urban working women was increased by those migrating from farming regions in search of work. The mechanisation of farming at the end of the nineteenth century not only reduced the need for a large workforce of farm labourers but ensured that farm work became a male preserve as the new technology was unsuitable for female operatives. All farm workers (male and female), as a percentage of the total labour force, fell from 53 per cent in 1870 to 37.5 per cent in 1900 and continued to fall sharply. For those who were left to live and work on the land, life continued to be challenging, particularly in the hostile climate of the Mid West.

Working-class married women, in need of money to augment the family income, were frequently exploited by devious and unscrupulous entrepreneurs who bought old tenement buildings and obliged their home workers to live there. These overcrowded apartments became sweatshops where women and their children worked for very long hours for little pay.

In fact, all women workers, along with men at this time, had no rights in law protecting them in the workplace. The federal and most state governments adopted a laissez-faire stance which left business enterprises unfettered by laws that had the potential to inhibit the creation of wealth.

Did changes in lifestyle for middle-class married women erode the ideal of home and family?

Whilst immigrant families were obliged to live in overcrowded, unhealthy and unsanitary ghettos in the cities, the late nineteenth and early twentieth centuries saw the expansion of an urban middle class of male clerical and professional workers. The development of city transport systems meant that these white collar workers on secure and steady incomes could move into better quality suburban housing. This transformed the daily lives of middle-class married women. The daily grind of cooking, cleaning, lighting fires and carrying out waste to external cess pits was exchanged for houses with indoor plumbing and central heating. Refrigerators, washing machines and commercial laundries further liberated the better off married women from the daily domestic grind.

Other changes within the family were also underway. Although farming families and those of immigrant families continued to be large (6–8 children), families of native white Americans were becoming smaller. By 1900, the average birth rate fell to 3.56 children from 5.42 in 1850. This was largely true of middle class families who clearly practised some form of birth control to ensure the reduction in family size. Immigrant families tended to be larger – especially those from Ireland and Italy who were largely Roman Catholic. At this time, religion will have certainly influenced attitudes to child-bearing.

Nevertheless, the fact that some women had fewer children to care for and that household labour had been reduced did not mean that all married women were looking for fulfilment outside the home. Less time spent on chores meant that more time was available to spend with the family and especially to support their children's education.

Better education equalled better career prospects for women?

By 1900, education was one of the key factors in creating better opportunities for women in the workplace. By 1900, half of high school graduates were female. The late nineteenth century had also seen an expansion of opportunities for women in higher education. However, many regarded a good education as merely a stage in their preparation for marriage and motherhood.

However, by the turn of the century, at least half of women graduates were delaying marriage and looking for career opportunities. A significant number found their way into teaching and social work. The traditionally male professions such as medicine and the law proved much more difficult to access. Nevertheless, there were signs of change. This was reflected to some extent **by the rise in the divorce rate** by 1900.

For those staunch supporters (both female and male) who continued to revere the ideal of 'separate spheres', this was an alarming development.

KEY EVENTS

The rise in the divorce rate In 1880, about one in every twenty-one marriages ended in divorce. By 1900, this had risen to one in twelve and continued to rise during the first two decades of the twentieth century.

1865–1914 A woman's place. To what extent were the rights of women a live issue in this period?

223

ACTIVISTS, REFORMERS AND CAMPAIGNERS 1865–1914

How were women influencing social reform?

Before the First World War, women in the US had no political power nor did the vast majority of them have any aspiration to achieve it. Nevertheless, they were prepared to protest and ensure that their voice was heard on those matters that really concerned them. A minority of mainly middle-class women asserted themselves in this period, predominantly to condemn what they perceived to be inequality or injustice in the treatment of particular groups of people or, alternatively, to condemn social evils that threatened the well-being of the family. For married women, this kind of activity outside the confines of the home, was considered to be socially acceptable and provided outlets for intelligent and energetic married middle-class women.

One example is the work of **Jane Addams** who established **Hull House in Chicago** in 1889 as a social centre to support the settlement of newly arrived immigrant families. Addams and her fellow workers came to act as an influential pressure group urging politicians to address a whole range of social issues but, most immediately, the problem of slum housing and evils that accompanied it.

Temperance was another area in which women's organisations relentlessly demanded reform and showed themselves as a force to be reckoned with. Action to curtail the proliferation of saloons began before the outbreak of the Civil War. Women believed it was their role to combat the evils of drunkenness that threatened and undermined home and family life. Temperance was the ideal of some; total **prohibition** the demand of others. Demand for action galvanised women into action in a way that the campaign for political and other rights was unable to do for some considerable time. This was achieved largely through active protest such as the **Women's Crusade** of 1873 and membership of pressure groups such as the **Women's Christian Temperance Union (WCTU).** When thousands of women in Ohio took to the streets in that year, they successfully closed the saloons and liquor outlets. The important role played by women in the campaign for prohibition and its subsequent repeal will be discussed specifically in Chapter 15.

KEY PEOPLE

Jane Addams (1860-1935) established the Hull House project on her return from travelling and was inspired by Toynbee Hall, a centre for charity work in the midst of London's slums.

KEY PLACES

Hull House, Chicago At Hull House, Addams and her volunteers provided classes for parents to care for their children. Men were helped to find jobs. English classes helped newly arrived Italian immigrants to overcome the language barrier. Day nurseries were provided for working mothers. The Hull House settlement attracted a host of well-educated women with expertise in a range of areas that equipped them to engage in the work of reform. Around 50 settlement houses had been established across the US by 1895.

KEY TERMS

Temperance in this context is the advocacy of drinking in moderation and the avoidance of excess.

Prohibition The banning of the manufacture, sale and transportation of alcoholic beverages was eventually embodied in the Eighteenth Amendment to the US Constitution in 1919 (see pages 242–48).

KEY TERMS

Women's Crusade of 1873 was the first mass movement of US women demanding the prohibition of the sale of intoxicating beverages.

How were women influencing reform in the workplace?

Some pressure was exerted, quite successfully, through the **National Consumers' League (NCL),** set up in 1899, to gain recognition for the rights of women in the workplace. This included:

- Pressure for the improvement in the wages of female sales clerks with local businesses.
- Pressure to secure protective legislation for women and children in the workplace and improve working conditions.
- Pressure on state governments to provide aid for mothers and improved facilities for children and young people – better schools and playgrounds, for example.

What was the impact of black women's clubs?

At the same time, black women in the southern states were also forming women's clubs pursuing similar issues, although here they were more directly concerned with their rights and equality. Much of this action was focused on the **National Association of Colored Women (NACW)** formed in 1896. By 1915 the NACW had 50,000 members. Unlike white women, black women suffered racial prejudice as well as gender discrimination (see also Chapter 3). Consequently, whilst there was a concern for social issues, the acquisition of civil rights was always a dominant feature of their campaigns. A key figure in the movement was Ida B. Wells (see also page 34) whose campaigns against lynching led her to be threatened and persecuted in the south.

CASE STUDY: VOTES FOR WOMEN 1865–1914

The campaign for the vote

The campaign for the vote for women, spearheaded mainly by educated, white middle-class women, dates back to the early decades of the nineteenth century. It became closely allied in the minds of early feminist reformers with the temperance and anti-slavery movements. Both before and during the Civil War, a number of largely middle-class women had been directly involved in political campaigns, although usually focussed on social issues. Many were married to male activists and frequently, though not

1865–1914 A woman's place. To what extent were the rights of women a live issue in this period?

225

exclusively, worked alongside them to press for reform. For example, from the mid nineteenth century, many leading feminists of the day such as **Lucretia Mott**, **Elizabeth Cady Stanton** and **Susan B. Anthony,** were actively involved in the campaign to abolish slavery.

The campaign for women's rights had begun specifically in 1848 when Stanton and Mott founded the Women's Rights Convention at Seneca Falls, New York State. The extension of the right to vote to all males contained in the Fifteenth Amendment (1870) (see page 13), infuriated feminist activists since it extended the franchise to all men irrespective of wealth, ethnicity or education whilst failing to establish the right to vote even for wealthy and well-educated women.

Opposition to the Fourteenth and Fifteenth Amendments effectively split the women's reform movement – a feature that was to become characteristic of women's campaign groups in the future. One section remained pledged to securing the vote for male African Americans whilst adopting a moderate approach to achieving the vote for women, initially at state level. This was the American Woman Suffrage Association (AWSA) formed in 1869 by **Lucy Stone**. The other section campaigned more aggressively for a federal constitutional amendment recognising the right of women to the vote. This was the National Women's Suffrage Association (NWSA) which was established, also in 1869, by Elizabeth Cady Stanton and Susan B. Anthony. In 1890, however, the two organisations merged to form the National American Woman Suffrage Association (NAWSA). Support from the mainstream of women was limited. By 1905 there were only 17,000 members nationally. By 1915 this had reached 100,000 but this represented only half of the number of women who were actively involved with temperance and prohibition groups.

In 1900, **Carrie Chapman Catt** took over from Susan B. Anthony as President of the NAWSA and organised a moderate campaign of lobbying politicians, distributing leaflets, holding marches and public meetings, steadily making headway, state by state. The women's movement developed a more radical wing on the eve of the First World War when **Alice Paul** formed a breakaway

KEY PEOPLE

Lucretia Mott (1793–1880) She organised the Women's Rights Convention at Seneca Falls in 1848 with Stanton. In 1866, she became a founding member of the American Equal Rights Association.

Elizabeth Cady Stanton (1815–1902) At the Seneca Falls Convention, she drew up a reform programme for women. She worked closely with Susan B. Anthony to secure the right to vote for women as well as property rights for married women and the right of divorced or separated women to have access to their children. She also campaigned for the liberalisation of the divorce laws.

Susan B. Anthony (1820–1906) She was a founding member of the American Equal Rights Association in 1866 and published a journal, Revolution, to promote the cause. In 1872, she challenged the terms of the Constitution by voting illegally in the presidential election of that year. She campaigned against abortion, which at that time was a threat to women's health and well-being.

Lucy Stone (1818-93) After studying for a degree, she began to give lectures condemning slavery and supporting women's suffrage. She edited the *Woman's Journal,* a feminist magazine.

'Shall women vote? No, they might disturb the existing order of things.' This cartoon is a caricature of political corruption depicting attitudes to women. The small drawings show examples of female persecution and the exploitation of labour.

organisation, the Congressional Union for Women's Suffrage (which became the National Women's Party after 1917) in 1913. She replicated the methods of the militant British suffragettes, organising mass demonstrations and, with a small band of like-minded women, picketed the White House on a daily basis. She received a seven month prison sentence in the US for illegally voting in a presidential election, during which she and others staged hunger strikes.

What was the impact of suffragist activity?

The policy of the NAWSA in focusing its campaigning at state level did yield some positive results. **By 1918 twenty states had given women the right to vote in state elections.** Public sympathy for the cause was also aroused by the treatment of suffragettes in prison. However, it was the part played by women on the home front in the First World which accelerated a federal response. Following **President Wilson's** call in 1918 for a constitutional amendment giving women the vote, Congress gave its approval in 1919. The Nineteenth Amendment to the Constitution was set in place in 1920 following its ratification by the requisite number of 36 states (i.e three quarters of the total).

1865–1914 A woman's place. To what extent were the rights of women a live issue in this period?

227

However, in America, as in Britain, the campaign for the vote never became a mass movement. Although some African American and immigrant women joined the NAWSA, it was largely a white middle-class organisation. The women's movement, if it can be called this at all at this point in time, was subsequently splintered into several areas of social action, as described earlier in this chapter, reflecting the divisions in women's attitudes to what constituted acceptable spheres of activity outside the home. It would, therefore, be fair to conclude that the interest of women in political matters was very limited. The extent to which the mass of American women actually valued the vote once it had been given to them is a matter of debate. This discussion will be continued in Chapter 15.

KEY PEOPLE

Thomas Woodrow Wilson (1856–1924) Born in Virginia, son of a Presbyterian Minister, Wilson had a successful academic career at Princeton University. He was elected President in 1912 and re-elected in 1916, introducing important economic and financial reforms concerning income tax and tariffs. He was not always a supporter of female suffrage but had changed his mind by 1918.

CONCLUSION

The period from 1865 until the outbreak of the First World War saw significant change in the American economy which enhanced opportunities for unmarried white women, most particularly those who were educated and middle class. Nevertheless, for the vast majority of working class, unmarried women who were predominantly of immigrant, African American or of other ethnicity, exploitation of themselves and often their children was the norm. Middle-class married women ventured out of their own homes to engage in the acceptable activity of social reform. Generally, these educated, middle-class women were a minority, as were those who became involved in pressure groups to bring about changes in legislation – mostly social. The exception to this was the ultimately successful campaign to achieve the vote for women. The overwhelming feature of this period was the centrality of home and family where women had real power and influence. The pursuit of rights, therefore, was only a live issue for a small minority who were not representative of the broad spectrum of American women.

QUESTIONS TO CONSIDER

1. In the period from 1865 until 1914, economic change and the expansion of education for women were the

most significant factors in creating opportunities for American women.

- Discuss why you might agree or disagree with this statement.
- Argue why one of these factors might be more important than the other.
- Discuss why your judgement might apply differently to different groups of American women.

2. What evidence is there, in this period, that the concept of 'separate spheres' was the most powerful force in shaping women's own beliefs about their role in society? Was this inevitably a barrier to progress in the pursuit of women's rights?

3. Discuss the extent to which women's rights were a live issue in this period.

1865–1914 A woman's place. To what extent were the rights of women a live issue in this period?

229

CHAPTER 15

1915–40 War, boom, bust and recovery

Change or continuity for women?

Hypothesis:

- In spite of the political and economic turmoil of this period, the position of women changed very little between the two World Wars.

Introduction

The experiences of the First World War did little to permanently change the position of the vast majority of American women. The extension of the franchise to women in 1919 failed to engage the majority with politics or interest them in participating in the democratic process. The rare exception was when there was a need for a political response to any threat to the integrity of home and family. The involvement of female pressure groups in social and moral campaigns caused divisions that continued to impede the formation of an identifiable, unified women's movement, although white upper- and middle-class women were able to exert significant pressure for change on issues of major national importance, in this case, the legal imposition of Prohibition and the subsequent repeal of the law.

WOMEN AND WORK 1915–40

Was the period of the First World War a turning point for women in the workplace?

The First World War opened up the opportunity for married women to legitimately enter the workforce. On the outbreak of the war in Europe in 1914, America expanded production of ammunition, goods and other supplies for the combatants. This industrial expansion increased job opportunities for unmarried women as well as for African-American workers who migrated in large numbers into the cities (see also Chapter 3, page 44).

However, America's entry into the war in 1917 increased the demand for labour and resulted in many married women coming out of the home to take the place of the men who had gone to fight. Women in farming areas still ploughed and harvested for their absent men-folk, but in the cities they went to work in heavy industry, drove streetcars and transport vehicles, delivered mail and all the other myriad of jobs normally done by men. In the process, many earned good wages for the first time, although they were still paid less than the men they had replaced for doing the same work. Approximately 11,000 women also served in the US navy as nurses, clerical workers and telephone operators. Between 1917 and 1918, one million women worked in industry.

Nevertheless, any lasting change that might have come about in the position of married women was insufficiently significant to substantiate any claim that the war can be seen as a turning point. Whilst it undoubtedly must have widened the horizons of unmarried women, the fact remains that it did little to change the accepted role of married women. There was, from the outset, a clear expectation that women who had left the home to support the war effort would return there when the men returned home. It must also be said that this was expected and indeed accepted by the vast majority of married women themselves.

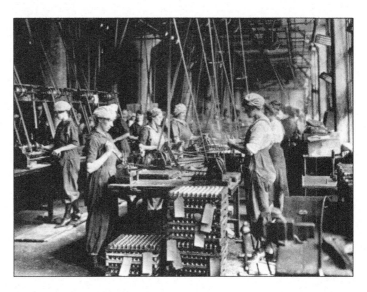

Female munitions workers during the First World War.

What was the impact of the post-war boom of the 1920s on the opportunities for and aspirations of women?

During the 1920s, the US underwent a massive expansion of manufacturing industry that created unprecedented prosperity. Mass produced, consumer goods proliferated so that those classified as luxury items in Europe, where they were associated with wealth and social status, became readily available to people of all classes in the US.

The boom created more jobs for unmarried women and the opportunity for an easier home life for married women. The availability of cheap, mass produced, labour-saving devices to buy on credit opened up the possibility to working-class families to own a car, a refrigerator, washing machine, vacuum cleaner and electric iron. The phenomenal increase in demand for these goods by 1928 is indicative of the impact they must have had on homes across the social spectrum. This is not to say that married women who were liberated from the daily routine of household chores consequently searched for new challenges beyond the home. Wives and mothers saw their lightened load as an opportunity to spend more time with their children and to support their education.

Nevertheless, the number of working class, married women in the workforce increased slightly in this period from 22.8 to 28.8 per cent. Further business expansion increased the demand for secretaries, typists and filing clerks. Overall, the number of women entering the workforce increased by two million. This represents an increase of jobs in shops and offices as well as factories. Women also continued to enter the lower level professions such as nursing, social work and teaching. Many of these would have been recruited from the increasing numbers of women moving into higher education. Opportunities in law and medicine were still limited.

Women still faced wage discrimination. In industry, work on the production line was still dominated by men, who showed resentment towards female factory workers. Women workers were seen both as a threat to jobs for men and to their wages which could be kept low whilst women were paid less.

Some working-class women did resort to union activity to defend their rights in the workplace but with limited impact. In 1929, a violent strike in North Carolina led to the deaths of six women. During the 1930s, the female membership of unions increased from 265,000 to 800,000. Where unions for women workers did exist, they were exclusively white (see also Section 2). The most exploited women workers – African American and Mexican American women – had no representation. The tendency continued for immigrant women, particularly those of Japanese origin, to enter into domestic service.

Was the Great Depression a major setback for the women in the US?

In October 1929 the years of plenty came to an end. The collapse of the stock market plunged the US into the deepest **depression** in its history.

The implications of this for working women – especially married working women – were significant. In the face of massive male unemployment, the apparent expansion of opportunities for women quickly receded. In 1936 a Gallup poll suggested that 82 per cent of Americans were opposed to women working. This ignored the fact that, in poor families, women worked to eke out the inadequate wages of the male breadwinner or supported their families when their husbands were unemployed. Twenty-six states introduced laws which banned married women from working although only Louisiana passed the law and then it was declared unconstitutional.

During the years of prosperity, the idea of increasing the spending power of working-class families with a second income had made it more acceptable for married women to go out to work (12 per cent of married women were working in 1930). The crash and its resulting high levels of unemployment resulted not just in women losing their jobs, but also in the expectation that those still in work (cheaper female labour being a preferable option for struggling companies) would give them up to make way for men. This was particularly harsh on female heads of households where they were the sole breadwinners.

By the end of the 1930s, more married women were drifting back into employment outside the home, largely out of dire necessity rather than from a drive to assert their rights. On the other hand, in contrast to the general picture, the female membership of labour unions trebled during the 1930s.

Were the rights of women at work advanced by Roosevelt's New Deal?

In March 1933 **Franklin Delano Roosevelt** was sworn in as President of the US. His mandate was to get America back to work and bring the Depression to an end. He promised the voters a 'New Deal' – a string of policies intended to stimulate the economy and support those who were particularly vulnerable and unable to help themselves. However, in practice, these policies were biased towards the male breadwinner and did little to raise the self-esteem and aspirations of women. Where women did benefit, it was not as a result of legislation or government action targeted at women specifically, but rather action intended to address wider social and economic issues. For example:

- **Social Security Act (1935)** helped to alleviate family stress by introducing welfare benefits for poor families. This benefited married women but was not designed specifically for them.
- **Aid to Dependent Children (1935)** helped women with young families who were unable to work and where there was no male head of the household. These benefits were largely given to white women who were obliged to go through a frequently humiliating process to get this aid.
- **The Fair Labor Standards Act (1938)** set new minimum wage levels. These benefited women but they still earned less than men doing the same job. A female teacher, for example, earned 20 per cent less that her male counterpart in 1939. Female **white collar workers** were paid at lower rates than male factory workers. The principle of lower pay for female workers had been firmly established by the National Recovery Administration in 1933 under the leadership of Frances Perkins (see page 237). The only real gains here for

KEY PEOPLE

Franklin D. Roosevelt (1882–1945) was a Democrat and President from 1933 until his death. He was very popular with the people, who believed that he could bring the USA out of the Depression. He was born into a rich family and educated at Harvard. He became Governor of New York State in 1928, in spite of being left crippled by polio in 1921. As president, he initiated a set of 'relief, recovery and reform' policies that came to be called the 'New Deal'. Their purpose was to bring the USA out of the Depression by getting people back to work and restoring prosperity.

KEY TERMS

White-collar workers Describes men and women in non-manual work; for example, clerical worker, banker, civil servants etc.

women were the reduction of their working hours, the abolition of child labour and the establishment of the right of all workers to join a labour union.

Throughout the 1930s, African-American and Mexican-American women continued to suffer as a result of discrimination and prejudice. This was particularly true of those living in rural areas where Roosevelt's policy of forcibly limiting levels of production to maintain prices adversely affected small landowners and especially **sharecroppers** in the south. When they moved to the urban areas, little work was available for men so their women sought domestic work. Native American women did, however, benefit from Roosevelt's personal interest in the plight of Native Americans. The Indian Reorganization Act (1934) gave Native American women formal political rights and provided them with training as domestic workers and seamstresses. There was also an interest in promoting native arts and crafts that provided work for Indian women (see Chapter 11).

WOMEN AND POLITICS 1915–40

On the eve of the First World War, opportunities for women in politics were probably greater in the states of the west. By 1918, twenty states in the west and mid-west had given women the vote. Jeanette Rankin of Montana had become the first woman to take a seat in the House of Representatives in 1917. In the states of the west and mid-west, women seized the opportunity for public office. This was, however, exceptional. Generally, politics was regarded by men (and many women also) as too dishonest and disreputable an activity for women, consequently, the numbers of women in politics increased only very slowly through the first half of the twentieth century.

Did American women appreciate the right to vote?
In 1920 the **Nineteenth Amendment to the Constitution** gave most American women aged over 21 years the right to vote. The exceptions were immigrant women who had not been **naturalised** and so remained disenfranchised. In

practice, African-American women in the south were unable to take advantage of their right to vote since they continued to face racial discrimination and intimidation. The immediate response of the majority of women to gaining political equality with men does not appear to have been enthusiastic. Evidence taken from surveys of subsequent voting patterns suggests that the majority of married women voted as their husbands did and showed little interest in the idea that the vote empowered them. For poor, working-class women, the reality of their lives was quite simply the daily struggle to survive. It was a way of life which, for the majority, left little time for political interest and one where it was difficult to appreciate the relevance of political activity.

A 'new deal' for women in politics 1933–40?

The new deal policies of President Franklin D. Roosevelt brought little change for the majority of women. For those aspiring to enter the professions and public office, nothing much was achieved. Only nine women had entered politics by 1939. **Nellie Tayloe Ross** became the first female Director of the Mint and **Florence Allen** the first woman judge on the US Circuit of Appeals. **Mary McLeod Bethune** was the first black woman to enter the government as Director of Negro Affairs. Roosevelt appointed the first female member of the Cabinet when **Frances Perkins** became Secretary of Labor in 1933. The negative reaction to this appointment highlighted the continuing and deeply entrenched prejudices of businessmen, labour unionists and politicians against women in positions of influence. These were particularly apprehensive of Perkins' reputation as a social reformer. However, whilst she actively promoted social reform, she did little to directly promote increased opportunities for women in politics.

American women did have a role model in the First Lady, Eleanor Roosevelt (see page 55). She successfully combined her role of wife and mother (she gave birth to six children of whom five survived) with active support for women's rights, civil rights for African Americans and political support for the New Deal policies of her husband. Before becoming First Lady, she had joined the League of Women

KEY PEOPLE

Nellie Tayloe Ross (1876–1977) trained to be a teacher. She married William Ross in 1902 and moved to Wyoming, where William was elected governor in 1922. Nellie continued to be involved in politics after his death. She became the first female governor of Wyoming – the first woman to serve as the governor of a US State. In 1933 she became the first female director of the US Mint.

Florence Allen (1884–1966) studied law at the Universities of Chicago and New York, gaining a law degree in 1913. She actively supported the women's suffrage movement and experienced at first hand the difficulty for a woman to make her way in the legal profession. However, by 1920, she had become a judge and in 1922 was elected to the Ohio Supreme Court. In March 1934, she was appointed by Roosevelt as a judge in the US Court of Appeals.

Mary McLeod Bethune (1875–1955) Both of her parents had been slaves. She became a teacher, eventually starting her own school for African American girls. It was a great success and by 1922 had 300 students. She was active in the campaign for civil rights, opposing 'Jim Crow' laws and demanding federal action on lynching (also see pages 29–33) She always voted, despite threats and intimidation from the Ku Klux Klan when it reappeared in the 1920s. She served in the administration of Franklin D. Roosevelt in 1936 and became vice president of the NAACP in 1940.

Frances Perkins (1882–1965) became a social worker and then a teacher in Chicago. In 1910, having gained a Master's degree, she became secretary to the Consumer's League. In this position, she came to the attention of a number of influential politicians of the day including Alfred Smith, who became governor of New York State in 1919. She was appointed by him to be chairman of the Industrial Board in 1924. From this position she was able to secure a reduction in the working week for women to 54 hours. In 1929 Roosevelt became governor of New York State and promoted Perkins to Industrial Commissioner. This made her the natural choice to become Labor Secretary in 1933.

Voters and the Women's Trade Union League (1921) and showed herself to be a woman of strong beliefs and independent thinking. She was also active in the Democrat Party, campaigning energetically for Democratic nominees for the presidency including her husband. Whilst she supported her husband's presidential policies, she, nevertheless, always stuck to her own principles. For example, she was a staunch supporter of the anti-lynching campaign even when the President's response was lukewarm.

ACTIVISTS, REFORMERS AND CAMPAIGNERS 1915–1940

Did the right to vote really empower women after 1919?

The answer to this question is probably 'No' in the context of all American women, since there is little evidence to indicate that the vote was used by women to promote significant change for themselves. For the minority of educated middle-class women who had campaigned for the vote, the Nineteenth Amendment represented a triumph. However, they failed to make further substantial change because they were divided as to how the vote could best be used to improve conditions for women and increase opportunities for them.

This division can be seen very clearly in terms of those educated women who upheld the sanctity of home and family and who continued to press for social reform as opposed to feminist groups who chose to take up the cause of equal rights for women and began to campaign for an Equal Rights Amendment (ERA) (see page 277) from 1923. For some educated, professional women, establishing the principle that women were equal in every respect to men was a natural extension of women's rights. Other feminist groups were opposed to this idea, as they saw the ERA as a threat to securing the right of women to be protected in situations where their physical and biological differences might be compromised, for example, in the workplace, where they could be required to undertake heavy work or where they might lose their personal privacy.

The most extreme opposition came from right wing anti-feminist groups who opposed equal rights and actively campaigned against the feminist movement using propaganda that portrayed them as spinsters and lesbians. Some of these actually formed an auxiliary branch of the Ku Klux Klan to promote anti-feminism. By 1969 the campaign for ERA had achieved nothing (see Chapter 17 for further discussion).

Meanwhile, others groups concentrated on specific social reforms, as described earlier. Their leaders (Jane Addams, for example) continued to campaign for essential legislation to regulate working hours and conditions for women, to abolish child labour and to improve living conditions for poor families, especially those in the tenements of the big cities. Educated African-American women such as **Mary Talbert**, led the campaign to prevent lynching, incidences of which increased in the 1920s following the re-emergence of the Ku Klux Klan (see page 52).

Yet even in the ranks of female social reformers, there were philosophical disagreements about what equality for women actually meant. Some argued that to press for legislation that in any way protected women or created special conditions for them in the workplace, only served to emphasise their differences and, implicitly, their weaknesses in comparison with men. During this period, success in the sphere of social legislation was very limited:

- A Women's Bureau was established in the Department of Labour in 1920 but was very limited in what it achieved, since its focus was on striving to improve working conditions and unfair treatment at work. This met with resistance from some employers and male labour unions.
- The Shepherd-Towner Act (1921) made funds available for maternity and infant health education but funding was terminated in 1929. In any case, it was limited in that the medical profession resisted the provision of medical care free of charge or financial aid to poor women.
- Legislation to ban the employment of children under 14 years and to introduce an eight-hour day for women was short-lived, as the concerted pressure of big business on

The Roaring Twenties was notable for its energy and dynamism. For this was the age of jazz, rag and 'boogie woogie' (see page 47), of the cinema, of radio, of mass advertising and consumerism. Above all, it was the age of the proliferation of the motor car, which provided young adults with unprecedented freedom.

the politicians proved overwhelming. The legislation was overthrown by the Supreme Court in 1922.

- However, female pressure groups who had been part of the temperance movement were influential in the successful introduction of prohibition in 1920 and ultimately in its repeal in 1933 (see the case study beginning on page 244 for further discussion).

Was there a 'new' feminist movement in the 1920s?

The '**Roaring Twenties**' in the US are characterised not only by the massive further expansion of consumer industry but also by the vast fortunes that enterprising speculators were able to amass through wheeling and dealing on the stock market.

In this affluent context the emergence of an identifiable group of, typically, young upper- or middle-class women, who ostentatiously threw off the standards and norms of their mothers and grandmothers, must have suggested that a feminist revolution was in progress. Characterised by

their bobbed hair, short clothes and sometimes outrageous and frequently promiscuous behaviour, the 'flappers' as they came to be known, searched, largely unsuccessfully, to find a new identity.

In reality, the flappers did not represent a social revolution. Nor did they present a unifying concept of the 'modern woman'. If anything, they were only united by their determination to rebel and, even then, they comprised only a relatively small proportion of the privileged, female population. Few others went beyond copying the hairstyles and the fashion. The majority of women (especially older ones) disapproved of their extrovert and permissive behaviour. Consequently, there was little erosion, during this period, of the

Flappers doing the 'Charleston'.

acceptance of 'separate spheres'. The world of the flappers, especially the wealthy ones captured in the novels of **Scott Fitzgerald**, was a transitory one and had little lasting effect on the position and aspirations of the mass of women in America at this point in time.

Further educational opportunities

Education remained an important part of the life of young women. The number of graduates from higher education continued to grow in this period. As a result, women became involved in research and the number gaining higher degrees and doctorates also expanded. However, there was still strong male resistance to women entering the professions, especially medicine and the law. Woman aspiring to these areas took up the struggle to gain access but this struggle was a relatively self-contained one and did nothing to improve the prospects of women generally.

The decade saw the expansion of opportunities for African-American women, who regarded education as the means to gain social and economic equality as well as the recognition of their rights. In 1921 **M. Carey Thomas,** an African-American woman, founded the Bryn Mawr Summer School for working-class women. Voluntary groups, such as the Young Women's Christian Association, created opportunities for young women of different cultural heritages to come together to discuss matters of common concern.

A WOMAN'S RIGHT TO CHOOSE – THE BIRTH CONTROL CONTROVERSY

Attitudes to birth control and accessibility of contraceptives

Whilst the majority of married women readily accepted their role, they had no right of choice when it came to child-bearing. Although the reduction in the size of mainly white middle-class families suggests that some form of birth control was in use, African American as well as poorer white families remained large. This may have been partly the result of ignorance about contraception. However, religious beliefs were also an important factor.

**The Comstock Laws
1873** were a collection of federal and state laws making it illegal to send any 'obscene, lewd and/or lascivious' materials by mail. Contraceptive devices, information about contraception and abortion, all came within this definition. The laws also made it illegal to prescribe contraceptives or even to provide advice on birth control. The last vestiges of these laws were finally overturned by the Supreme Court decision in the case of *Griswold* v. *Connecticut* in 1965 that the use of contraceptives rested within a couple's 'right of privacy' within the terms of the Constitution.

Contraceptives Condoms and diaphragms made from vulcanised rubber had been available for purchase since 1838. These were available be purchased in pharmacies by the end of the nineteenth century until this was made illegal by the Comstock Laws.

For Roman Catholics and some Protestant communities, relationships within marriage were believed to be for the purpose of procreation. Consequently, artificial methods of birth control were regarded with distaste. Some even considered them to be immoral.

These attitudes and beliefs were reflected in some State legislatures, whose laws made the acquisition of contraceptives extremely difficult. A major obstacle was the **Comstock Laws (1873)** that effectively made the sale, advertisement and distribution of **contraceptives** illegal. Prior to this legislation, they had been on sale in pharmacies. These laws drove contraceptives 'under the counter' which meant they could be bought, but at a price. For poor families particularly, they were expensive. Poorer women were obliged to resort to illegal abortion as a means of contraception, when they were either weary of relentless child-bearing or unable to cope with another mouth to feed.

Margaret Sanger and the American Birth Control League.

Margaret Sanger believed passionately in a woman's right to choose if and when she would bear children. She devoted most of her life's work to making birth control advice available to women, especially those who were poor. Her crusade began in 1912 with newspaper articles giving contraceptive advice to women in defiance of the Comstock Laws. She promoted the right of every woman to be *'the absolute mistress of her own body'*. Her first birth control clinic, opened in Brooklyn, New York in 1916, was closed by the police. She subsequently served thirty days in prison for her action. Undeterred, she went on to establish the **American Birth Control League (ABCL)** in 1921 and in 1923 established the first legal birth control clinic with financial backing from John D. Rockefeller.

The extent to which the vast majority of married women were liberated at the time as a result of Sanger's work is debatable. She was, in many respects, ahead of her time in her thinking about contraception and she faced powerful opposition from religious organisations and from politicians. Although by 1924, the ABCL could boast

27,500 members, there were still only ten branches in cities across just eight states.

The Comstock Laws were effectively ended in 1938, when the federal ban on birth control was lifted; however, state legislatures enforced their own laws on contraception. There was no recognition of the right of women to make a choice about child-bearing and, as suggested above, those who benefited from the relaxation of the law were those who could afford to pay for contraceptives. Illegal, back-street abortion, therefore, continued to be a common form of birth control for poorer women.

CASE STUDY – AMERICAN WOMEN AND THE PROHIBITION CAMPAIGN

In December 1917, the Eighteenth Amendment to the Constitution was passed, banning the sale, import, transport and manufacture of alcoholic drink – the era of prohibition had begun. The Twenty-first Amendment repealing this was finally **ratified** in 1933 bringing the era to a close. In both instances, different female pressure groups had played a significant part in the campaigns leading to these conflicting pieces of legislation. The issue of prohibition provides a good example of the fundamental divisions that existed in the early decades of the twentieth century between women's groups who used the same arguments to achieve opposite outcomes. It is also indicative of the strength and influence of the female voice when focused on issues identifiable with their traditional 'sphere' within which they were regarded as the moral authority. In determining the influence of women in the successful enactment of prohibition legislation, it is important to take into consideration:

- the significance of women's organisations and their leadership;
- the power of home protection as a justification for action by women;
- the impact of the alliances they made with other groups pursuing similar goals;
- the social, political and economic context at critical points.

KEY PEOPLE

Margaret Sanger (1879–1966) was born in New York. Her later crusade was based on the experience of her own mother, a devout Roman Catholic, who endured 18 pregnancies producing 11 live births, of which Margaret was the sixth. Her own life was steeped in controversy, not only because of her birth control campaign but also as a result of some of her other extreme views, for example, on the subject of eugenics (selective breeding to improve genetic qualities). She was opposed to abortion because of the dangers to the mother's health. In the 1950s she raised money for the development of the Pill (see pages 268–69).

KEY TERMS

The American Birth Control League (ABCL) was founded by Margaret Sanger in 1921 and gained legal recognition in New York state in 1923. The League's purpose was to educate through the distribution of written materials, conferences and lectures. It also collected information relating to the negative social effects of unlimited child-bearing and organised field workers to disseminate, educate and establish birth control centres across the US.

Ratified Constitutional amendments could only become the law of the land when they had been formally approved by three-quarters of the total number of states.

Frances Willard (1839–98) gave up her position as a professor of English to help to organise the Chicago Woman's Christian Temperance Union (WCTU) (see page 224) and to devote herself completely to the temperance crusade. In 1891 she was elected president of the World Woman's Temperance Union. In 1880, she began a crusade to win the right of women to vote so that liquor could be banned. The activities of the WCTU expanded to include welfare work, prison reform and public health. By 1890 the organisation had 150,000 members.

KEY TERMS

The Anti-Saloon League was established in 1893 and became the main organisation lobbying for Prohibition. It gained most of its support in the southern states and the rural North. It was particularly well supported by Protestant ministers and their congregations – Methodists, Baptists and Congregationalists. Successful in 1919, it was overwhelmingly defeated by anti-Prohibition groups in the early 1930s.

Non-partisan Not aligned to any political party or point of view.

Lobbying tactics refers to the practice of gaining the attention of politicians or other people of influence in order to persuade them to support a particular cause.

What was the contribution of women to the passage of the Eighteenth Amendment?

Middle-class women's groups had been involved in the temperance movement since the early decades of the nineteenth century. From 1874, the campaign was dominated by the Women's Christian Temperance Union under the powerful leadership of **Frances Willard**. Willard demonstrated many leadership qualities, not least the appreciation of enhancing the appeal of the movement with an emotive image and a uniting purpose. Consequently, the argument for promoting temperance was firmly rooted in the protection of the home. In the early days, women took to the streets to protest, handing out leaflets in saloons, lobbying saloon keepers, holding prayer meetings and vigils.

The turning point came in 1893 with the formation of the **Anti-Saloon League (ASL).** The League was also a **non-partisan** organisation and, following the death of Frances Willard in 1898, quickly allied itself with the Union to push for prohibition measures. By 1913 their successful combined **lobbying tactics** and joint campaigns had resulted in prohibition laws being enacted in nine states across the US, with more to follow as the campaign gained momentum.

By 1917, when the US entered the First World War, twenty-six states had prohibition laws, in some, home-made liquor remained legal, for example, California. The ASL and WCTU recognised that if the evils of drink were to be removed there had to be consistency and this could only come from national prohibition laws. At this point, they used all the experience they had gained from their earlier campaigns to use propaganda and pressure to achieve their goal. Congress passed the prohibition amendment in 1917. By 1919, the required number of state legislatures had ratified the amendment. The passage of the prohibition amendment through legislatures in at least ten states was assisted by the fact that members were eager to attract the female vote.

However, there were other factors that created a political climate favourable to the passage of the Eighteenth

Amendment at this point in time. These need to be considered when evaluating the impact of the female lobby, although it must be said that both the ASL and the WCTU used the following factors as propaganda to speed up the successful outcome of their campaign:

- **Nativism** was rife in the 1920s
- The outbreak of the First World War led to increased hostility towards those of German immigrant origin. Many of the major breweries in the US were owned by Germans.
- The 'wets' (those opposed to prohibition) failed to unite and organise themselves against the prohibition lobby. These included the brewery owners themselves who had failed to respond to pressure from temperance groups to clean up their saloons in order to make them more salubrious places.

Why had the attitudes of women to prohibition apparently changed by the late 1920s?

Whilst women were clearly influential in the passage of the Eighteenth Amendment, they were equally effective in the decision of Congress to repeal it. There had always been a body of female opinion that did not support prohibition. However, by the late 1920s and early 1930s, there was evidence of a fundamental change of attitude amongst a significant number of women who had once supported prohibition but who now joined the pressure to repeal the law. This was particularly true of former rank and file members of the WCTU who, by the late 1920s, were joining the opposition in increasing numbers. It was not difficult to produce persuasive evidence to support any claim that this law had not been effective in protecting home and family. The anti-prohibition campaign reveals the extent to which women were deeply and often bitterly divided in how to achieve their priorities and how effectively the same arguments and methods could be used to achieve opposing goals.

Early attempts by some women to oppose prohibition had failed to gain a mass following. In 1922, for example, the Molly Pitcher Club, led by **M. Louise Gross**, was formed in New York City in an effort to organise a female protest

'**Speakeasies'** were illegal
liquor shops or drinking
clubs. They appeared in all the
big cities in the US during the
prohibition period. They were
usually owned and operated
by gangland bosses or
organisations.

Racketeering refers to
illegal business deals and
involvement in related
criminal activity which was
rife during the 1920s.
Gangland bosses became
wealthy and gained power and
influence by corrupting local
politicians and officials.

KEY PEOPLE

**Pauline Sabin (1887–
1955)** belonged to a wealthy,
political family. Both her
grandfather and father held
political office in the
Democrat and Republican
parties. She was involved in
local politics from 1919 in the
ranks of the Republican Party,
from which she defected in
1924 when President Hoover
supported prohibition. She
inherited a fortune in 1934
and continued to be active in
local politics until her death
in 1955.

movement against the introduction of prohibition. Its
impact, however, was limited. It was, and remained, a
localised response. Its arguments were based on the claim
that prohibition limited personal freedom. Although
personal rights and freedom were dear to the hearts of all
Americans, this did not have the same powerful appeal as
the threat to home and family life. In the face of the moral
arguments presented forcefully by other anti-prohibition
organisations, its cause was weak.

Prohibition had spawned a whole new culture of violence
and immorality, which was perceived as a threat to home
and family by women who saw themselves as the guardians
of the 'separate sphere'. The illegal importation and
production of alcohol and its consumption in equally illegal
'**speakeasies'** contributed to the growth of organised crime
on a grand scale, including **racketeering**, prostitution and
drug trafficking. Law enforcement, especially in the major
cities of the US, was paralysed, either because the extent of
crime and violence was overwhelming or because key
officials and officers were on the pay roll of wealthy gangland
bosses. Violence was a fact of life and, according to anti-
prohibition propaganda, the willingness of all classes of
people to blatantly flaunt the law was providing young
people with poor role models for acceptable adult behaviour.

> '*The young see the law broken at home and upon the
> street. Can we expect them to be lawful? To-day, in any
> speakeasy in the United States you can find boys and
> girls in their teens drinking liquor and this situation has
> become so acute that the mothers of this country feel
> something must be done to protect their children.'*
>
> Pauline Sabin

It was in this climate that the Women's Organization for
National Prohibition Reform (WONPR) was formed in
1929 under the charismatic leadership of **Pauline Sabin.**
She had been a supporter of prohibition but had become
convinced of its failure. By this time, the reality of
prohibition meant that the arguments used by the WCTU
and the ASL no longer had the same power and credibility
as they had in the campaign for the Eighteenth

Amendment. This is not to say that prohibition and temperance were no longer high profile issues. Rather, that the legislation was not effective in achieving the goal of abstinence: people could still obtain alcohol quite easily.

For these reasons, the repeal of prohibition was probably the most controversial issue of the time. The leadership of WONPR was so powerful and well-organised that it could quickly capitalise on women's disillusionment with prohibition to add weight to the drive for repeal of the amendment. By 1931, it had 1.5 million members nationwide – the biggest organisation pressing for repeal. In spite of this, Sabine and other high profile women in the repeal campaign were frequently subjected to abuse from women who continued to believe in prohibition. The fact that the leadership of WONPR presented an image of wealth and privilege did not go unnoticed by those women opposing repeal.

> 'No one could see your meetings...and not be impressed with the number of women of wealth present...Are we not right in saying that it is not the protected woman of wealth but the women who toil who will suffer should the old conditions return – the wives of labouring men, the mothers of little children.

> Extract from a letter from a supporter of prohibition to Pauline Sabin.

Why was WONPR successful in achieving its goal?

Firstly, WONPR's underpinning rationale for its campaign was the protection of home and family as opposed to the protection of personal freedom. It made much of the argument that prohibition had promoted, rather than eliminated, excessive drinking. The task of amassing support from women who had already passionately supported prohibition on the basis of strong moral principles, was a challenging one. The u-turn was achieved by convincing arguments that prohibition had demonstrably failed to achieve its goals and that the only true path to home protection was that of temperance. The home protection argument was a highly emotive one in male dominated political circles.

Secondly, its leadership and core membership was upper class and highly organised at state and national levels. By the late 1920s, the WCTU had become increasingly a working-class organisation and, as a result, no longer had the same capacity or opportunity to influence policy. On the other hand, Sabin and the core membership of WONPR were upper class and well connected. Their husbands were already members of the all-male **Association Against the Prohibition Amendment (AAPA)** formed in 1918.

Thirdly, WONPR very effectively harnessed the same arguments and methods used by the WCTU and the ASL to secure prohibition, to bring about its repeal. WONPR relentlessly lobbied and pressured congressmen. They held rallies and conducted an intensive campaign of home visits to gain support. National leaders supported more hard-to-win areas of the country where support for prohibition was especially strong – the southern states, for example. Unlike the WCTU, WONPR did not claim any strongly religious affiliation or philosophy. This broadened its appeal. In spite of the obvious political connections of the leaders, WONPR promoted itself as a non-partisan organisation and, consequently, sought and gained allies in the ranks of Republicans and Democrats.

Whilst it cannot be argued that women were necessarily pushing against an open door over the repeal issue, it must be said that doubts about the value of the prohibition legislation were increasing, especially amongst male politicians. In addition to the social evils that it created, a powerful argument was the significant loss of tax revenue as a result of the liquor ban. In the period of the Great Depression of the 1930s, as Roosevelt struggled to restore the shattered US economy and address unprecedented levels of unemployment, the potential income from the tax on liquor and the job opportunities that would accompany its production were attractive possibilities. Furthermore, the case for the repeal of the Eighteenth Amendment was supported by a number of high profile public figures,

KEY TERMS

The Association Against the Prohibition Amendment (AAPA) was formed to oppose the passage of the prohibition amendment. Its membership was largely made up of wealthy businessmen and bankers who had close associations with the breweries. This led them to be treated with some degree of suspicion by others involved in the anti-prohibition movement.

including powerful business interests. All of these factors clearly helped WONPR's cause by creating the climate for repeal. The Twenty-first Amendment ending prohibition finally became part of the US Constitution on 5 December 1933. No-one doubted that the female campaign had been decisive in bringing this about.

What did the campaigns for prohibition and then its repeal achieve for women in the US?

- The campaign for prohibition and then for its repeal established very clearly that women were a force to be reckoned with in bringing about change when they were well-led, highly organised and fighting for such an emotionally charged cause as the protection of home and family. It is important, however, to recognise the exceptional nature of prohibition and its power to harness mass female support. It is probably fair to argue that few other issues, at this time, were comparable.
- The divisions that existed between women who remained faithful to the WCTU cause and those who came to support the WONPR exemplify differences that continued to impede the formation of a united women's movement in the twentieth century, the campaign for the Equal Rights Amendment being a good example.
- The WCTU and the WONPR did nothing to further the cause of rights for women or to improve the position of working-class and poor women, who had been the focus of their pro- and anti-prohibition propaganda.
- The prohibition campaigns clearly show that protection of the home continued to be the most powerful cause and the one that most concerned the mass of American women.

CONCLUSION

Overall, the extension of women's civil rights made little discernible progress during this period. To some extent, this was the outcome of external pressures, not least the resistance of male employers and politicians to change, but also the lack of support from the mass of American women for demands for equality. In fact, what emerges clearly in this period is the continuance of the centrality of home and family and, most importantly, the compulsion to protect it at all costs. This is well demonstrated in the campaign for prohibition laws and, subsequently, for their repeal. This campaign is also significant since it demonstrates that women, when acting collaboratively and exerting their right to protest, presented a forceful pressure group that could not be ignored. It also serves to illustrate the deep divisions in the perception amongst women themselves of their position in society and in their aspirations. This continued to thwart the formation of a really powerful women's movement.

The acquisition of the vote meant little to the mass of American women partly because there was, as yet, no real recognition of its potential to change the status quo for women. This was not helped by those very few women who did enter state or federal politics but failed to use their positions to promote women's issues. Moreover, since married women tended to vote in the same way as their husbands, there was no compulsion on male politicians to win the female vote by addressing women's issues. Feminists pursuing women's rights were a minority and, having achieved the vote, even they subsequently had divided priorities.

Whilst the involvement of the USA in the First World War clearly created unprecedented opportunities for women in the workplace, as did the post-war boom of the 1920s, the treatment of women workers at the end of the war and during the Depression clearly demonstrates that the expansion of opportunities for women remained tenuous and did not represent a fundamental change of attitude either of male employers or of a sizeable proportion of women themselves.

QUESTIONS TO CONSIDER

1. What were the most significant factors limiting the opportunities for women in the period between the wars?

2. Was the period from 1915 until 1940 one of continuity or change in the extension of rights for women?

3. What can be learned from the involvement of women in the prohibition campaign and that for its repeal?

CHAPTER 16

1941–69 A challenge to the 'cult of true womanhood'?

Hypothesis:

- The combination of socio-economic change and the 'new' feminism represent a turning point in the pursuit of rights and opportunities for women.

Introduction

The concept of 'separate spheres', reinforced by the media in the post war years, remained a powerful barrier to significant change for women and polarised opinion amongst American women about their roles. The contribution made by women to the war effort did nothing to encourage recognition of the right of married women to go out to work. However, the 'new feminism' and the civil rights movement were becoming important agents of change for women by the 1960s. By 1969, women had achieved important rights and women's issues were influencing politicians and their policies.

WOMEN AND WORK 1941–69

The Second World War – change or continuity for women?

Again, as in 1915, the war made huge demands on manufacturing industry that could not be met entirely by the male workforce. When the men went to fight, women responded to the call to replace them in the workplace. Consequently, they entered every conceivable area of work. By 1945, there were five million more working women than in 1940. Many of these were married women. Unlike the First World War, 350,000 women joined the armed forces. Yet, even in these circumstances, the huge contribution of women to the war effort was represented by the media as a short-term extension of their domestic role. One newspaper article wrote of the, '...*deep satisfaction which a woman of today knows who has made a rubber boat which may save the life of her aviator husband or helped fashion a bullet which may avenge her son.*' Moreover,

Female engineer working on an aeroplane during the Second World War.

only a small proportion of people sampled in an opinion poll during the war agreed with the idea of women working.

Nevertheless, in contrast to the situation in 1919, by 1945 there was evidence that women's attitude to work was changing. Those women who had served in the armed forces had broadened their horizons. Whereas the majority of married women on the home front had been happy to return to their domestic roles in 1919, after 1945 around 75 per cent wanted to remain in paid employment. In particular, married women had shown during the war years that they could take care of their homes and children as well as work. This was in spite of the fact that federal grants for day care centres for working mothers in the armaments industry, awarded under the Lanham Act, were gradually withdrawn between 1942 and 1946 until only three states continued to fund child care.

In the immediate aftermath of the war, large numbers of women were laid off to make way for the returning soldiers. This was a clear indication that the concept of 'separate spheres' had certainly not been eradicated. Indeed, in the post-war years, the media played an important part in reinforcing the long-held belief that a 'woman's place' was very much in the home:

- Countless magazine articles elevated the ideal American family and portrayed domesticity as the ultimate and most rewarding role for American women. Beauty, cooking, homes and gardens were the common themes. It was a popular image.
- Dr Benjamin Spock published his famous, *Common Sense Book of Baby and Child Care* in 1946, emphasising the important role of mothers in the home. It became the bible for child-rearing parents and a best seller – over 23 million copies were sold over the next thirty years.
- Any sign of instability in the family was blamed by the media on married women trying to fulfil the dual role of wife and mother with that of employee. The divorce rate rose significantly to 18.2 per cent in 1946 (from 10.2 per cent in 1940). When the rate of juvenile delinquency also began to rise, women were accused of deserting their homes and abdicating their responsibilities. Both men and women who valued the traditional image of home and family were alarmed by these trends. This concern was also reflected in the attitudes of many male politicians in both political parties.

For unmarried women, job opportunities in the **service economy** continued to expand. Many of these jobs were now open to African American and, increasingly, to more immigrant young women, who were entering the US in increasing numbers after 1945.

Was there an expansion of opportunities for women in the professions?

The war may have offered opportunities for work but, in its aftermath, opportunities for women to enter professional occupations were reduced. The G.I. Bill of Rights, as it was popularly known (its actual title was the Servicemen's Readjustment Act 1944), established the right of ex-servicemen to access higher education and provided funding to enable this to happen. The result was a massive increase in the numbers of men entering colleges and universities after the war. In the mid-forties, for example, the normal annual enrolment of 4,500 students at the University of Indiana, was massively increased to over 10,300. This incredible growth was replicated across the US as universities and colleges expanded and new ones were established. Although more women were entering higher education, the number of men was increasing at a much faster rate as a result of the generous grants provided for them by the federal government. This had a knock-on effect on admission to professional positions. Women made very little headway in the post-war years but the number of men in these occupations increased by 40 per cent. Even social work, which had traditionally been the preserve of middle-class women, was taken over by male university students and graduates undertaking research into social issues, sometimes to inform government policy.

The 1960s – a new age for women in the workplace

By 1960, there were twice as many **working women** as in 1940. For the most part, they worked in relatively low prestige jobs for wages that remained significantly lower than those of men in similar occupations. What accounts for this increase? Certainly it cannot be simply explained in terms of an increase in the number of working mothers forced into the workplace though extreme poverty. Such women had long been forced to work to sustain their families.

Closer examination of female employment records for the early 1960s indicates a changing pattern of female employment:

- An **increase in the number of well-educated wives entering the workforce** from households with a comfortable income provided by the male breadwinner.
- Indications that the idea of a second income was becoming acceptable. This enabled better-off families to

Working women in 1960
40 per cent of all women over 16 years were working and 30 per cent of women workers were married. The number of working mothers had risen from 1.5 million in 1940 to 6.6 million by 1960.

Increase in the number of well-educated wives entering the workforce
By 1964, 42 per cent of married women in the workplace were from households where the male income was in the $7,000 – $10,000 bracket. 37 per cent of women came from homes where male earnings were below $3,000 per annum.

enjoy the good things of life in an increasingly consumer orientated society or to be able to purchase a more comfortable, suburban home.

- The tendency for women over the age of 35 years to go out to work when children were growing up and their maternal role was contracting.

Increased employment opportunities for women?

The enormous increase in the number of working women must also be seen in the context of economic change in the USA. During the 1950s, the service industry overtook manufacturing in generating the majority of the national income. Such an economy became virtually dependent on female labour, in part because it was cheaper and consequently expanded profit margins.

The successful launch of the Russian *Sputnik* in October 1957, followed by *Sputnik II* in November of that year marked the beginning of the 'Space Race'. The US recognised the need to harness all its talents and abilities to be ahead of the game – female as well as male. This resulted in a further expansion and reappraisal of educational provision, particularly in universities. Although the impact of this may not appear statistically significant in terms of women in higher paid, highly technical occupations in comparison with men, it did mark recognition of what women could offer and resulted in the creation of greater opportunities in higher education, which were to the advantage of increasing numbers of young women.

Did the expansion of opportunities for married women indicate a waning of traditional attitudes and values?

Throughout the 1950s and early sixties, there is no evidence to suggest that women were putting work or a career before their potential or actual roles as wives and mothers. Young middle-class girls still went to college in the hope and expectation of finding an eligible husband. In the uncertain days of the **Cold War**, Americans **married younger and had more children**. What is clear is a change of attitude, at least within the better off American families irrespective of their ethnic origins. By the late 1960s, the

The **Cold War** describes the period between 1945 and the late 1980s when relations between the USSR and its allies and the USA and its allies were hostile. It engendered an atmosphere of suspicion and fear, the latter generated by the amassing of nuclear arms by both sides with the capacity to destroy the world.

Married younger and had more children In 1950 the average number of children was 3.09; in 1957 it was 3.77, falling to 3.65 children per family in 1960. Marriage rates in the 1950s reached an all time high. The age of young people marrying in 1950 was at its lowest (median age for men was 22.8 years; median age for women was 20.3 years).

opportunities that a second income provided for the family to enjoy a better lifestyle and enriched leisure time, outweighed any earlier concept of the necessity for the male to be seen to provide. This resulted in a greater merging of the male and female roles and responsibilities in the home. It was not, however, a trend that was replicated in the homes of lower-income families where the inability of the male breadwinner to provide for the family continued to be seen as failure.

Surveys of the children in better-off families with working mothers contradicted the assertions of their critics. Such children appeared more confident, independent and self-assured. Daughters of working mothers in the 1950s and 60s were more likely to name their mothers as the person they admired the most, unlike girls whose mothers stayed at home. More importantly, they grew up with higher expectations for themselves, intending to be well-educated and to establish themselves in a career before considering marriage. The impact of this became clear in the 1970s when the number of single women in the workforce increased. There was, by this time, a growing tendency for middle-class and some working-class women to marry later and produce fewer children. In this respect, the 1960s may be seen as a turning point in the position and role of women in American society.

ACTIVISTS, REFORMERS AND CAMPAIGNERS 1941–69

In January 1968, a group of young feminists demonstrated their rejection of traditional womanhood in a ceremony of sorts in the national military cemetery at Arlington, Virginia. This involved the ritual burying of what they saw to be the weak, submissive and dependent woman, so long admired. The 'ceremony' followed a march on Congress to demonstrate against the war in Vietnam (see pages 81–82). This may be seen as a defiant manifestation of the 'new' feminism that had been growing during the late 1950s and early 1960s.

> '...we were attempting to organise ourselves on the basis of power...the so-called power of wives and mothers.

KEY CONCEPTS

Opportunities that a second income provided
A survey in Illinois in the late 1960s showed that middle-class families with a second wage spent 45 per cent more on gifts and recreation, 95 per cent more on restaurant meals and 25 per cent more on household goods than those that relied only on the paternal income.

That this power is only a substitute for power, that it really amounts to nothing politically, is the reason why all of us attending this funeral must bury traditional womanhood tonight. We must bury her in Arlington Cemetery...for in Arlington Cemetery, our national monument to war, alongside Traditional Manhood, is her natural resting place.'

Extract from the 'funeral' oration given at the 'Burial of True Womanhood' in Arlington cemetery, January 1968

What were the origins of the 'new' feminism?

During the 1950s and early 1960s, there was an emerging group of women who were clearly focused on the pursuit of their rights and prepared to challenge robustly the accepted status of women in American society. Undoubtedly, this new wave of more aggressive activism might be seen to have been inspired by what might be described as the spirit of the age. The campaign for black civil rights was gaining momentum and national attention, as well as providing inspiration for other groups who believed that they too suffered from prejudice and discrimination. The reaction to the war in Vietnam after 1964 also fuelled the inclination to protest at home.

Its emergence was also a response to the failure of government to respond positively to the demands for equal rights and particularly for equal pay that had been the quest of earlier feminist campaigners following the successful acquisition of the vote for women back in the 1920s. In fact, in the 1950s, politicians had no incentive to respond to these demands for equality. They had no reason to court the female vote. It presented no great threat to their political positions since women were not united in pursuit of specifically female goals and, therefore, did not vote 'en bloc'.

To some extent, therefore, the 'new' feminism may well have been born out of disillusionment with the achievements of the 'old'. This was exacerbated when the policies of **President Kennedy** (1961–63) failed to deliver what they at first promised. Kennedy was the first President to appear to consider seriously the status of women in the

KEY PEOPLE

President John F. Kennedy (1917–63) was elected a Congressman in 1945 and a Senator in 1952. In 1961 he became President of the USA, the youngest ever elected. Great reforms were anticipated when he talked of a 'New Frontier'. He was slow to take up the cause of civil rights, but became determined to introduce a Civil Rights Bill early in 1963 after the troubles on the Freedom Rides and the protests in Birmingham, Alabama. He was prevented from seeing the final result by his assassination in Dallas, Texas, on 22 November 1963.

USA after he was elected in 1961. This encouraged activists. But when the President's Commission on the Status of Women reported in 1963, the message it gave out was a mixed one. On the one hand, the resulting Equal Pay Act embodied the principle of equal pay for women. On the other hand, the commission also promoted special training for young women for marriage and motherhood. The message was clear – women were first and foremost wives and mothers. This was to some extent further emphasised by Kennedy's refusal to respond to the pressure from Margaret Sanger (see page 241) to recognise the need for the provision of birth control to be the responsibility of government.

Further disappointment followed. Feminist groups had been active in the black civil rights movement and been inspired by it. The Civil Rights Act of 1964 (see pages 74–75) prohibited discrimination on the basis of gender but the **Equal Employment Opportunities Commission,** set up to enforce its terms, failed to satisfy sufficiently the demands of feminists for equality. As a result, radical feminists (for the most part young, educated women) began to campaign more forcefully for women's rights.

What was the 'new' feminism and how did it differ from earlier feminist activity?

One of the most notable characteristics of the emerging 'new' feminism in the 1960s was its total rejection of the protection of home and family as its raison'd'être' for action. It was more aggressive in the methods it used and, in the closing decades of the century, its demands were radical, controversial and became inextricably bound up with national politics and policy.

To some extent, this radical reaction may have been inspired by the plethora of books and propaganda that emerged on the subject of women's liberation from the 'separate sphere' in the 1960s. One of the most influential feminist writers of the early 1960s was **Betty Friedan.** In her book, *The Feminine Mystique* (1963), she argued that married women were yearning to escape from their *'comfortable concentration camps'* (i.e. their suburban homes) in order to discover their own identities. She urged them to

KEY TERMS

Equal Employment Opportunities Commission is a federal agency with the responsibility of ensuring that the terms of the 1964 Civil Rights Act and the Equal Pay Act are followed, and to deal with complaints about the failure of employers to observe these. The Equal Pay Act, in particular, stated that there should be no discrimination in the pay of men and women in situations where they are undertaking the same work.

KEY PEOPLE

Betty Friedan (1921–2006) was born to Jewish parents and campaigned against the discrimination and injustice experienced by Jews. Following her successful university studies she became a journalist for left wing and union newspapers. A survey carried out in 1957 amongst her fellow college graduates suggested that she was not alone in her frustrations with domesticity. From 1966 until 1970, she was president of NOW. Amongst her many extreme views, she showed a distaste for lesbianism and was anxious to protect feminism from being tainted with its association. Following her death in 2006, she was described as one of the most influential feminists of the twentieth century. *'She changed the course of history almost single-handedly. It took a driven, super aggressive, egocentric, almost lunatic dynamo to rock the world the way she did.'*

Carl Friedan (Betty's husband) in the *New York Post*, 5 July 2006

adopt a '*new life plan*', playing a full role in the public sector. The book challenged existing social attitudes to women and was successful, amongst mainly middle-class women, in preparing the way for ideological change about their position in society. Nevertheless, Freidan's influence is recognised to have been pivotal in instigating the 'new' feminist movement. There was clearly a sufficiently significant critical mass of women who were inspired by the more extreme feminist arguments of Friedan and others to support the movement.

In 1966 Betty Friedan and other activists who had previously supported the civil rights movement, formed the National Organization for Women (NOW) to press for equality using all the available means of protest – lobbying members of the US Senate, filing lawsuits against discrimination and generally seeking to gain the support of public opinion. Involvement in civil rights protests and in the anti-Vietnam War campaigns gave women increasing confidence in their ability to protest effectively. A new word – 'sexism' – entered their vocabulary, descriptive of another aspect of discrimination similar to that of racism.

Surprisingly, perhaps, feminists were slow to accept the emergence, in the late 1960s, of the contraceptive pill, given its potential for advancing the cause of women's right to choose their number of children. Their opposition, however, was not founded in a distaste for the concept but was rather based in concern for the risks, which some critics in the medical profession claimed, to the health of women. They did, however, act as a pressure group to bring about more research and modifications to the product that was released in the late 1960s.

By 1968, NOW had became more aggressive and passionate in pursuit of its objectives – undoubtedly a reflection of Friedan's own personality and style. Its members extended their protest to publicly throwing away their high-heeled shoes, bras and curlers. But it was its action to press for the right of women to abortion that resulted in a wholesale loss of support (see Chapter 17). In 1969, Friedan was a co-founder of the National

Organization for the Repeal of the Abortion Laws (NARAL). As this new wave of feminism became increasingly radical in its demands for the rights of women, the divisions between these feminists and those women upholding traditional values became deeper. As a result, anti-feminism became a potent force which, by the 1970s, was also commanding political support.

WOMEN AND POLITICS 1941–69

It can be argued that, in this period, the influence of women on the political scene diminished and that the apparent gains of the New Deal period were lost or eroded. Although women gained certain rights from the passage of the Civil Rights Act of 1964, this was not enacted exclusively in response to the demands of the female, equal rights lobby and many of these were dissatisfied with the outcome. It is fair to say that, in the post-war period, there was little sympathy in political circles for distinctly female issues. Men generally, and those in politics particularly, opposed the demand for the Equal Rights Amendment. The number of women members of Congress increased very slowly so that by 1969 there were only eleven and not all of these actively promoted women's rights. Women could not, therefore, rely on 'inside' support.

Moreover, the traditional area where women had once been in a position to influence policy (social reform to address poverty) was no longer exclusively theirs. The Depression of the early 1930s and the need to find solutions to social problems had engaged the minds of mainly male researchers and academics in universities. By 1940 an increasing number of men were becoming social workers, displacing women who had previously dominated this area of activity. This tendency increased in the post-war years as education reforms favoured returning soldiers and the numbers of men in higher education increased quicker than the number of women. The introduction of social insurance as the answer to problems of poverty caused by unemployment, poor health or old age was welcomed. Furthermore, as the economy became more robust and unemployment significantly reduced, the opportunities for female pressure groups to exert influence on policy became virtually non-existent.

The emergence of the new feminist movement and the extreme nature of some of its demands would change this situation in the closing decades of the twentieth century and bring distinctly women's issues into the centre of the political arena.

CONCLUSION

It would be inaccurate to say that little had been achieved by the end of the decade. Pressure for equal rights, particularly in jobs and pay, did have the support of increasing numbers of women. Many gained inspiration and confidence for mounting their own campaign from their involvement in civil rights protest and in opposition to the war in Vietnam.

In August 1970, for example, a Women's Strike for Equality held to mark the fiftieth anniversary of women's suffrage, brought thousands of women onto Fifth Avenue, New York. Moreover, the march brought together radical and more moderate feminists and attracted full national media coverage from both television and newspapers. They demanded not only the right to equal opportunities in employment but also the right to safe, legal abortions.

The emergence of a more radical and aggressive feminist movement, openly attacking the traditional role of women and the concept of the 'separate sphere', might well be seen as an erosion of traditional values. However, the fact that there remained a significant body of female opinion strongly supportive of home and family and that political policy still protected this concept would indicate its continuing importance. A survey in 1968 indicated that 65 per cent of girls aged 15–19 years, wanted to be housewives by the age of 35 years.

By 1969, some indications of a movement towards a more equal status were evident:

- Single and married women were able to obtain credit in their own name.
- Advertised jobs were no longer under 'Male' and 'Female' headings.
- The provision of federal funding provided an incentive to large business corporations to adopt equal rates of pay and to avoid discrimination when employing workers.

However, the numbers of women entering highly paid, professional occupations increased only slowly. The majority of female workers (especially married women) were content to work in lower prestige, service occupations if these provided them with a reasonably comfortable lifestyle. In any case, there was little support from male workers to advance the cause of equality in the workplace, although this was beginning to change after the mid-1960s. Women were still dependent on male politicians for whatever changes were introduced. In 1969, there were still only eleven women in national politics. Women, therefore had the vote, but no powerful political voice. Very little progress had been made to eradicate poverty, a condition that deeply affected the lives of thousands of American women irrespective of ethnicity.

QUESTIONS TO CONSIDER

1. The two world wars can be seen as turning points in the expansion of opportunities for American women. Was one more significant than the other in bringing about changes in the position of women?

2. Identify the evidence that you would provide to argue that each of the following were agents of change that advanced the cause of equality and opportunity for women:

   - The Second World War
   - Economic change
   - The 'new' feminism
   - The civil rights movement.

   - Compare the relative importance of these agents of change in the period from 1945 until 1969.

3. How accurate is the hypothesis at the beginning of this chapter?

4. Would you agree that the rate of change in the position of women accelerated in the period from 1940 until 1969?

CHAPTER 17

1969–92 A triumph for radical feminism?

Hypothesis:

* Radical feminism failed to unite American women in the further pursuit of their rights.

Introduction

In the closing decades of the twentieth century, feminism and its antithesis, anti-feminism, assumed unprecedented importance, particularly in the political sphere. Women's rights had a higher profile in the policies of the Democratic and the Republican parties largely as a result of the issue of abortion. This caused deep divisions, not only between politicians but also between women themselves. The latter proved to be the biggest obstacle to the acquisition of rights for all American women. Ultimately, women were more effective in securing their rights in the social and occupational spheres than in politics. It can be argued that the real gains that were made by 1992 owed more to civil rights legislation than to feminist pressure groups.

WOMEN AND WORK 1969–92

Was gender discrimination eliminated by equal opportunities legislation?

By the early 1970s, laws against gender discrimination and stereotyping did open up some areas of work to women that had previously been reserved exclusively for men and vice-versa. Women could now become telephone engineers; men could become telephone operators. Women now had the opportunity to join the police force and fire services or to become engineers and construction workers; men could become nurses. More courses in higher education were made available for women, partly as a result of the ending of exclusively male colleges. Between 1970 and 1980 gender segregation in employment had decreased by 10 per cent. Whilst this appears a negligible amount, it was, nevertheless, an unprecedented rate of change taking the twentieth century as a whole. It is an indication, however,

NOW law suit An example of this was when in 1979, NOW successfully pursued the case of a female employee in the Iowa City fire brigade when the fire chief refused her permission to feed her baby at work during her time off. The city authorities also threatened her with disciplinary action if she breastfed her baby in the fire station.

that discrimination and inequality were by no means eliminated. Even where equal opportunities existed, they were not accompanied by equal pay for the same work. Not surprisingly, therefore, men were less willing to take those jobs which were previously the preserve of women.

Irrespective of the equal opportunities legislation, **NOW** and other women's groups found it necessary to engage in **law suits** to force employers to implement the law appropriately. Particularly sensitive areas were those around pregnancy and child care, in situations where women were now working in traditionally male jobs. Increasingly, working women themselves became organised and began to pursue their rights in the workplace through trade union activity (see Chapter 9).

Nevertheless, discrimination in the kind of opportunities available to women did continue. By 1970, women made-up 42.8 per cent of the total workforce and 47 per cent of all women had a job. Moreover, by this point in time, married women in the workforce outnumbered single ones. By 1989, 73.2 per cent of married women with children aged between 6 and 17 years were working outside the home. A large proportion of these were well-educated and middle class. In spite of this, very few women entered skilled work or the professions. During the 1970s, only 4.8 per cent of America's three million managers and executives were women. The majority remained in low prestige jobs – clerical or service occupations. This is explained to some extent by the fact that in the 1970s and 1980s, the advantages that women might have gained from the expansion of opportunities for them in higher education, especially those who might have been pursuing higher degrees in business and management, had yet to impact in high prestige occupations. It was suggested that there existed a 'glass ceiling' – an invisible barrier that prevented women (and also ethnic minorities) from reaching the top jobs in big companies irrespective of equal opportunity legislation. However, by the mid-1990s there is evidence that the picture was improving, particularly for middle-class, white American women but also for the better off African-American, Native-American and Japanese-American woman. By this time, the wage gap had virtually closed for young, educated women, who were now earning approximately 98 per cent of men's rates of pay. Yet class divisions continued amongst white and ethnic minority women and these divisions remained characterised by poverty as well as employment opportunity.

In addition to issues of inequality in job opportunities and rates of pay, the refusal of the federal government to legislate in favour of paid maternity leave and the lack of child-care facilities, remained obstacles for married women in the workforce. By the mid-1980s, only five states provided partially paid maternity leave. Women who were the sole breadwinners in the family were particularly hard hit by wage discrimination. They faced poverty as a result of low wages that meant they were unable to afford private child care and struggled to support their families on meagre earnings. This particularly, though not exclusively, affected African American women who, by the 1960s, accounted for the largest proportion of the marked increase in the number of unmarried mothers – 73,000 rising to one million by 1980 and 2.9 million by 1990.

By 1992, there was still no federal law requiring employers to provide paid maternity leave in spite of pressure from the female lobby. The substantial increase in the number of working women, together with the discrimination they faced in work opportunities and unequal pay, help to explain why feminist organisations in the 1970s and 1980s gained so much grass roots support from some, though by no means all, working women.

To some extent, the self-awareness, confidence and assurance that had emanated from the feminist movement had begun to have some impact for educated women by the mid 1990s. Women were emerging from universities and colleges with qualifications that were at least as good as and often exceeded those of men. It is noteworthy that, whilst women may have been discriminated in business enterprises and public services, an increasing number of women were making their own way in the business world as a result of their own enterprise. By 1996, statistical surveys indicated that American women owned 7.7 million businesses employing around 15.5 million people and

A pro-abortion rally.

generating many millions of dollars. An estimated 3.5 million women owned home-based businesses and employed several million workers both full and part time. Many of these women had also had homes and families.

ACTIVISTS, REFORMERS AND CAMPAIGNERS 1969–92

What was the impact on American society of radical feminism?

The momentum gained by the feminist movement in the late 1960s continued undiminished into the early 1970s and became more radical in the rights it demanded as well as the methods of protest that it used. However, the proliferation of feminist groups, many with different and sometimes conflicting areas of focus, ensured that feminist campaigns would be fragmented and their achievements, therefore, limited. For example, by the mid-1970s, at the far edge of the spectrum, '**The Feminists**', a group of women in New York, called for the abolition of marriage whilst the **Radicalesbians** claimed that women could only be really liberated through lesbianism and joined other, more extreme members of NOW in demanding abortion rights for women. In 1969, Betty Friedan, as the president of NOW, declared abortion to be '*a woman's civil right*'. This campaign reached a climax in 1973 when the Supreme Court established a woman's right to abortion as a result of its judgement in the case of *Roe* v. *Wade* (see pages 271–75 for further discussion of this case and its significance). Without doubt, this was probably the most significant achievement of radical feminism and also its most controversial.

By the mid-1970s, radical feminism had reached its peak. Pressure for action on women's issues passed to more moderate feminist groups who pursued their goals less aggressively. However, the abortion issue galvanised the opposition of women who maintained traditional values of home and family as well as powerful elements in Church and state. As a result, a recognisable anti-feminist movement emerged to challenge feminist assertions of what constituted women's rights.

The challenge posed by radical feminists to the traditional image of womanhood clearly influenced the thinking of younger women. This was prompted, to some extent, by the media coverage given to meetings and public outpourings of the often extreme views by feminist groups as well as by the writings of leading radical feminists such as Betty Frieden. In January 1972, the first edition of the feminist magazine **'Ms'** was published. Edited by **Gloria Steinem,** it promoted feminist ideals and quickly became popular. By the end of the year, it had a circulation of 200,000 copies. This publication was important in providing a sympathetic balance to the often highly critical and derisory approach of male dominated publications.

Organised campaigns raised awareness amongst women of the inequality and discrimination they experienced in their lives. Popular culture in the 1970s – popular music (for example, **Helen Reddy's** *'I Am Woman')*, films, books, fashions, education and more liberal lifestyle opportunities, led teenage girls to think about their future roles and to reject those characteristics that, it was argued, had traditionally determined femininity and exposed women to exploitation and degradation by men. For example, back in 1968, national news coverage had been attracted by groups of radical feminists from Boston, New York, Detroit, Florida and New Jersey who publicly crowned a sheep at the Miss World competition as a protest against what they saw to be the degradation of women involved in the contest.

Certainly, surveys carried out in the 1970s and 1980s suggest that the attitudes of young women towards the 'separate spheres' were indeed changing although the reasons for this change cannot necessarily be attributed exclusively to the influence of radical feminist propaganda. In 1968, for example, 65 per cent of girls between the ages of 15 and 19 years wanted to be housewives by the time they had reached the age of thirty-five. By 1978, only 25 per cent had these aspirations. Whilst this might be explained in terms of increased opportunities and feminist propaganda that increased awareness of alternatives to marriage and motherhood, a further contributory factor was the availability of the contraceptive Pill. During the

Ms magazine The term 'Ms' first became popular in the early 1970s when it was adopted by women who did not wish their marital status to be known or who retained their maiden names on marriage. *Ms* magazine was first published as an insert in *New York* magazine in 1971. It gained notoriety when it published the names of women who admitted to having had illegal abortions ahead of the *Roe* v. *Wade* decision. Unlike other magazines for women, it did not contain the usual mixture of fashion and recipes but attracted controversy by exposing the extent of rape and the reality of domestic violence by publishing, in 1976, a front page picture of a woman with a bruised face.

Gloria Steinem (1934) Her support for women's rights was influenced by her mother, Ruth, a highly intelligent, well-educated woman, who was forced to give up a successful career in journalism when she married Gloria's father. He divorced her when she became ill. Gloria opposed the view that women should have to choose between a career or marriage and became politically active in the feminist movement in the 1960s.

early 1970s, the Pill became available to all young women (unmarried as well as married) who had reached the 'age of majority', which by this time was 18 years of age. For those who were in a position to take advantage of access to the Pill, it was liberating since, for the first time, it gave women themselves total control over child bearing. Sociologists have argued that it explains the growing tendency for young woman to marry later and to take advantage of educational and career opportunities to an unprecedented extent. At the same time it alarmed those who upheld traditional values surrounding marriage and the home since it appeared to encourage promiscuity.

In 1980, 40 per cent of women in higher education had their sights set on a career compared with just 21 per cent a decade earlier. By 1986, 56 per cent of women in the USA considered themselves to be feminists and the vast majority were beginning to recognise that they had the right to make choices. Increasingly, it became clear that home and family were neither the exclusive nor the only option for American women.

The demise of radical feminism?

By the beginning of the 1970s then, it appeared as though the momentum and attention that the feminist movement had gained had made it well-placed to bring about fundamental changes in American society. In 1970, only 37 per cent of white American women and 60 per cent of African American women supported the efforts of feminists to improve the status of women. By 1985, this had risen to 72 per cent and 78 per cent respectively. However, the fact that many of these fundamental changes did not happen may be attributable to a number of factors,

- So extreme were some of the pronouncements of radical feminists that they invited suspicion, disgust and rejection, not just from those women who, by the mid-1980s, still rejected radical change but also from the male population. In a survey carried out in 1972, 33 per cent of men supported gender equality. By 1990, this had only risen by 7 per cent. As Congress and State legislatures were still male dominated, this was a significant statistic.

- Whilst feminist propaganda may have conveyed the messages to some middle-class women that they wanted to hear, a significant proportion of poor, working-class women, who comprised a sizeable proportion of the population, were of the view that much of what was said bore little resemblance to the reality of their own lives. There was, therefore, no mass support for the feminist position.
- Its potential impact nationally was further weakened by the fact that radical feminist groups, including local branches of NOW, operated predominantly at the grass roots level by responding to local priorities – for example, setting up rape centres, self-defence classes, providing contraception or health centres for women and girls. These priorities were not always NOW's national priorities. This kind of local response, therefore, diluted the potential impact that NOW might have had if it had been able to harness the united support of all the membership across the US.
- By the mid-1970s, some radical feminists were in the process of re-thinking their beliefs, especially about the meaning of equality.
- From the mid-1970s, a plethora of more liberal feminists emerged to pursue their own very specific agendas, often related to social and welfare issues such as child care facilities, discrimination and women's earnings.
- By the mid-1970s, feminist pressure groups were more representative of America's ethnic diversity. These were pursuing objectives very specific to their own situations and therefore divided priorities in the pressure groups. African-American, Mexican-American and Asian-American women, for example, all formed groups to oppose the continuing racial discrimination they suffered in their lives and the economic circumstances that forced so many of their women to live in poverty. In 1977 a National Conference of Women was held in Houston, Texas. The 2,000 delegates of mixed age and ethnicity who attended the conference were focused on the campaign for equality in work and pay.
- For many women, their priorities had already been met by the rulings of the Equal Employment Opportunity Commission in the 1960s and by other legislation

relating to women's rights in the same period (see page 258).

- The highly organised, anti-feminist backlash most seriously undermined what radical feminists were seeking to achieve, together with their failure to establish a foothold in politics. (The latter point will be discussed further below.) American women who clung to traditional values associated with home and family had always opposed those whom they believed devalued the role of mother and homemaker. In the 1970s, anti-feminist organisations opposed those issues which radical feminists pursued most rigorously with equal vigour – the right to legal abortion and the Equal Rights Amendment (ERA).

CASE STUDY: *ROE* V. *WADE* AND THE ABORTION RIGHTS CONTROVERSY 1973

Why was *Roe* v. *Wade* significant in the history of women's rights in the USA?

The decision in the case of *Roe* v. *Wade* was a landmark in the history of the pursuit of women's rights. It was a test case that effectively ensured the establishment of a women's right to a legal abortion during the first six months of pregnancy and, most specifically, her right to make that decision independently. For the traditional defenders of home and family, it struck at the root of what they held most dear. It was almost certainly the most controversial, as well as most significant event, since it was underpinned by arguments relating to a woman's right to control her own body and to make decisions on child bearing. (It is significant that it was not until 1965 that the constitutional right of married couples to use contraception was established by the Supreme Court. This right was extended to unmarried couples in 1972.) Earlier campaigns to legalise abortion had focused on the pain and misery that was caused when women were forced, from desperation, into having an illegal, 'back street' abortion. By the early 1970s, abortion had become the burning issue in establishing the extent of women's rights, in this case the right of choice.

Organisations such as the New Women Lawyers, the National Abortion Action Coalition and the Women's Health and Abortion Project filed numerous lawsuits in individual cases. The fundamental argument was that women who had unwanted pregnancies or became pregnant as a result of rape were discriminated against since they were forced by the law to share their bodies with another living organism against their will. Women lawyers also argued that, '*despite the fact that both men and women are responsible for any pregnancy, it is the woman who bears the disproportionate share...of the burden*'. There were, therefore, issues of equality as well as of discrimination. Moreover, there were no protective rights for working women who most commonly faced dismissal when they became pregnant and were denied career opportunities. Men were not threatened in the same way.

The case

The Supreme Court ruling in the case of *Roe* v. *Wade* was delivered in 1973. Until this point in time, it had been the responsibility of the state legislatures to rule on the legal status of abortion. In the majority of the states, abortion was illegal except in the case where the life of the mother was threatened. These laws had been passed in the nineteenth century and remained on the statute books. In 1970, Norma McCorvey, a poor, single, working-class woman from Dallas, Texas, sued the Dallas County District Attorney, Henry Wade, under the name of Jane Roe, for the right to have an abortion. Although her life was not in danger, she argued that she did not want to bring another child into the world that she could not afford to raise.

Roe's lawyers – **Sarah Weddington** and **Linda Coffee** – argued that the abortion laws in Texas violated her rights under the Constitution of the USA. The judges in the case decided in her favour but only as a one-off case. This did not satisfy Roe's legal team who had wanted this to be a test case that would ensure that District Attorney Wade could not prosecute any other women in Texas who wanted a legal abortion and that funding would be made available to poor women seeking an abortion. In fact, the court would only rule on this specific case. As a result, Roe's legal team appealed to the Supreme Court.

Justice Harry Blackmun (1908–99) His decision in the case of *Roe v. Wade* established the constitutional right to abortion in the USA. In spite of the death threats that followed the decision, he remained committed to abortion rights as essential to women's equality.

The right to privacy The Supreme Court's role is to ensure that the terms of the Constitution and its Amendments are properly interpreted to safeguard the freedom of the individual. It was argued that the right of a woman to make decisions on child-bearing was encompassed by the right to privacy and freedom within the Fourteenth Amendment.

The Supreme Court first heard the case in 1971. It finally decided in Roe's favour in January 1973. The judgement was arrived at by **Justice Harry Blackmun** after due consideration of the sensitive issues surrounding abortion. His decision was that Roe's **right to privacy** was protected by the terms of the Fourteenth Amendment and that this encompassed a woman's decision to have an abortion. This was in spite of urgent appeals that the right of the unborn child should also be considered in reaching the decision.

Reaction to the *Roe* v. *Wade* ruling

The repercussions of the ruling of the Supreme Court in 1973 were significant and enduring. Abortion became a huge and divisive issue and the *Roe* decision in particular unleashed an unending stream of criticism, both in terms of its legality as well as its morality. It was challenged by state legislatures which refused to implement the ruling, leading to a plethora of appeals to the Supreme Court in the ensuing years against state imposed restrictions on the availability of abortion. Although it did initially strike down many of the decisions made by state authorities, the Court responded in the ensuing years by granting states the right to impose some restrictions on the availability of abortion. These typically related to the provision of counselling as an essential pre-requisite, the termination of pregnancy for teenage girls and the determination of where the procedure should take place. The provision of funding for abortions was a recurring source of controversy and became the subject of review in 1976, after which Congress passed the Hyde Amendment banning the use of federal funding for abortion.

But for the supporters of women's rights and those who had long campaigned for the legalisation of abortion, *Roe* was a triumph. The National Abortion Rights Action League came into being after the *Roe* decision, to support the rights it recognised. On the other hand, staunch opposition came from many quarters. Religious leaders in the Catholic Church condemned the decision and decreed that abortions would not be performed in Catholic hospitals or by Catholic doctors. Evangelical Protestant churches and some Jewish groups also opposed *Roe*. The only acceptable justification for abortion for these groups remained the threat to the life of the mother.

As suggested earlier, abortion rights galvanised anti-feminists into organised opposition under the leadership of **Phyllis Schlafly**. To them, women who presented the kind of arguments that were used to support abortion rejected their natural instincts and were not 'real' women. Attacks on abortion clinics and, at the most extreme, incidents involving violence towards, and even the murder of, doctors who performed abortions were manifestations of the depth of opposition from some sectors of the public. A number of pro-life organisations came into being, most notably the **National Right to Life Committee.** Pro-life campaigners focused on the point at which life begins, believing that this is at conception. Others who opposed abortion but were prepared to compromise, focused attention on the time frame in which termination should take place, believing that after six months the unborn child is a living being. This remains a hotly debated issue.

The political implications of *Roe* v. *Wade*

It was inevitable that such a controversial and emotive subject as abortion would become centre stage in the political arena. It was also ensured by the changing voting patterns of female voters. An important outcome of the feminist movement was the growing political awareness amongst the critical mass of women, which contrasted sharply with the apathy displayed by many women voters around the middle of the century. The 1970s showed a marked upturn in the number of women voting in state elections as well as those for Congress. Politicians, anxious to win the female vote, had to give some recognition to female issues. Clearly, this in itself presented a dilemma, since women themselves were significantly divided on the subject of abortion.

Support and opposition to abortion became polarised between the two main political factions although, in terms of privately held views on abortion, it cut across party lines. In terms of public policy, the Republicans strongly opposed abortion. In 1976 and again in 1980, they called for a Constitutional amendment to ban abortion. Whilst President Nixon (1969–74) failed to express a view, his Republican successors – Ronald Reagan (1981–89) and George H.W. Bush Snr. (1989–93) – were strongly

KEY PEOPLE

Phyllis Schlafly (b. 1924)
A Republican supporter, born in 1924 in St Louis, Missouri. In the 1960s she gained a reputation as a political activist. She criticised the US government's arms' control agreements with the Soviet Union during the 1960s and wrote and lectured on national defence. In the 1970s she gained a reputation for her anti-feminist campaigns. Her critics noted that it was ironical that this woman, who had a demanding career as well as a husband, home and family, should have so vehemently advocated the fulfilment of being a full-time wife and mother. She was, however, a Roman Catholic by religion which has influenced her attitude to home life and abortion in particular.

KEY TERMS

The National Right to Life Committee was established in 1973 in response to the *Roe* decision. Its fundamental purpose is to secure the right of the unborn child to be protected by the Constitution. It is a non-sectarian organisation. Its Board has representatives from all of the 50 states.

opposed. The gender gap that emerged in voting patterns – 47 per cent of women voted for Reagan in 1981 and 55 per cent of men – caused concern for some Republicans that the party was taking too hard a line. Reagan and Bush attempted to deal with the pro-abortion responses to cases brought before the Supreme Court by appointing judges known to be anti-abortionists. Yet, in spite of five such appointments across the two presidencies, *Roe* remained largely intact. However, Republicans generally tended to focus on the female middle-class voters who were largely anti-feminist anyway.

In spite of numerous challenges and with some modifications, the *Roe* v. *Wade* judgement has remained in place. Anti-abortion demonstrations are still held annually to mark its anniversary. Abortion remains one of the most contentious issues facing American society in the twenty-first century. The abortion issue galvanised the opposition of women who maintained traditional values of home and family, as well as powerful elements in Church and state.

ANTI-FEMINISM AND THE ATTACK ON THE EQUAL RIGHTS AMENDMENT

As suggested earlier, the action on abortion produced a massive, anti-feminist backlash from those women who supported traditional values. Radical feminism, linked to the legalisation of abortion, drove many women who continued to believe passionately in the 'separate sphere', to join or form anti-feminist protest groups. The impact of anti-feminism on the national scene can be attributed to the ability, drive and conviction of Phyllis Schlafly, who organised and led the anti-feminist reaction. She was able to use skilfully arguments that praised the traditional role of women whilst dismissing radical feminists as, '*a bunch of anti-family radicals and lesbians*' and, in so doing, was able to attract support from a wide range of women who were readily convinced that women's liberation did not have all the answers to furthering their rights. She believed that the role of wife and mother was what was truly liberating. In her book, *The Power of the Positive Woman,* published in 1977, she virtually re-packaged the philosophy of the

Phylllis Schlafly campaigning against the Equal Rights Amendment in the rotunda of the Illinois State Capitol 1978.

'separate sphere' to appeal to a broad spectrum of women who had rejected feminism. As NOW and the more radical feminist groups were pinning all their hopes on ERA, the destruction of the Amendment became her target.

> *'The Positive Woman starts with the assumption that the world is her oyster. She rejoices in the creative capability within her body and the power potential of her mind and spirit. She understands that men and women are different and that those very differences provide the key to her success as a person and fulfilment as a woman.'*

Quote from *The Power of the Positive Woman,* Phyllis Schlafly, 1977

The campaign for the ERA began its life in 1920 in the wake of the Nineteenth Amendment that gave women in the USA the vote. At that time the suffragist and feminist, Alice Paul, believed that the vote alone would not guarantee women equal rights (see page 227). The ERA presented to Congress repeatedly between 1923 and 1970 but rarely made much progress. It was narrowly defeated in the Senate in 1946 and accepted in an amended form in 1950. This was unacceptable to its supporters. Opposition to the ERA came from labour unions that were apprehensive of the implications of an influx of female labour, with equal rights to the jobs and pay of male workers. Some feminists also believed that women needed gender specific legislation to protect their interests in the workplace which the ERA would supplant.

The ERA was finally passed by Congress in 1972 and was sent to the state legislatures for ratification. Its progress was fairly rapid but then slowed dramatically so that, by 1979, it was clear that the three-quarters majority required for it to become a constitutional amendment was unlikely to be achieved. By this time, even some radical feminist supporters were beginning to re-think their views about the true meaning of equality. The ERA treated men and women as equal and identical rather than recognise their distinctive qualities. In fact, what radical feminists wanted by this time was equal treatment not to be treated as equal *per se*. A further argument was that most of the goals of ERA had been achieved by the Civil Rights Act of 1964, by the Equal Employment Opportunity Act of 1972 and by the clause in the Fourteenth Amendment that provides equal protection under the law for all citizens of the United States.

In 1972 Schlafly established the National Committee to Stop ERA in 1972. She was able to use powerful arguments about the implications of the ERA if it became a constitutional amendment to generate support for its rejection in the remaining states. Women were alarmed, for example, that they could become subject to the military service and would have to use unisex bathrooms. They were also likely to lose the protection needed by women working in heavy industry. ERA became caught up in the abortion controversy as opponents of the *Roe* v. *Wade* decision recognised the potential impact of equal rights. The most powerful argument of all was that ERA posed a threat to home and family. Equal Rights could also remove the obligation of divorced men to provide financial support for their offspring. It is important to appreciate that, even by the end of the twentieth century, this remained a highly emotive issue and clearly influenced, not only anti-feminists, but also the politicians in state legislatures. This explains to some extent their reluctance to ratify the ERA after it had been passed by Congress in 1972 even as late as 1982.

Schlafly's experience of using lobbying tactics helped to ensure that no more states ratified the ERA after 1977. The timescale for ratification ended in 1982. Although some radical feminists attempted to gain an extension, by this time support had waned significantly and it was allowed to lapse.

WOMEN IN POLITICS 1969–92

What progress had women made in politics by 1992?

In spite of the fact that women's issues gained a higher profile in Congress and in state legislatures in the closing decades of the twentieth century, by 1992 women had not yet established a sufficiently secure base in the political system to be able to make a significant difference to policy or to influence the attitudes of male politicians to women's issues. This is not to say that progress had not been made but rather that it had been limited. There are a number of factors that help to account for this. Some of these can be explained by the attitudes of male politicians; others are the responsibility of women themselves.

Certainly, women were more politically aware, as is suggested by the increase in the number of women using their vote. However, the number of women who saw political office as a desirable career was possibly comparatively low. Political influence was a means to an end rather than an end in itself. That said, there was a marked increase in the number of women putting

Shirley Chisholm (1924–2005) was born in Brooklyn, New York to West Indian parents. After graduating from college, she worked in a childcare centre in Harlem. Following her marriage in 1949, she became involved in local politics along with her husband. In 1964 she won a seat in the New York State Assembly, where she pressed for the provision of day care centres for children. In 1968 she became the first black woman to be elected to Congress, where she made a point of hiring all female staff and supported action on civil rights. In 1972, she became the first woman to stand for presidential nomination at the Democratic Party Convention. She served in the House of Representatives until she retired in 1982.

Geraldine Ferraro (b. 1935) was born in New York to Italian American parents. Before entering politics she was a teacher and a lawyer. She was elected to the US Congress in 1978. During the early 1980s she unsuccessfully campaigned for election to the Senate. She served as the US Ambassador to the United Nations Commission on Human Rights from 1993.

KEY TERMS

The National Women's Political Caucus was dedicated to increasing female participation in government through training and support. It was founded in 1971 by Gloria Steinem (see page 268).

themselves forward for election. In 1968 only 20 women across the nation put themselves forward for election to both houses of Congress. By 1990 this had increased to 78. In 1972 **Shirley Chisholm** became the first black woman to campaign for presidential nomination. There was a slow increase in the number of women elected to the House of Representatives between 1970 and 1992, but it was not until 1992 that women took up seats in the Senate in significant numbers.

What is clear from the statistics is that, although numbers were still small, there was an upward turn and a marked increase in the female composition of Congress by the early 1990s. This increase may be seen as a measure of the success of attempts by women in politics to organise themselves in order to encourage more women to stand for election. In 1971, the **National Women's Political Caucus** was established to encourage and prepare women to stand for election. The number of women actually standing for election for Congress and state legislatures doubled between 1974 and 1994. In 1984, **Geraldine Ferraro** ran for election as Vice President.

	Female members
House of Representatives 1970-1992	
1970	12
1980	19
1992	47
The Senate	
Before 1992	1 or 2
1993	7
1995	55

Women did make progress in state and local government in the same period. In 1974, Ella Grasso became the first woman to be elected to the position of state governor in New Hampshire. By 1990, seven more states had female governors. In 1978, Diane Feinstein became mayor of San Francisco; Jane Byrne followed in Chicago the year after. By 1992, 19 out of 100 of the US's big cities had female mayors.

Whilst there is evidence of increased female participation in politics, even by 1992 the numbers were small, given

1969–92 A triumph for radical feminism?   279

that women formed the largest percentage of the total population. However, attitudes were changing. In 1978, a Gallup poll claimed that 76 per cent of women said they would vote for a female president; only 19 per cent said 'no' – a significant increase on similar polls taken in the 1960s. By 1991, this had risen to 86 per cent with only 9 per cent saying 'no'. This enthusiasm was not reflected in male opinion polls. Generally, however, until the 1990s and the huge opportunities provided by **President Clinton** following his election in 1992 (one third of his 500 appointments were female), ambitious women tended to pursue their careers in such areas as business and law rather than politics. Moreover, the interests of women were in pursuing their rights in the workplace or campaigning for reforms that would benefit women. Women were very effective lobbyists and preferred to work through the courts to pursue women's rights. The *Roe* v. *Wade* case is a good example of this. On the other hand, there is evidence that more women in Congress could have made a difference. For example, in 1980 the Congressional Caucus for Women's Issues did help to ensure that older women, in particular, were more financially secure by the provision of pension plans.

Undoubtedly, women wishing to enter politics faced obstacles that were mainly placed there by men. Whilst the number of women standing for election might have risen, the number of vacancies in both houses of Congress did not. Removing the existing male incumbents was no easy task. Republicans especially remained suspicious of the women's lobby with its particular issues that they saw as prejudicial to family values. Consequently, their interest in female voting power was a somewhat negative one. For example, they focused particularly on winning the votes of white middle- and working-class women whom they believed were hostile to the feminist left. The Republicans saw themselves as the party that supported and upheld traditional American ideals of family life and, therefore, opposed on principle any actions that appeared to threaten the family even though others would have seen it as support. For example, even though some state legislatures had passed laws requiring employers to provide paid maternity leave, President Bush **vetoed** a federal bill providing paid parental leave, indicating some degree of hostility to working mothers. By the early 1990s there was still no federal law establishing the right of working women to be paid maternity leave.

The Democrats, on the other hand, appreciated female support – in 1986 the female vote helped them to win control of the Senate. Earlier, in 1974, they had passed the Equal Credit Opportunity Act banning discrimination in access to bank loans, mortgages and credit cards. In 1972, when the Democrats were dominant in Congress, they ensured the passage of a Child Development Act, setting up a national system of day care centres to support working mothers. However, the Republican President, Richard Nixon, vetoed the Act on the basis that such a provision would be damaging to family well-being. Even in the closing years of the century, home protection continued to be of supreme importance and, in some respects, a handicap to the progress of married women.

CONCLUSION

It could be argued that the period from 1969 until 1992 saw more rapid improvement and progress in equal opportunities for women. Radical feminism contributed to this development and may, in some respects, have accelerated changes that were already in progress. There were, however, other contributory factors:

- The continuing expansion and development of the economy as well as its technological advances provided a wider range of jobs for women, many with clear career pathways.
- The expansion of higher education and the ending of gender discrimination attracted a greater proportion of women than men and meant that by the late 1980s, the female workforce (married and unmarried) was becoming much better educated and more ambitious.
- The Women's Liberation Movement that emerged and gained momentum in this period clearly challenged many women to reflect on their role and communicated assertiveness and confidence even though many rejected

the more extreme assertions and arguments of radical feminism. Women's rights had largely been secured by the Civil Rights Act of 1964 and subsequent legislation relating to equal opportunities. This accounts to some extent for the diminished support of women for the ERA.

- The case of *Roe* v. *Wade,* based as it was in the context of the right of women to choose, was clearly a landmark victory for women's rights even though the controversy surrounding it continued throughout this period.
- Women became more politically aware and came to appreciate the power of the vote. Politicians recognised the importance of attracting the female vote during this period, even though their numbers in Congress remained small in proportion to the size of the female population.
- There is some indication that, by the early 1990s, women were poised to move forward at an accelerated rate.

However, obstacles to equality remained. Women continued to face discrimination in their pursuit of managerial jobs or in reaching the higher echelons in their chosen careers. Obstacles continued to be placed in the way of married women. These reflect the continuing importance of home and family which it was felt must be protected above all else. This presented barriers to securing affordable child care and paid maternity leave, essential if mothers were intending to pursue careers. By the late 1980s, 50 per cent of the most successful women were childless. It also meant that female activists were treated with suspicion because they were perceived as a threat to traditional family values. Above all, American women were divided about their priorities. They were also separated by class and ethnicity. These were important factors that prevented them from becoming a really powerful force for change by the closing decade of the century.

QUESTIONS TO CONSIDER

1. What evidence can you provide to support an argument that gender discrimination in employment had ended

by 1992? In what ways should this argument be modified?

2. Was the 'new feminism' a help or a hindrance to furthering the cause of rights and equality for all American women?

3. To what extent was anti-feminism a more powerful force than radical feminism during the 1970s and 1980s?

4. Evaluate the impact of Pauline Sabin, Betty Freidan and Phyllis Schlafly on the progress of women's rights.

5. Was the result of *Roe* v. *Wade* really a landmark decision for the recognition of women's rights?

6. Reflecting on the period from 1865 to 1992, how much did women owe to politicians for what had been gained by 1992?

EXAM STYLE QUESTIONS

1. To what extent can the 1960s be seen as the most significant turning point in the position and role of women in the USA between 1865 and 1992?

2. Assess the view that the Second World War was the most significant turning point in the quest for women's rights in the USA between 1865 and 1992.

3. To what extent did the federal government hinder the development of women's right in the USA in the period 1865 to 1992?

Exam Café

Relax, refresh, result!

Relax and prepare

Laura

I found it useful, as I finished studying each of the four sections, to spend some time reflecting about the changes that had taken place and the progress that had been made by the groups we have been studying over the hundred year period. I tried to weigh up whether they had made progress or just stayed the same at different points in time. Then I tried to think of explanations for my opinions. I think it is really important to try to get to grips with what was actually happening to all of these people at different stages between 1865 and 1992. But the more difficult part is putting all of this together over the 100 year period.

I'm planning to make a time chart that I can use to highlight what I think are the key developments. Then I can collect around these the key information that I might need to explain their importance or significance. I'm always worried about the dates I should learn – there are so many dates! I think that my time chart will help me to identify the important ones that I really need to know.

Student tips

Pardip

I think that, to be able to answer the exam questions well, we need to be able to identify the events or developments that made a real difference, those things that were obstacles to improvement and those periods of time when things just stayed the same. I knew it would help me to have a visual picture of the whole period, so I have drawn graphs for each of the four groups to cover the 100 years and plotted on the peaks, troughs and plateaux in the progress towards gaining their rights. Then I've annotated the graph to identify and explain the changes – whether they were political actions, economic developments, the results of protest, actions of individuals or groups, such as the effects of war. I have found that these completed graphs give me a helpful basis for writing answers to exam questions. They are also helping me to identify the factual information to support the assertions I am likely to make when I answer questions in the exam.

That's a good idea. My notes are very detailed so I need to get the information they contain into a form that I can learn from for the exam. The graph would help to link the chapters together so that I can see the developments over time and the patterns of change. I am also making two sets of pocket-sized cue cards. One will have the main facts across the period. The other set will summarise the main arguments that we have discussed during the course. The cue cards will give me a quick and easy reference point as I revise and a way of checking that I really know and can recall everything I need to answer the questions well. I've always done this for exams. I sometimes think through possible questions when I'm travelling to school and things like that so, if I find I can't recall something I know I've learned, I can just pull them out of my pocket and check. This reinforces my learning.

Harry

We are certainly going to be asked questions that will require us to recognise the significance of a particular event, series of events or actions in bringing about progress towards the acquisition of rights over the whole 100 year period, so we will need to be able to look backwards and forwards from the event or action to be able to weigh up its importance. I think your graphs will help with this, Pardip. We will need to have thought through how we might respond to the different kinds of questions that we will be set so that we can go into the exam with our thoughts organised and our arguments ready for whatever question might come up, so I like the idea of the cue cards as well, Sanjot. It helps me with the exam nerves if I am confident that I really know the topics that I might be asked to write about.

Discussion points:

- Are your concerns about the exam similar to those of these students?

- What do you think about the ideas suggested here?

- What other strategies would you suggest for dealing with revising for questions which will cover 100 years?

- Are there ways in which you can work together to prepare revision aids?

Before you begin to look again specifically at each of the sections in this book, it is useful to ensure that you are clear in your mind about the meaning of some of the terms that are likely to be used in the questions on your exam paper. For example,

- **Turning point** – this term is usually used to describe an event or development that marks a complete change of direction or the reversal of a trend. This would involve a break with what has gone before and make a sustained difference afterwards. An event or development might still be seen as a turning point even though its full impact may not be seen for some time, provided that there is no return to what existed before the event or development.
- **Significance** – an event or development can be judged to be significant if it is seen as an achievement or as something remarkable at the time. It is especially significant if it is seen to make a real difference that affects people or particular groups of people or brings about change and improvement that is lasting or leads to further development.
- **Judging extent** – is another way of asking 'how far?' This involves examining the events or developments identified in the question and deciding on their strengths and limitations in bringing about progress or preventing it. An important part of making this judgement will be the identification of other factors that might have been as effective as, or possibly more effective than, the event or development identified in the question. When answering a question covering a period of 100 years, it is important to remember that an event or development can be more significant at one point in time than another.

The first stage of your revision is obviously to work through either the sections of the book or your detailed notes on these; also, any other notes you have made as a result of your wider reading. Below is a check list of what you should know and understand as a result of your revision and learning.

When you have completed the first stage, the next is to track the different threads that run throughout each section to provide a picture of change across the period: for example,

- Government and Presidential policy.
- Legal cases.
- Economic factors.
- The role of individuals, activists and pressure groups across the period.
- Solidarity and unity of the group across the period.
- The impact of the world wars.
- The impact of individuals.
- The strength of the opposition.

These are some of the factors that **might** form the focus of an exam question.

You then need to look across the whole of the 100 year period and identify,

- the points in time when each group made the most progress,
- the points when there was the least progress or even regression.

In each case, you need to be able to place these developments into the context of the period from 1865–1992 and be able to provide explanations.

African Americans

By the end of Chapter 1, you should be able to:
- Judge the extent of liberation for former slaves in 1865 and how far the radical Republicans were responsible for it.
- Examine the white reaction to black freedom.
- Understand why Reconstruction came to an end in 1877.

By the end of Chapter 2, you should be able to:
- Appreciate the varying nature of black economic and social conditions in both south and north.
- Consider the main reasons for the development of Jim Crow segregation.
- Assess the strengths and weaknesses of Booker T. Washington as a black leader.

By the end of Chapter 3, you should be able to:
- Realise the full impact of the First World War on black civil rights.
- Judge the importance of organisations such as UNIA and the NAACP in the struggle for black civil rights between the world wars.
- Analyse the reasons for the limited progress in the field of black civil rights in this period.

By the end of Chapter 4, you should be able to:
- Examine whether this was the most important period for the importance of the Supreme Court and the Presidency in encouraging civil rights.
- Look at the importance of Martin Luther King's leadership of the civil rights movement in the context of the whole 100 years.
- Analysing how far white resistance to black civil rights was less successful in this period.

By the end of Chapter 5 you should be able to:
- See the importance of Black Power in the context of the previous campaigns for civil rights for African Americans.
- Appreciate the significance of economic and social progress in the achievements of black civil rights.
- Be able to discuss of the extent of black civil rights by 1992.

Trade Union and Labour Rights

By the end of Chapter 6, you should be able to:

- Recognise and explain the obstacles to progress in the development of labour and union rights in the late nineteenth and early twentieth century.
- Reach a decision about the contribution of the new immigration to the slow development of organised labour in the period.
- Identify other factors inhibiting the development of labour rights such as attitudes of employers.
- Understand how significant the Pullman and Homestead strikes were in the quest for recognition of labour rights before 1914.

By the end of Chapter 7, you should be able to:

- Judge whether the 1920s and 1930s can really be described as the heyday for organised labour and gather together the evidence for your judgement.
- Assess the importance of the New Deal legislation in establishing trade union rights.
- Recognise the link between the health of the economy and industrial unrest.
- Understand the role of employers in industrial relations in this period.
- Consider the extent to which the period between the two world wars (1914–45) was one of change, continuity or regression in the struggle for labour rights.

By the end of Chapter 8, you should be able to:

- Consider if post-war prosperity and economic change effectively undermined the power of organised labour before 1969.
- Judge the significance of the 1964 Civil rights Act in expanding labour rights.
- Assess whether the changing focus of the federal government in the 1960s seriously undermined the power of the labour unions.

By the end of Chapter 9, you should be able to:

- Recognise the significance of political and economic factors in reducing the power of labour unions in the closing decades of the twentieth century.
- Explain the decline in trade union membership by 1992.
- Assess the significance of the apparent rejection of trade union membership by large numbers of workers by 1992.

Native Americans

By the end of Chapter 10 you should be able to:
- Identify and understand the significance of all the factors that contributed to the destruction of the traditional way of life of the American Indians (Native Americans) before 1900.
- Understand and assess the impact of government policies of assimilation between 1865 and 1900.
- Assess the importance of the Dawes Severalty (Homestead) Act (1887) and the policy of allotment.
- Identify the factors that contributed to the limited ability of the American Indians to maintain their right to self-determination.

By the end of Chapter 11 you should be able to,
- Critically evaluate the early attempts by Native Americans themselves to resist government policies and preserve their right to self-determination.
- Assess the impact of the First World War on Native American soldiers.
- Assess the impact of the Indian Citizenship Act of 1924.
- Understand the effectiveness of changes in government policy by 1945.
- Decide on the extent to which the work of John Collier and the Indian Reorganisation Act (1934) represent a turning point in the quest of Native Americans for self-determination.
- Assess the importance of the National Congress of American Indians.
- Decide what progress had been made by Native Americans in their resistance to assimilation by 1945.

By the end of Chapter 12 you should be able to:
- Understand the impact of urban life on Native Americans who moved from the reservations to live in the city.
- Assess the importance of direct involvement by Native Americans in pursuing their rights between 1945 and 1969.
- Understand the importance of the changes in government policy towards the Indians between 1945–69.
- Judge the significance of changing government policies in securing rights for Indians.
- Understand the extent to which Native Americans were still struggling for self-determination by 1969.
- Recognise the significance of the black civil rights movement and the growth of Native American protest, especially of 'Red Power', in securing rights for Native Americans.
- Understand the significance of the work of NARF and the appeals to the Supreme Court in gaining rights for Native Americans.

By the end of Chapter 13 you should be able to:
- Assess the significance of Richard Nixon and subsequent US Presidents between 1970 and 1992 on the recognition of Native American rights.
- Judge the impact of 'Red Power' on government policy.
- Understand the role of the Supreme Court in the pursuit of Native American rights.
- Assess the extent of Native American gains by 1992.

Women in the USA

By the end of Chapter 14 you should be able to:

- Understand the economic factors that were increasing opportunities for some women in the workplace before 1914.
- Appreciate the impact of the ideal of home and family on women's attitudes to the pursuit of their rights and the extent to which this was changing by 1914.
- Identify the areas in which women were bringing about change by 1914.
- Evaluate the strengths and weaknesses of the campaign for the vote by early feminists.
- Identify those factors that limited progress in securing equal rights by 1914.

By the end of Chapter 15 you should be able to:

- Weigh up the impact of the First World War on opportunities for women and reach a view as to whether or not it can be seen as a turning point.
- Assess the impact of the passage of the Nineteenth Amendment on women and judge the extent to which the vote made a real difference to the majority of American women.
- Understand the contribution made by the fluctuating economic situation on opportunities for women.
- Understand the significant features of the Prohibition and Anti-Prohibition campaigns and what can be learned from this about the attitudes and values of women at this point in time.
- Decide how far the New Deal advanced the cause of civil rights for women.
- Understand the extent to which women were divided on their aspirations for themselves and their future, and the impact of this on their quest for the extension of their rights.
- Identify the factors that inhibited progress by 1940.
- Assess the progress made by women by 1940.

By the end of Chapter 16 you should be able to:

- Recognise the impact of the Second World War on opportunities for women and especially its aftermath.
- Evaluate the extent to which the post-war growth in the economy affected opportunities for women.
- Understand the factors bringing about changes in the lifestyle and expectations of women, both married and unmarried.
- Understand the conflict between changes in the aspirations of women and traditional values of home and family.
- Assess the impact of the 'new feminism'.
- Recognise the factors that impeded progress by 1969.
- Evaluate the progress made by women towards equality by 1969.

By the end of Chapter 17 you should be able to:

- Recognise the impact of civil rights legislation on extending women's rights.
- Assess the extent to which women had achieved equality in the workplace by 1992.

- Evaluate the impact of radical feminism and the mobilisation of the Anti-feminist movement on advancing the cause of women's rights.
- Understand the significance of Roe V. Wade in the context of women's rights.
- Recognise the factors leading to the failure of the campaign for the Equal Rights Amendment.
- Evaluate the extent of the progress made by women to establish equality of opportunity and status by 1992.

Get the result!

Examiner's tips

Preparing to answer exam questions

The chapters in this book have been written in such a way as to help you to develop the thinking skills that you need to address the kind of questions you are likely to be set on the examination paper. If you have worked through the 'Relax' and 'Refresh' sections, you should now have organised your thinking and assembled your ideas so that you are ready for the essay questions.

A typical question will identify one particular factor or one point in time in the 100 year period and ask you to evaluate its contribution to bringing about progress for any of the four groups of people in this study. It is important to remember that this means you need to look at what has happened **before** and what happened **afterwards** as well as at the impact **at the time** in order to evaluate the contribution of the focus of the question. As you arrive at your response to the question, remember to think about these points:

- The relative importance of one particular factor over time is likely to vary. For example, the policy of a President or actions of the federal government might be very important at a particular point in time but, before or afterwards, other factors might be more significant in promoting progress.

- In some instances also, the progress achieved may be only short term as changes in policy or contextual circumstances can limit or even reverse it.

Before you begin to write, have a clear idea of the argument you are going to present and the information you will need to draw on to support the assertions you are going to make. Make sure that you present a **balanced and well-supported response** that shows a clear understanding of change, continuity and progress over the 100 year period and the factors bringing this about.

Before you start to write, it is really important that you spend a few minutes planning how you are going to answer the question – by drawing a mind map or flow diagram, for example.

Below there are four exemplar questions (one for each of the four areas of your study) with commentaries to help to illustrate some of the points that are made above and to provide basic models which can be adapted to suit your response to a variety of questions.

African Americans

What was the importance of African-American leadership to the achievement of black civil rights in this period?

Gathering material for the answer:

What type of question is this? At AS level you are often asked for the reasons/causes of an event or a development. However, at this level, you will have to do more than merely produce a list of reasons for, say, the achievement of black civil rights. One factor that helped cause the development will be identified. Then you will frequently be asked to assess its relative importance. Thus your skill in handling relevant material and how well you can select appropriate and relevant examples will be tested.

For instance, here in this essay you should be able to show that in the earlier part of the 100+ years African-American leadership would have been weak because slavery had only just ended. White radical Republicans made the running. Then black leadership either played down the importance of civil rights (Booker T. Washington) or faded after a promising start (Marcus Garvey and UNIA). The role of the NAACP needs examination as it developed black leadership in an unspectacular, though important way. Then there is the dramatic leadership of the SCLC and Martin Luther King and the Malcolm X inspired Black Power campaigns. In the final years the role of the NAACP needs further examination as well as other leaders such as Jesse Jackson. Does your definition of black civil rights include social and economic equality and was that still struggling to be fulfilled at the end of the period?

You need to produce an analytical answer which adopts a thematic approach and does not merely go through the whole period chronologically. It is also important to decide how much time you will give to factors other than African-American leadership. This needs some attention even if you decide African-American leadership is the most important factor. For instance, did white opposition weaken in the later part of the period? How significant were federal government institutions, Congress, the Presidency and the Supreme Court, in bringing about change? Clearly these factors overlap and you will have to sort material in an essay plan before you begin.

Here is an extract from Pardip's answer: here he is considering the limitations to black leadership in general and his theme in particular is the role of Congress in achieving or resisting civil rights and, within that, the contributions of the African-American leadership.

Pardip's answer

African-American leadership was much less strong inside Congress. Yet, because of the nature of the American political system it was always likely that Congress, a federal institution, would be called upon to help enforce black civil rights. However, black representation in Congress in the late 19th century was not numerous and rarely effective. When progress came it was because radical white Republicans such as Stevens and Sumner were getting their own way in the late 1860s and enforcing a clear set of civil rights through acts of Congress. Significantly, the mood of Congress changed to become more negative in the 1870s and African Americans in Congress, such as Senators Hiram Revels and Blanche K. Bruce, were unable to prevent the end of Reconstruction and a slide into segregation in the south through the Jim Crow laws and watched with indifference by a Northern Congress.

Moreover, between about 1900 and 1960 as the Jim Crow laws were rigidly applied, black representation in Congress was almost non-existent and few white sympathisers were prepared to speak out. In 1926 Oscar de Priest was the first black representative in Congress for a quarter of a century and there were few others. In the 1950s and 1960s Adam Clayton Powell was an effective representative for Harlem and achieved reform in the area. But he was not a good team player and never led a national movement.

The effective campaigns of Martin Luther King in the 1960s were successful by organising mass black support from below which then put pressure on the federal government and the Presidency. However, Congress, with its large number of southern white representatives and senators, was still reluctant to pass civil rights legislation. In the end it was President Johnson's political abilities and previous experience of Congress, rather than black leadership, that was crucial in getting through the civil rights Act of 1964 and the Voting Rights Act of 1965. Nevertheless, the campaigns of King and the SCLC had provided him with the circumstances that made it possible for him to use his skill in this way.

Trade Union and Labour Rights

To what extent were divisions within the trade union movement itself a major obstacle to the development of trade union and labour rights in the years from 1865 to 1992?

This focus of this question is the exploration of divisions within the trade union movement as a factor inhibiting progress towards the acquisition of trade union and labour rights across the whole of the 100 year period. This also implies consideration of all the other factors affecting the development of these rights and assessing the extent of their significance. As with any of the questions that you meet on the exam paper, you are free to reach your own conclusions about this question. The important thing is that you attempt to arrive at a judgement which is supported by the evidence that you have assembled and takes into account the changing situation at key points within the 100+ year period. Hopefully, you will already have developed your ideas about this as a result of your studies and revision. The first stage is to decide on the line of argument that you are going to follow through your essay. For example, you might take one of the following:

- Divisions within the trade union movement were a major (i.e. the biggest) obstacle to the acquisition of labour rights.
- Divisions in the trade union movement were significant but there were other factors that were equally and, at some points, more important during the period from 1865 until 1992.
- Other factors (e.g. economic or political) were more important in preventing the development of trade union and labour rights.

This is the opening paragraph of Laura's response to this question.

Examiner says:

Laura begins her answer well. She states her argument clearly, agreeing with the question but showing awareness that other factors were important. If she continues this argument throughout her essay and supports it with evidence, examining all the factors she will gain good marks.

Laura's answer

It can be argued that at key points in the period from 1865 until 1992, there was a lack of unity and solidarity amongst workers and their trade unions. This was particularly the case before 1955 when the AFL and CIO combined in order to combat falling union membership at a time when employers seemed to have the upper hand. In this period, it is clear that the lack of solidarity impeded progress in securing union rights even though these had effectively been established in law in 1935. However, other factors also contributed significantly to the slow progress, for example, the changing economic situation, the lack of political support for much of the period and, particularly, the determination of powerful employers to resist the unionisation of their workforce.

Native Americans

To what extent was the policy of the federal government the most important factor inhibiting the progress of Native Americans to achieving their civil rights between 1865 and 1992?

In this question the main focus is on the impact of federal government policy and actions. A further significant aspect of the question is the term 'most important'. This requires you to pay some attention to other factors and to suggest why these were more or less important. The first stage in answering it is to decide upon the line of argument that you are going to take in your answer. You either need to agree or disagree with the assertion in the question or you could partially agree and partially disagree.

The important thing here is that you make a decision as to how you are going to approach this question, make sure that you cover the period from 1865–1992 and support your arguments with factual information. Hopefully, you will have considered possible questions such as this as part of your revision and will have come to the exam with your ideas already formulated. Give yourself a few minutes in an exam situation to recall and organise your thoughts and plan your answer. You might sketch out a mind map to help you with this process. Your answer will be more impressive if you approach it in an analytical manner. It is easy to drift into writing a chronological account, especially when you are covering a specified period of time.

This is Harry's opening paragraph in his answer to this question.

Harry's answer

For much of the period from 1865 until 1992, the status of Native Americans was in the hands of the federal government. Of all other organisations, it had the biggest impact on the lives of the Indian tribes. Certainly, until the 1930s and again between 1945 and the early 1970s, through its attempts to assimilate them into US society, it can be argued that the rights to self-determination that they claimed were blocked by federal action. On occasions, this undermined their human as well as civil rights. However, it must be said that Native Americans largely owed the rights that they had gained by 1992 to the federal government. At the same time, it can be argued that, before the 1960s, Native American peoples were not united in pursuit of their rights and this also impeded progress throughout much of the period.

Examiner's comments

Harry has made quite a good start to his essay here because he has set out quite clearly at the very beginning how he is going to address this question. He has shown awareness of the fluctuations in the progress of Native Americans as a result of changing government policy. By his use of dates, he has been able to demonstrate that he has placed the question in the context of the whole period from 1865 until 1992 and also that he is aware of key points within the period where government policy changed and had impact. He has alluded to the fact that there were other factors impeding progress. As a result of his introduction, the examiner will be clear about the line of argument that he is going to take in his essay. However, the mark that he is actually given will depend very much on how he develops his answer.

Women in the USA

The questions on this section may well prove to be the most challenging, because the aspirations of women throughout most of this period were diverse and fragmented. Bear in mind that the rights that women claimed in this period can probably be best summarised under the heading of equality, remembering that, with the possible exception of the right to vote, not all women wanted these rights and some were fiercely opposed to certain aspects of the campaigns that were undertaken to achieve them during this period. At no point throughout the period from 1865 until 1992 was there what could be called a women's movement commanding the united support of a significant proportion of the female population of the USA. Let's see how this works out in the context of the question below.

To what extent was feminism a significant force in enabling women to gain their civil rights and to increase the opportunities open to them between 1865 and 1992?

The key words and phrases in this question are **'to what extent'** and **'a significant force'**. By using the words 'significant force' the question is suggesting that women themselves played a major part in achieving their civil rights and the extension of equal opportunities. You will need to decide if you agree with this, whether it was true at some times rather than others or whether there were other factors that contributed to advancing the position of women that were more important. An evaluation of what feminism actually achieved will help this discussion. You could follow this line of argument,

- Throughout the period from 1865 until 1992, some feminists were very effective in making their presence felt, by campaigning on a range of issues associated with women's rights. However, divisions and conflicts of interest ensured that they had limited direct impact on the rights that women gained during this period. It can be argued that the gains that were made largely came as a result of other factors, most notably economic growth and political policy.

- Early feminists were a minority of educated, middle-class women who actively promoted a number of important social issues and aimed to establish women's rights in the workplace; others joined the campaign which had been going on since the end of the eighteenth century for a constitutional amendment extending the franchise to women.

Let's have a look at an essay plan Sanjot has completed. Do you agree with what he has done? Are there any other points that you need to add? Would you change the order in which he has written them? He has not come to a conclusion about the relative importance of feminist campaigns and other factors in bringing about change – what is your conclusion? Now try to write the essay.

Sanjot's essay plan

Introduction: mainly agree but were other significant factors. Women in the USA were never united in pursuit of their rights and significant numbers of them actively opposed feminist causes. This weakened their effectiveness in bringing about change.

Examples of the diversity of feminist groups before 1945:

- Jane Addams and the Hull House project focus on settlement of immigrants.
- Campaigns aimed at protection of the home and family e.g temperance and prohibition, were also used to promote women's suffrage – Elizabeth Cady Stanton and Susan B. Anthony, Frances Willard – Women's Christian Temperance Union 1874.
- Campaign to fight for women's rights in the workplace (reasonable hours, safe working conditions, fair pay) – Florence Kelley and the National Consumers' League focussed campaign on state legislatures.
- Black feminists active in pressure for rights and equality for African Americans – National Association of Colored Women campaigned for the vote for black women and pressed for equality before the law e.g. Ida B. Wells and the campaign against lynching.
- Campaign for the vote took different approaches:
  - Elizabeth Cady Stanton, Lucretia Mott, Susan B. Anthony, Carrie Chapman Catt, National American Woman Suffrage Association (1890) – worked to extend the vote state by state
  - Alice Paul and the Congressional Union for Women's Suffrage (1913) – more militant wing using methods similar to those of suffragettes in the UK.

Achievements of early feminists:

- raised awareness of issues
- had some success at state level (women had the vote in 11 states by 1914);

BUT:

- decision to pass the 19th Amendment was more as a result of women's work during the First World War than campaigns for suffrage, although the treatment by the authorities of more militant suffragettes such as Alice Paul aroused public sympathy.
- the acquisition of the vote was not immediately appreciated by the majority of American women, especially African Americans and Hispanics, who were prevented from registering their votes.

From 1960s onwards feminist groups more radical and agressive:

- impact of the 'new feminism' – Betty Frieden and the activities of NOW; Gloria Steinem;

- The campaign for women's right to choose - Margaret Sanger and contraception; radical feminism, the right to legal abortion and the case of Roe v. Wade and its impact,
- Women trade unionists (sometimes referred to as 'trade union feminists') pressed for equal rights for women in the workplace, especially for equal pay.

BUT aroused fierce anti-feminist opposition

- Phyllis Schlafly and anti-feminism,

What had the 'new' feminism actually achieved by 1992?

- had some impact on the attitudes and expectations of a greater number of American women than previously and accelerated changes that enhanced women's rights e.g. some success in the workplace
- Roe v. Wade (1971) was a landmark decision in extending women's right to choose in matters of child-bearing; raised awareness of alternative opportunities for women besides marriage and family.

Failures:

- Passing of Roe still contentious today; abortion was a particularly contentious issue as a result of Roe v. Wade (1971).
- The campaign for the Equal Rights Amendment (1923) — progress on this by 1972 — reasons for its failure.
- Still not total equality in workplace or in political power.

Other factors extending the opportunities for and rights of women:

- Industrialisation, economic growth and expansion as well as improved educational opportunities were largely responsible for expanding opportunities in the workplace, especially from the 1950s onwards.
- Social and economic change, especially from the 1950s onwards; change of attitude to home and family life
- The federal government advanced the cause of women's rights through legislation and increased opportunities, especially in politics— e.g. 19th Amendment (1920); aspects of New Deal legislation — especially the Fair Labor Standards Act (1938); opportunities created for women in politics under Roosevelt (e.g. Frances Perkins, Florence Allen, Mary McCleod Bethune, Nellie Tayloe Ross); women gained their civil and equal rights as a result of the Civil Rights Act(1964); Equal Employment Opportunities Commission (1964) set up by President Johnson; 1972 Equal Employment Opportunity Act.

Conclusion

BIBLIOGRAPHY

General Histories

Richard M. Abrams, *America Transformed: Sixty Years of Revolutionary Change, 1941–2001,* 2008

J. M. Blum, *Years of Discord: American Politics and Society 1961–74*, Norton, 1992

W. H. Chafe, *The Unfinished Journey: America since World War Two*, Oxford University Press, 6th edn, 2007

G. Gerstle, E. Rosenberg and N. Rosenberg, *America Transformed: A History of the US since 1900*, Harcourt Brace, 1999

M. Jones, *The Limits of Liberty: American History 1607–1980*, Oxford University Press, 1983

African American civil rights
Original source books

A Testament of Hope: The Essential Writings of Martin Luther King, Harper Collins, 1991

Autobiography of Malcolm X, Penguin, 2007

W. E. B. Du Bois, *The Souls of Black Folk*, Oxford World's Classics

Henry Hampton, Steve Fayer, Sarah Flynn, *Voices of Freedom: An Oral History of the Civil Rights Movement from the 1950s through the 1980s,* Bantam, 1991

Booker T. Washington, *Up from Slavery,* Dover Thrift

General civil rights

R. Cook, *Sweet Land of Liberty?* Longman, 1998

A. Fairclough, *Better Day Coming? Blacks and Equality 1890–2000,* Penguin, 2002

Ron Field, *Civil Rights in America 1865–1980,* Cambridge, 2002

E. Foner, *A Short History of Reconstruction 1863–1877,* Harper Perennial, 1990

Vincent P. Franklin and Bettye Collier-Thomas (ed.), *Sisters in the Struggle: African-American Women in the Civil Rights and Black Power Movements*

J. H. Franklin and A. Moss Jr., *From Slavery to Freedom: A History of African Americans*, Alfred A. Knopf 7th edition, 2000

Colin Grant, *Negro with a Hat: Marcus Garvey*, Jonathan Cape, 2008

Gilbert Jonas, *Freedom's Sword: The NAACP and the Struggle Against Racism in America 1909–1969,* Routledge, 2007

Peter Ling, *Martin Luther King*, Routledge, 2002

Bruce Perry, *Malcolm X,* Station Hill, 1991

Kevern Verney, *Black Civil Rights in America*, Routledge, 2000

C. Vann Woodward, *The Strange Career of Jim Crow*, Oxford University Press, 1974

J. White *Black Leadership in America: from Booker T. Washington to Jesse Jackson,* Longman, 1990

Websites

Civil Rights in Mississippi Digital archive go to Civil Rights movement

African American World (History section)

Native American rights

C. Bolt, *American Indian Policy and American Reform*, (Unwin, 1990)

D. Brown, *Bury my heart at Wounded Knee* (Vintage, 1970)

Vine Deloria Jr. & Clifford M. Lytle, *The Nations Within, The Past and Future of American Indian Sovereignty*, University of Texas Press, 1984

Peter Iverson, *'We Are Still Here' American Indians in the Twentieth Century*, Harlan Davidson Inc., 1998

Jack Page, *In the Hands of the Great Spirit: The 20,000 Year History of American Indians*, Free Press, 2003
Philip Weeks (ed.), *'They Made Us Many Promises': The American Indian Experience 1524 to the Present*, Harlan Davidson Inc., 2002

Women's rights

Vicki L. Crawford (ed.), Jacqueline Anne Rouse and Barbara Woods, *Women in the Civil Rights Movement; Trailblazers and Torchbearers 1941– 1965*, Indiana University Press, 1990

Sara M Evans, *Born for Liberty: A History of Women in America*, Free Press, 1997

N.E.H. Hull & Peter Charles Hoffer, *Roe v. Wade: The American Rights Controversy in American History*, University of Kansas Press

Kenneth D. Rose, *American Women and the Repeal of Prohibition*, New York University Press, 1996

S. Rowbotham, *A Century of Women: The History of Women in Britain and the United States*, Penguin Books, 1999

GLOSSARY

Affirmative action A policy began under Johnson which continued into Richard Nixon's Presidency. It was to affirm the rights of African Americans to have equal opportunities in areas where, because of the discrimination against them in the past, they might still be seen to be at a disadvantage. It particularly applied in employment and education.

The Amalgamated Association of Iron and Steel Workers (AA) was a labour craft union formed in 1876. It represented skilled iron and steel workers.

Amendment to the Constitution This was any addition to the original Constitution and Bill of Rights (1783) that interpreted the original law and established the extent of individual or collective rights of the United States of America. The subsequent amendments, in some cases, clarified the existing law or defined it in response to social and political change.

The American Birth Control League (ABCL) was founded by Margaret Sanger in 1921 and gained legal recognition in New York state in 1923. The League's purpose was to educate through the distribution of written materials, conferences and lectures.

The Anti-Saloon League was established in 1893 and became the main organisation lobbying for Prohibition. Successful in 1919, it was overwhelmingly defeated by anti-Prohibition groups in the early 1930s.

The Association Against the Prohibition Amendment (AAPA) formed in 1918 to oppose the passage of the prohibition amendment.

Black consciousness Acute awareness of your black racial identity partly caused by a society that treated people inferiorly because of their racial background. It led many to investigate their own racial roots and to emphasise their own cultural heritage.

Bifurcation The splitting of the black community in two – by the 1980s the wealthier black middle class were becoming increasingly prosperous while the very poorest African Americans were becoming relatively poorer and poorer in comparison with the rest of the nation. So they developed correspondingly different social and political attitudes.

The Black Panthers A Black Power group that started in Oakland, California in 1966 and soon received national attention by armed parades of 'self defence' (against 'police brutality') in a distinctive uniform that included berets and dark glasses.

Blue-collar workers are wage earners in manual, industrial jobs.

Boll weevil The insect which attacked the cotton plant, feeding on its buds and flowers. It first appeared from Mexico in Texas in 1892, and gradually spread north and east to all cotton growing districts by the 1920s, proving resistant to treatment.

Bourbons The ruling group of southern politicians from the Democrat party, dominant between the end of Reconstruction and the political upheavals of the 1890s. They favoured control rather than liberation of black people.

The Brotherhood of Sleeping Car Porters and Maids (BSCP) was a labour union organised by the predominantly African-American Pullman Porters. It began in 1925 and struggled for twelve years to win its first collective bargaining agreement with the Pullman Company. In 1935, it was the first labour organisation led by African Americans to be accepted into the American Federation of Labor.

Bureau of Indian Affairs The name given to the Office of Indian Affairs after 1947. In 1949, it was transferred from the Department of War to the Department of the Interior. This federal government organisation controlled the money allocated for the development of Native Americans and was responsible for their education as well as for the reservations.

Carpetbaggers When military rule was imposed on the south after the Civil War, those who came from the north to implement the policies of Reconstruction became known as carpetbaggers because of the bags made of cloth they carried. Many southerners viewed them as people who would take away many of the valuable goods of the south in their bags.

Closed shop A term used to describe a factory or workplace that is dominated by one trade union and where all workers are obliged to belong to that union.

Commission on International Co-operation (CIC) This was set up to campaign for dialogue and understanding between the races. It raised money for education for blacks and condemned lynching and **peonage**.

Confederacy The eleven states that tried to secede (break away from) the United States: Alabama, Arkansas, Georgia, Florida, Louisiana, Mississippi, South and North Carolina, Virginia, Tennessee and Texas. They formed their own system of government giving each state some independence but combining militarily in an attempt to beat off northern forces in the Civil War.

Congress The federal legislature (parliament or law-making body) of the USA. It consisted of two houses with near equal powers, the democratically elected House of Representatives with numbers proportionate to population, and an indirectly (until 1913) elected upper house, the Senate, which had two representatives per state regardless of population. For legislation to be successful both houses had to pass any proposal.

Congressional Caucus An organisation of elected members of Congress who are normally Democrats and are always African Americans, set up in 1970/1. They act as a kind of pressure group for black interests.

Congress of Industrial Organizations (CIO) Originally the Committee for Industrial Organizations, this was formed in 1935 by eight unions from within the AFL. In 1936, the AFL expelled the CIO unions within its ranks. It subsequently broke away and formed a rival union organisation. This split weakened the labour movement until 1955 when the AFL and the CIO amalgamated.

Contract system involved the employment of workers that could be laid off in slack periods.

CORE – Congress of Racial Equality This was set up in 1942 to protest against *de facto* racial segregation in northern cities. It was revived in 1961 from a moribund state by one of its founders, James Farmer. It was an important organisation for the next few years but then split over support for Black Power in 1966. After 1968, when Roy Innis took over the running of CORE, it focused on economic themes rather than political ones and moved back to a more moderate position, stressing the importance of black community self-development.

Crop-lien system The profits from harvesting a crop would be used to pay back loans and supplies given on credit by local shopkeepers. Lenders often insisted the crop be cotton because its sales were seen as the most reliable.

Daughters of the American Revolution An all women's group comprised of descendents of those who were 'patriots' in the War of Independence: originally (though no longer) an all-white group.

Deep South Usually refers to the states where segregation was most embedded, Mississippi, Alabama, Georgia and South Carolina.

De facto means the actual position in reality.

De jure means the official position in law.

Emancipation Proclamation This was issued by President Lincoln and gave freedom only to those slaves in rebel-held territory in the south. Slaves in states loyal to the Union were not freed.

Enfranchised Being given the right to vote.

Equal Employment Opportunities Commission is a federal agency with the responsibility of ensuring that the terms of the 1964 Civil Rights Act and the Equal Pay Act are followed and to deal with complaints about the failure of employers to observe these.

Equal Rights Amendment is the title of a proposed amendment to the Constitution that would guarantee equal rights in law to all Americans irrespective of gender.

Fair Labor Standards Act 1938 was amended between 1949 and 1996 in each case to increase the minimum wage. In 1961, the application of the minimum wage legislation was also extended to employees in schools, hospitals and nursing homes.

Federal system A federal system is a form of government where there is more than one source of authority; in the case of the USA, a combined government for all the states in Washington and governments within the states themselves, each having their own defined areas of authority over citizens. This is in contrast to a unitary system where all power flows from the top.

Federal territories were the new lands opened up for settlement in the mid and far-west. As territories they became subject to the laws of the US and were administered by officials appointed in Washington DC. When the population of the territories reached 60,000, they could apply to become a state. This gave them the right of some degree of self-determination. They had their own elected state assembly and governor, and were given authority to make their own laws.

Feminists In this context, feminists were mainly middle-class women who were concerned with securing equal rights for women. In this period, they focused their attention on the rights to vote and were very much a minority movement.

The Feminists This was a radical feminist splinter group of NOW that existed in New York between 1968 and 1973. Its alternative title was *A Political Organisation to Annihilate Sex Roles*. It promoted the view that, to be truly liberated, women needed to separate themselves from men in every aspect of their lives. They were particularly opposed to marriage.

The five civilised tribes The five tribes were the Cherokee, the Chickasaws, the Choctaws, the Seminoles and the Creeks.

Freedmen Originally referring to African Americans who had obtained their freedom before the Civil War, the term came to embrace all former slaves who were freed by President Lincoln's Emancipation Proclamation in 1863.

Ghetto A section of a city occupied by one social or racial group.

Harlem Renaissance An out-pouring of artistic talent by blacks, many from Harlem, in the 1920s and 1930s in literature, the visual arts, theatre and music.

The Indian Rights Association (IRA) was a social activist group founded in Philadelphia in 1882. The group was devoted to the cause of assimilating the Native American peoples. It was influential in the formation of Indian policy in the 1930s.

Indian Vocational Training Act 1956 established vocational training for American Indians, including adults, so that they could obtain a 'marketable skill'. This training was provided with federal funding for all those who applied, provided that they lived near to reservations and were under the jurisdiction of the Bureau of Indian Affairs.

Jim Crow Originally a character in an early nineteenth-century minstrel act, the term became a mildly offensive way to refer to black people in a rather stereotyped way. The term then became more fixed towards the end of the century to describe the segregation in the southern states.

Ku Klux Klan (KKK) A terrorist organisation, mainly in the southern states, which advocated white supremacy. The first Klan dissolved in 1871 but was then revived in 1915.

Laissez-faire The belief that there should be no government interference in the organisation and operation of business and commercial concerns.

Lobbying tactics refers to the practice of gaining the attention of politicians or other people of influence in order to persuade them to support a particular cause.

Manifest Destiny A belief held by white Americans that God had chosen them to populate the lands from the Atlantic seaboard to the Pacific Ocean.

The melting pot The idea that all the different peoples living in the United States would minimise their differences in cultural, racial and religious background to integrate harmoniously, producing an American identity.

Migrant farm workers were mainly labourers without permanent employment who moved around in search of largely seasonal farm work, such as harvesting or fruit picking. At other times of the year they struggled to survive.

Municipal The equivalent of local council workers in the UK.

NARF (Native American Rights Fund) began as the California Indian Legal Services and in 1970, as a result of a grant from the Ford Foundation, was able to establish a base in Boulder, Colorado.

National Association of Colored Women (NACW) was established in Washington DC in 1896 – an amalgamation of several smaller groups led by educated black women. It was focussed on the achievement of the vote for women but also campaigned to stop lynching and discrimination and to improve educational opportunities, especially in the southern states. By 1918, its membership had increased to 300,000.

National Association for the Advancement of Colored People (NAACP) Founded in 1909, it was the first successful, nationwide civil rights organisation to campaign systematically for black civil rights and gain a large membership of both black and white supporters. Its successes were rarely spectacular but it played a significant long-term role in the fight for the legal end of segregation.

National Congress of American Indians (NCAI) was formed in Denver, Colorado in 1944 by a group of 80, mainly educated Native Americans, representing fifty tribes.

The National Consumers' League (NCL) was a pressure group established in 1899 by a group of women associated with Hull House under the leadership of Florence Kelley. The NCL focused its attention on securing fair working conditions for women and children. This included safety at work, reasonable working hours and fair pay.

National Indian Youth Council (NIYC) was founded in 1961 in New Mexico to pursue civil rights for American Indians. In particular, it attempted to preserve Indian's fishing rights in the north west.

National Labor Relations Board (NLRB) 1935 was (and remains) a government agency responsible for addressing unfair labour practices in private sector employment.

National Negro Congress Founded in 1935 to act as a pressure group to ensure that African Americans received their fair share of New Deal benefits. After a well-supported start it gradually declined to become an organisation limited to Communist support. It was disbanded in 1947.

The National Right to Life Committee was established in 1973 in response to the *Roe* v. *Wade* decision. Its fundamental purpose is to secure the right of the unborn child to be protected by the Constitution.

National self-determination The belief that peoples of Europe should be able to determine for themselves (by voting) to which country they would like to belong.

The National War Labor Board (NWLB) was established in 1941 by the federal government in response to the willingness of unions in essential industries to forego strike action for the duration of the war. Its function was to control wage increases.

National Women's Loyal League was established in 1863 by Anthony and Stanton. It acted as a pressure group to urge Congress to introduce an amendment to the US Constitution that would end slavery. Following the passage of the Thirteenth Amendment in 1865 that ended slavery, the group was disbanded. Its membership subsequently focused on the campaign for female suffrage.

The National Women's Party (1917–) In 1917, the Congressional Union changed its name to the National Women's Party (NWP) which focussed its efforts on obtaining the vote for women by means of a constitutional amendment and generally working to advance the cause of women's rights. After the passage of the Nineteenth Amendment it campaigned for an **Equal Rights Amendment** to the Constitution. The NWP continues to fight for women's rights today.

The National Women's Political Caucus was dedicated to increasing female participation in government through training and support. It was founded in 1971 by Gloria Steinem.

Nation of Islam The Nation of Islam (also known as the Black Muslims) was a group founded in 1930 by Wallace Fard who led it until his disappearance in 1934.

Native capitalism was intended to reduce the burden on federal or state expenditure by the development of profit-making enterprises by Native Americans themselves.

Nativism means the hostile response of one cultural group seeking to preserve its inherent characteristics in the face of increasing ethnic diversity.

Naturalisation The procedure that conferred American citizenship on foreign immigrants and the rights and freedoms that accompany this status.

Negro The commonly used word for the African American up to the 1960s. 'Negro' was originally seen as a politer name to the vulgar alternatives, but black consciousness in the 1960s and 1970s felt that 'negro' had too many associations with slavery, oppression and segregation, and so replaced it with 'black'. More recently African American has been used as a means of indicating a person's ethnicity while emphasising shared heritage.

Peonage This was when labourers were forced to work for a master until their debts were paid off.

Populist Party An alliance of farmers and poor whites against the old landowning planter class who had dominated southern government.

Primaries An American electoral feature whereby preliminary voting in an election is undertaken by voters registered for one of the parties – and sometimes the electorate more generally. The precise rules vary from state to state.

The Progressive Movement The Progressives represented a wide coalition of interests in the US who believed that aspects of American society (especially corruption among the very rich) needed reforming.

Prohibition The banning of the manufacture, sale and transportation of alcoholic beverages was eventually embodied in the Eighteenth Amendment to the US Constitution in 1920.

Pullman coaches were the more comfortable and luxurious passenger carriages on a train occupied on lengthy journeys for day or night travel.

Racketeering refers to illegal business deals and involvement in related criminal activity which was rife during the 1920s. Gangland bosses became wealthy and gained power and influence by corrupting local politicians and officials.

Radicalesbians An organisation formed in 1973 and combining women's liberation and gay liberation. It campaigned for a genderless society where people could relate to each other as people, unimpeded by gender roles and expectations.

Reconstruction The name given to the period 1865–77, a time of rebuilding or reconstructing the society and infrastructure of the southern states after the devastation they suffered through the Civil War.

Redemption Governments Democrat controlled governments that developed in the southern states from 1870 onwards to replace governments imposed by the north after 1865. They were said to have saved or 'redeemed' the traditional south.

Reservations were the lands designated by the US government for occupation by the Native American tribes. The process began in the 1850s but accelerated in the 1860s.

Scalawags co-operated with African Americans and carpetbaggers to impose Reconstruction on the south. They were very unpopular and the word (originally referring to poor livestock or a worthless person) was intended as an insult.

Service economy Examples of the service sectors are the leisure industry, retail outlets, eating places, real estate, secretarial and professional services.

Sharecropping was when landowners divided up their plantations into small tenancies of between 30 and 50 acres.

Social Darwinism The application of Darwin's biological theory of evolution to sociology by arguing that the survival of the fittest can be applied to the development of races and societies. Human society, it was argued, operated on scientific principles in a similar way to the natural world.

Southern Christian Leadership Conference (SCLC) This was formed in 1957 to widen participation in the civil rights movement. Black clergymen were particularly prominent and Martin Luther King was president. Later the organisation was led by Ralph Abernathy, from 1968–77, and then Joseph Lowery 1977–97.

'Speakeasies' were illegal liquor shops or drinking clubs. They appeared in all the big cities in the US during the prohibition period. They were usually owned and operated by gangland bosses or organisations.

State legislature The parliament or law–making body elected in each state of the USA. In the federal system it has the right to pass laws on a wide range of domestic affairs.

Student Non-Violent Co-ordinating Committee (SNCC) Set up as a result of the sit-ins, the organisation maintained links with SCLC (on whom it sometimes relied for funding) but was largely independent in its decision making. Disbanded in 1970.

The Taft-Hartley Act (Labor Management Relations Act) 1947 was enacted to restore the bargaining power to employers in unionised industries that had been lost by the terms of the Wagner Act. To achieve this, it established rules of conduct for unions in their negotiations with management.

The Teamsters Union (International Brotherhood of Teamsters) was established in 1903. It became one of the largest unions in the USA and remains so today. In modern times teamsters are truck drivers.

Temperance in this context is the advocacy of drinking in moderation and the avoidance of excess.

Universal Negro Improvement Association (UNIA) Led by Marcus Garvey, UNIA campaigned for equal rights and for the independence of the black race rather than it being absorbed into an equal melting pot in the US.

Veto To have the power of veto is to use one's position to reject a proposal that the majority support. In the American Constitution a President can veto a law passed through Congress if he dislikes it. However, this veto is limited. If both Houses of Congress re-pass it with a two-thirds majority, the President has to accept it. This is what happened to President Andrew Johnson a number of times in 1866/7.

White Citizens' Councils An organisation set up to maintain segregation. The earliest ones date from 1955 and aimed to maintain strict segregation in as many areas of life as possible.

White-collar workers Describes men and women in non-manual work, for example, clerical worker, banker, civil servants etc.

Wild cat strike A strike undertaken by workers without the agreement of their union leaders.

The **Women's Christian Temperance Union (WCTU)** was a mainly middle-class organisation founded in 1874 by Susan B. Anthony and Elizabeth Cady Stanton, partly to promote the cause of women's suffrage but also to combat the evils of excessive drinking.

'Yellow dog contract' The derisory term used by a trade union leader to describe the contracts signed by workers that prevented them from joining a union. Although this practice had been common since the end of the nineteenth century, the term itself wasn't used before 1921.

Galbraith, J.K. 135
Garvey, Marcus 48–9
ghettos, black 29, 45–6, 77, 95
glass ceiling 265
Grant, Ulysses S. 11, 21, 24

Harding, Warren 54
Harlem 29, 45–6, 47, 138
Hayes, Rutherford B. 24–5
Haymarket Affair 101, 102, 104–5, 107
Homestead Act (1862) 166, 219
Homestead strike 107, 111–15
Hoover, Herbert 54, 126, 186
housing 78, 82

'I have a dream' speech 73, 74
immigration 1, 100, 101, 105–7
    by country 1, 2, 105, 106
    from Asia 148–9
    and women's work 221–2, 253
Indian Agents 171
Indian Bureau 168, 175, 187, 190
Indian Citizenship Act (1924) 183–4
Indian Claims Commission 195
Indian Education Act (1972) 206
Indian Removal Act (1830) 164
Indian Reorganization Act (1934)
    186–90, 192–3, 235
Indian Self-Determination and
    Education Assistance Act (1975)
    193, 207
Indian Territory 164
Industrial Workers of the World 104
industrialisation 99–101, 219

Jackson, Jesse 69, 92–3
Japanese Americans and Indian land
    191
Jim Crow laws 29–30, 36
Johnson, Andrew 12, 13, 14–15, 19
Johnson, Lyndon B. 24, 62, 74–5,
    76, 85, 89, 139–40,
    and Native Americans 196–7, 199,
    205

Kennedy, John F. 71, 72, 89, 138–9,
    199, 257–8
King, Martin Luther 59, 69, 70,
    72–5, 79, 80, 81–2
Knights of Labor 101–2, 110, 113
Ku Klux Klan (XXX) 23, 49, 52–3,
    66, 238

labour market changes 1950s 136–7
laissez-faire capitalism 108, 118
Lakota Sioux 169, 209
land
    and African Americans 18–19, 25,
    27, 28

Native American 165, 166, 168–9,
    173, 176–9,
    206, 211–12
life expectancy: Native Americans
    198
Lincoln, Abraham 9, 10, 11
Little Rock Central High School
    67–8
Los Angeles: 1965 riots 77, 82
    1992 riots 94–5
lynching 33–5, 42, 50, 51, 57, 238

McCarthy, Joseph/McCarthyism
    2–3, 61
Malcolm X 79–81, 82
Manifest Destiny 169
Marshall, Thurgood 63–4
maternity leave 266, 281, 282
melting pot 45, 180–1, 213
Meriam Report 185–6
middle-class 220, 222–3, 225, 228
    black 47, 50, 58, 93–4, 95
    Native American 214
Military Reconstruction Act (1867)
    13
military service 45, 60, 62, 191, 251
Mississippi v. *Williams* 32
Molly Maguires 106–7
Montgomery bus boycott 68–9
Mount Rushmore, occupation of 209

National Association for the
    Advancement of Colored People
    38, 40–2, 43, 51–2, 57, 63–4,
    111
    legal strategy 54, 55–6, 58, 61, 65,
    76, 87
National Association of Colored
    Women 225
National Congress of American
    Indians 191–2, 199–200
National Consumers' League 225
National Industry Recovery Act
    (1933) 127
National Labor Relations Act (1935)
    127–9
National War Labor Board 131
Native American Rights Fund 211–
    13
Native Americans *1865–1900* 160,
    162–79, 289
    loss of tribal life 162–3, 167–8,
    170, 173–5
    tribes and battles 164, 165–6
    and westward expansion 163–4
Native Americans *1900–45* 180–93,
    214, 289
    pressure groups 191–2, 193

voting rights 183–4, 192
Native Americans *1945–69* 194–
    204, 289
    assimilation policy 183, 185, 188–
    90, 192–3,
    195, 198–9, 213
    and civil rights movement 199–
    201
    government policies 195–9, 295
Native Americans *1970–92* 205–16,
    289
    child welfare 208
    protests 209–11
    religious freedom 208, 211
native capitalism 208
native sovereignty 201, 211
nativism 120, 244
New Deal 54–5, 126–30, 133,
    234–5
    and Native Americans 186–8, 192
New Deal Order 4, 5
Niagara movement 38, 40
Nineteenth Amendment 5, 227, 235,
    237
Nixon, Richard 85–7, 89, 141, 150,
    274, 281
    and Native Americans 197, 205–7
NOW 258, 259, 265, 267, 270, 276

parallel businesses 28
Parks, Rosa 68
party system and black civil rights
    23–4
Perkins, Frances 234, 236, 237
Plessy v. *Ferguson* 31, 54, 56, 63, 65
political system 3–4
poverty 27–8, 78, 137–8, 158
    black 45–6, 57, 77, 89
    Native Americans 171, 172, 178,
    203
    and women 262, 266
Powderly, Terence V. 101–2
Progressive era 4–5
prohibition campaign 224, 239,
    242–8, 249
Pueblo Indians 184, 185, 198
Pullman Company 122–5
    strike 108, 115–17

racial uplift 49–50
racketeering 245
radical feminism 258–60, 261, 264–
    78, 281
Randolph, Philip 52, 62, 83, 110–
    11, 122–5, 132
Reagan, Ronald 89–90, 144–6, 151,
    208, 274–5
Reconstruction period 4, 8–26
Red Power 200–1, 209–11, 213
Red Scare 2, 120

Printed in Great Britain
by Amazon

27507579R00176